A RESURRECTION LIKE CHRIST'S

DAVID. W. COOKE

WESTBOW
PRESS®
A DIVISION OF THOMAS NELSON
& ZONDERVAN

WestBow Press books may be ordered through booksellers or by contacting:

WestBow Press
A Division of Thomas Nelson & Zondervan
1663 Liberty Drive
Bloomington, IN 47403
www.westbowpress.com
844-714-3454

ISBN: 978-1-6642-8939-0 (sc)
ISBN: 978-1-6642-8941-3 (hc)
ISBN: 978-1-6642-8940-6 (e)

Library of Congress Control Number: 2023900671

Print information available on the last page.

WestBow Press rev. date: 01/13/2023

My Prayer

Heavenly Father, I pray that if what I write is not truthful, that you would bring correction to myself, and bury my words in the depths of the sea, no more to be read. For I do not desire to harm your church by bringing division or false teaching, but only to reveal what your scripture declares to be the correct view of our resurrection. Amen.

Your Prayer

Heavenly Father, grant to me discernment and understanding of the resurrection, by the power of your Holy Spirit, as revealed in your holy and perfect word. Amen

The two great Days spoken of in the New Testament are the "Day of Salvation" and the "Day of Judgment. The framework of my thought and this book is formed by acknowledging that they are different days and separating their events.

CONTENTS

Preface ix

Introduction xv

Part 1: A Framework for Understanding the Inaugurated View . . 1

   1. The Body. 3

   2. A Matter of Days. 24

   3. Building the Kingdom's Temple 43

Part 2: Exegetical Basis for the Inaugurated View 61

   4. Old Testament Typology. 63

   5. Gospels. 82

   6. Resurrection of the Body in 1 Corinthians 15 94

   7. Resurrection of the Body in 2 Corinthians. 126

   8. Christ's Coming and Judgment Day in 1 Thessalonians . . .159

   9. The Revelation of Jesus Christ in Paul 175

   10. The Revelation of Jesus Christ in Peter. 202

Conclusion 227

PREFACE

I found out last year my heritage is 55% Scotch-Irish, confirming what I had been told when I was young, and I can see some of these genetic traits in me. My Presbyterian and Scott-Irish heritages have come home to roost, as God was sowing seeds throughout my childhood. Scotch-Irish have a reputation for being strong willed or hardheaded or clear thinkers depending on who you ask. I have found my Presbyterian heritage, but you will soon discover I have a doctrinal issue with the Westminster Confession and pretty much every Christian I know. I believe most of the Christian world has an incorrect view on the bodily resurrection.

A little of my family history first. I grew up without a strong Christian foundation. I was not raised by my parents, but had visitations with my father and my grandparents, as my father lived at their home. My grandfather was a regional superintendent for the railroad. I have many memories of being at their home with my father and them driving their Rambler to visit us. Grandmother used to take us to church as kids. Shortly before her passing, when I was 20 years old, she looked at me and asked me, "David are you going to church?" I wasn't at the time, but that moment and question were embedded in my mind. Small things sometimes have large impacts.

My father was a barber by trade, handsome, a tremendous athlete, and a marine Sergeant who served in the Pacific during WW2. He was also an alcoholic who died when I was 15. A clean shaven, well-dressed alcoholic. He was a member of the Presbyterian Church, but I am not sure it wasn't partly to satisfy his bride's family—beautiful women can be very persuasive, and he married the most beautiful girl in McLean County Illinois after returning home from the war. She was the only child of an upper middle-class family. Her name was Betty. I have a picture of him from his service in the Pacific before they were married, standing next to a plane with "Betty brown eyes" written on the side. Her family had a beautiful two-story home, and I spent a lot of time at it growing up. They got married at First Presbyterian Church in Bloomington when dad returned from the war. A short while later, pregnant with her first child, she was driving back to her mom's home to retrieve a roll of wallpaper and was killed by a drunk driver. My father never recovered. He told my sister as much. Betty was not my mother, but her mother considered us hers after Betty died, and that is how I had two grandmothers on dad's side. After her death my father married my mother. She was also an alcoholic, which is why I ended up in foster care.

My first foster mother was a Mennonite and used to take me to Sunday school. She liked to tell me "as a twig is bent so goes the tree", referring to her early influence in my life. I never asked what kind of tree I was, but I like to think it was an oak. After first grade I moved to another foster home in Dwight, Illinois. I received no spiritual guidance from my foster parents, but my siblings and I would go to the small First Baptist church. God was molding me even then.

I was saved when I was 22 years old. I had dropped out of college and returned to my childhood home devastated. My life was a mess, and I was frustrated. My hopes and dreams were not materializing, and life felt like swimming upstream against a strong current. Many of my high school friends had somehow left me behind. They were returning or moving on after finishing college. But there I stood, and no Martin Luther was I. Reading the Bible led to my conversion. One night I picked up a King James Bible in my bedroom and began reading. I instantly knew it was true. The desire to read the Bible and understand more about this God was immediately a priority for me. My views on moral issues changed instantly. I was a different person overnight. I felt clean for the first time in a long time. I obtained an unwavering conviction that I was not alone in determining my path forward. Life became very exciting. The darkness was gone. The future was bright.

There was a lot to learn, but how does one determine what is true? There are many different Christian churches. What makes them different? My thinking was, with so many differing views, why not read the scripture myself? Then I could properly determine the right course and separate the wheat from the chaff. How hard can it be I mused?" There was plenty of youthful naivety in my thinking about the time it would take to grasp the breadth of the redemption story. It was much more complex than I anticipated, yet simple at the same time. I don't generally count patience a strength—it is probably the thorn in my flesh—fortunately, at the time I was unfamiliar with Moses' time spent in Egypt and Paul's life in Judaism, how God takes his time preparing his children for service. I just "started walking" so to speak, not realizing the path was more of a marathon than a dash. God doesn't count time the way I would like, but he has a way of tempering and crafting our strengths and weaknesses for his use, producing an excellent product in time.

But the basic premise of the scripture being the standard by which all matters would be adjudicated, was not open for discussion. I was an early fan of the Reformation before I knew that the Reformation highlighted Sola Scriptura. Why can't I read the text of scripture and commentaries from those gifted to teach in order to further my education? Is not this the preferred method, where a student can shorten the time to grasp difficult concepts by not having to figure it out alone, but learn from another's time and effort? Teachers were given for this reason. I didn't have in person teachers, but I had their written thoughts.

Books have been a huge part of my Christian life and I know there are no coincidences for the elect. A few books had a major influence on my thinking. Everyone knows the enormous volume of Christian books available and looking back I can see God directing my education. I had considered going to a Bible College, then Seminary. I visited two colleges after starting a career in nuclear power but could never take that step and give up my secure job. That decision remains a mystery for me, but I also knew God had given me this job. I tried to read the most advanced books I could, a sort of "training on the cheap" program. The first book that had a huge impact was Charles Hodge's *Systematic Theology*. This was my first exposure to an Augustinian (Reformed) position on the means of salvation. I had been a Christian six years and immediately recognized this construct conformed to scripture. It made the soteriology puzzle piece fit. And an important doctrine was brought into focus. The second book was Martin Luther's *Bondage of the Will*. Luther described this book, of all the pages he wrote, as being his most important. His descriptions of unregenerate mankind as dead, blind, and enslaved spiritually, as well as his clear insight into how one's *nature* determined the will not vice versa, became immovable tenants of my doctrine. I liked his fire and command of the scripture. These books laid a critical foundational, in my understanding of Christian doctrine. I was all in. They saved me from years of reinforcing false premises.

The third book that influenced the book I am writing now, is ironically one I had set aside for quite a few years, rarely reading: John's Revelation. I had become frustrated in what I had been taught and read about Revelation. My church experience had taught Dispensationalism. It never made sense to me, and seemed more like a current form of Gnosticism, where one needed a secret knowledge to understand the code. John describes Revelation as delivering a blessing to those who read it, and I was not feeling "blessed". I needed help. I could not push the "I believe" button on dispensationalist expositions—the puzzle pieces just would not fit and I refused to smash them in. I see this as another example of providence protecting me from error.

Much later on, I discovered Martin Lloyd-Jones, and listened to one of his Friday night sermons on Revelation. I felt like God had brought the magic key and delivered it to me, for it made perfect sense. The structure of the book was unfolded, and the pieces suddenly fit. This leads me to the book which led to my writing this book. A friend, who is a former Presbyterian minister, called to ask if I knew someone who would be interested in a commentary on the Old Testament, by Keil-Delitzsch, as he was thinning his library. I had a renewed interest in the Old Testament, having read some of the works of Meredith Kline who had been professor of Old Testament at Westminster in Philadelphia, Gordon-Conwell, and Westminster Seminary in California. Karl Keil and Franz Delitzsch were two 19th century German theologians. Their commentary on the Old Testament is considered one of the most comprehensive and is still held in very high regard. I told my friend I would take the books. I went to pick them up, and suddenly realized just how comprehensive they were because I needed a couple trips to my car to load the ten thick volumes. I began reading volume nine on Daniel and Ezekiel and was immediately impressed. I finished Daniel and began Ezekiel. A particular section in Ezekiel immediately caught my attention. It was unexpected. It was a position on the bodily resurrection which is contrary to anything I had ever heard taught. By this time, I had read enough of his work to realize, that Keil was a powerful scholar, but it was such a brash statement.

> According to the distinct teaching of the Christ and the apostles, the popular opinion, that the resurrection of the <u>dead as a whole</u> will not take place till the last day of this world, <u>must be rectified</u>.[1]

The above quote is from the additional commentary on Chapters 40-48, attached at the end of his verse-by-verse exposition of Ezekiel and not included in many online commentaries. I wonder how many people have read this section or just passed by this incredible theological statement. It planted a seed in my mind to determine if Keil was correct. I believe he is, and this book is my endeavor to prove that our bodily resurrection mimics Christ's resurrection, and there is not an intermediate state for the saints in heaven, where we are bodyless. When we die, we then proceed to heaven in our new glorified body. We do not enter heaven without a body, like some disenfranchised soul.

---

[1] C.F Keil and F. Delitzsch, *Commentary on the Old Testament*, (Grand Rapids: Eerdmans, 1973), 9: 410.

INTRODUCTION

Rom. 6:5 *"For if we have been united with him in a death like his, we will certainly also be united with him in a resurrection like his. ..."*

The simple premise that upon death the saints will be transformed from our mortal bodies to our glorious bodies as we enter heaven, the location synonymous with glory because it is the residence of our glorified Lord, should not be a topic of debate, but it is because of the doctrine of the *Intermediate State*. This doctrine teaches that a believer enters heaven at death as only a soul which will be united with its glorious heavenly body at the end of time on Judgment Day. I wrote this book to prove the fallacy of this doctrine. The title, *A Resurrection like Christ's,* was chosen to show that as Christ died, rose from the dead, and ascended into heaven in body and soul to be glorified—so do his saints: our resurrection to heaven is exactly like his. We do not enter heaven as "bodyless souls".

To understand my approach to the topic of resurrection as seen in Scripture, it is crucial for the reader to understand the timeline I am working from, beginning with Christ's first advent. I advocate that, upon the death of the elect, an immediate continuing resurrection to life in heaven in our glorious bodies occurs during the gospel era, between Christ's first advent and his final coming to Judgment on the Last Day. The second major point which follows from the saints being resurrected to heaven at their death is that only the unbelievers who rejected Christ, will be resurrected to judgment on the Last Day Judgment. Those who rejected Christ were cast down to the realm of the dead at death, awaiting the final wrath of God on Judgment Day.

Here is my timeline:

1. Christ's first advent and return to heaven.
2. Believers' resurrection (body and soul) to heaven during the gospel era (Day of Salvation), which day ends upon the final believers being taken to heaven via the Glory Cloud on the Last Day of the gospel era, when Christ appears in the air.
3. Judgment Day or the Last Day arrives, initiating Christ's coming to the earth to execute final judgment on the Satanic Kingdom and the lost. The resurrection of the dead without Christ occurs.
4. Renewal of heaven and earth.

My timeline may not be yours or even familiar to you. That said, it is my hope that you will consider my approach throughout this book and test it to see whether or not you believe it to be accurate.

The Inaugurated view

I have named my view of believers' resurrection the *inaugurated view* to enable me to contrast it with the traditional view which argues for an "intermediate state". The single point of this book is that our resurrection follows the pattern of Christ's resurrection—as his full glory was restored upon entry to heaven, so too is ours. The book is divided into two parts. Working backwards, Part 2 is an exegetical look at the biblical depictions of this specific transition period, from death to heaven, and whether it teaches a transition from one body into another at physical death (inaugurated view), or teaches an immediate state, where the saint is awaiting resurrection life for the body until the Last Day or Judgment Day (traditional view). This section will detail the period of the Messiah's work from his first advent through the building of his temple in heaven, which ends upon his final coming to judgment and destruction of the kingdom of Satan. Because the inaugurated view is so different from the traditional view, it will be helpful to give a broad overview of my views on the redemption pattern for the elect and the judgment pattern for the lost before entering into the exegesis of the scripture. Part 1 will build a framework will tying these thoughts to the supporting biblical texts.

My view is that the redemption pattern for the elect is new spiritual life in Christ through regeneration, witness for Christ on earth in our mortal body, death of our mortal body and resurrection to heaven in our glorified body. Thus, for the individual elect, there is a continuing resurrection of the entire person at their death until the full number of the elect is reached, signaling the completion of the heavenly Temple. The lost remain in a state of death due to their rejection of Christ, and upon death their mortal body returns to the ground, and their souls are held in the realm of the dead until their resurrection on Judgment Day. Unlike the traditional view which holds to a common resurrection of the body for both on the Last Day or Judgment Day, I believe there are separate timeframes for the resurrection of the elect and the lost. My view acknowledges more than just a first and last advent (coming) of Christ, recognizing a continuing coming of Christ through his Spirit whereby he brings new spiritual life to his people and which, at death, results in resurrection life in heaven in a glorified body.

I believe we must differentiate *regeneration*—where we are given new life and endowed with the Holy Spirit but remain on the earth in our mortal bodies—from our *resurrection* to heaven at death and transition from our earthly body to our glorified heavenly body. Resurrection means glorification, but regeneration only results in inner glory through the Spirit, while we are on earth exiled from our glorious heavenly home. Therefore, resurrection must be understood as completed only upon the receipt of our glorious body when we are residing in heaven. This view understands the comings of Christ via his Spirit to his people as the uniting of heaven and earth in part to allow for their witness to the world, where we are the light of Christ to the dark world. The end of this Day of Salvation, or time period of the gospel, results in his final removal of any elect still on earth who are unique in that they do not experience death before they are resurrected into the glory cloud, receiving their outer glorious body. This final removal of any light of Christ on the earth results in the earth returning to a state of complete darkness. Christ returns on this Day of Darkness to judge the lost and destroy Satan's kingdom on earth, resulting in the new heavens and earth. The Messiah's redemptive work having been completed, Christ will return the purified cosmos to God the Father as recorded by Paul in 1 Cor. 15:28:

And when all things have been subjected to Him, then the Son Himself will be made subject to Him who put all things under Him, so that God may be all in all.

The Intermediate State

The intermediate state is the doctrine which instructs the church that for the believer, at death only the soul goes into heaven, and the reuniting of the soul with the body does not occur until the common resurrection of the bodies of both the elect and unbelievers at the Final Judgment on the Last Day. This creates a temporary stage, or intermediate state, where the soul and body are separated. This view is illustrated by Dr. Kim Riddlebarger:

> We often say something such as "Grandma is in heaven," hoping to comfort confused and sad little ones who are dealing with a topic that even learned theologians do not fully understand. Yet, while "Grandma is in heaven" is certainly not a wrong answer if Grandma was a believer in Jesus Christ, the answer is incomplete and may even be misleading. To put the matter in biblical perspective, if Grandma was a believer, she is now in the presence of the Lord, awaiting His return and the resurrection of her body.[2]

I agree with Riddlebarger that this is *"a topic that even learned theologians do not fully understand", however,* I believe, this 'definition" of the intermediate state shows the tragedy of this doctrine on the church. The church cannot confess "Grandma is in heaven" as it may be misleading because she is currently only a disembodied soul awaiting the uniting of her soul with her body. That is not the Gospel. The unbeliever becomes a disembodied soul when their mortal body dies (per Adam's curse), and they have not obtained resurrection life in the immortal body Christ won for his people. I believe that to ascribe this curse to the elect is to deny the gospel.

It has been over 500 years since the Reformation when the 5

---

[2] Kim Riddlebarger, "The Intermediate State," *Tabletalk*, April 2020, https://tabletalkmagazine.com/article/2020/04/the-intermediate-state/

"solas"—Sola Scriptura, Sola Gratia, Sola Fide, Solus Christus, and Soli Deo Gloria were born and embedded in Protestant teaching. They traced massive fault lines in areas of Christian theology between Protestants and Rome, forever establishing their supremacy over church edicts and Christian thought for Protestants. Protestants seem to enjoy bringing up the sins of Rome and cannot fathom how Catholic doctrine tolerates the idea of Purgatory, but I submit that Protestants have not clearly broken from Rome in the area of the resurrection of the body. The church, both Rome and Protestant, holds on to a view of resurrection as being a reuniting of soul and body on the Last Day. For example, one Reformed pastor commented in his teaching series on Romans 8, that there is very little information concerning the Intermediate State in the Bible. He is correct but perhaps cannot see that the reason is that the Bible doesn't teach it. Certainly, the ultimate result of the entire redemption plan and one of the two pillars of the gospel, the death and resurrection of Christ, is not left obscured in any fashion. If obscurity exists it is due to us. I am convinced saints receive our spiritual bodies at death. Certainly, the God who created us body and soul, brings us back to his presence body and soul, and does not allow for a separation in the interim. Perhaps the Protestant church has more reforming to perform. Protestants and Catholics teach a judgment at death where one knows their eternal destiny, but the bodily resurrection for the elect and the lost is delayed until the final judgment. It is the validity of this intermediate state, which is the focus of this book. The error of the doctrine of the common resurrection of all mankind on Judgment Day is tied to the Intermediate State as they support each other.

Initial Comments on Resurrection

Christ died, rose again, then entered into heaven. But we are taught to believe that our pattern is different, that we enter heaven as souls, separated from our bodies, to be reunited with these bodies on the Last (Judgment) Day. No one can dispute this type of resurrection is different in time from Christ's. In this model we receive our glorified or resurrection body, not upon entering heaven, but at the end of this world. It also differs in that Christ was never without a body. Doesn't it seem strange to be in heaven, with our Lord and his glorified body, yet without our glorified body? How exactly does that work? Spiritual beings without bodies seems more like a depiction of evil spirits in horror movies than Christian doctrine taught in scripture. There are those who don't care about this matter. They are content with the assurance that eventually we get bodies, so why does it matter? But truth matters, scripture matters, and correct doctrine matters. I thought it was clear in scripture that our earthly body must return to the dust, for they bear the punishment and corruption of our old natures. Therefore, I consider it contrary to scriptural statements that we must somehow get this body again in any form like the old. All things become new. We are a new creation. I will be glad to rid myself of my current body, and Paul shared the same excitement. Why would I want any part of it back, as I have been fighting it for years?

Certainly, a topic critical to everything Christianity rests upon—the death and resurrection of Christ—has been made clear. Perfectly clear. The problem, as always, is with us. The church devotes much of its gospel focus on the cross. But the gospel is both his death and resurrection, death and life, one with the other. They are tied together repeatedly, with no mention of a separation in scripture, but we are told a separation does occur when we die: a resurrection life for the soul but not for the body. Without the resurrection the cross is worthless, for resurrection is what reunites us with heaven—the place where God dwells—from our exile on earth. A redemption that only removes the penalty of death for the soul at our death but does not provide new resurrection life to the body at the point of death, removes the unity of the gospel (Christ's death and resurrection) and assigns the bodily resurrection's power to the Last Day, which is unlike Christ's resurrection. It is important to get this doctrine correct. Does the traditional view of resurrection and its declaration that we enter heaven only having obtained half of the gospel message where we have new life for the soul but not a body to house it conform to scripture?

We are to follow Christ and be like him in all things, so why would God order our resurrection to be different than Christ's? I don't think he did. Christ and the Apostles didn't leave a teaching as central as the resurrection without clear instruction, we have partially abandoned it. I think ground zero for determining this issue includes four elements. First, a doctrine contrary to Christ's example must clear a very high hurdle in in order to deviate from his pattern. Should we not be cautious when deviating from Christ's resurrection pattern? If he entered heaven in a glorified body, we should assume that so do the saints until proven otherwise. Second, scripture must have clear explicit statements that our resurrection differs in this manner. There are multiple places in scripture where this topic is discussed in detail. These passages presented perfect opportunities to state this difference in clear terms. There is not one.

Third, most interpretations of the timing of the resurrection of the saints use texts containing the final judgment or the Last Day. The Last Day is also known by many other descriptions: second death, the resurrection of the dead, and Judgment Day. Those assigning this Last Day to the resurrection of the saints are mistaken. They fail to take into account that this is the day for the final conquest and elimination of the rebels—that is the design and primary theme of Judgment Day. Although Judgment Day has significance for the saints, it is not a day for their judgment, but their vindication. It is the last day of the Kingdom of Satan (this is covered in more detail later).

Fourth, one must reconcile how Christ's redemptive work is truly complete now when the traditional view states that there is more work for him to do on the Last Day, after we arrive in heaven at death. Are there more commands that he must give on the Last Day in order to bring us to perfection in the place of perfection, heaven, where we already had been dwelling since our death? Paul uses present tense descriptions to describe our current condition: "in heaven", "in Christ", "a new creation", a "part of his body". When Paul describes our resurrection to heaven, he calls it a release, a removal of our earthly body, and a transition to our final spiritual condition. Our inner glory via the new creation is no longer hidden or veiled by our fallen mortal body (cf. Rom. 7:22-23, 2 Cor. 4:16-17, Eph. 3:16, 1 Tim 3:16-17. Paul compares our inner man with our outer man and asks in Rom. 7:24 (NIV),

> Who will rescue me from this body that is subject to death?

The answer is: Christ will at our death when he gives us our new spiritual body, through the power of the indwelling of the Spirit of Christ. This is the redemption of our body. Rom. 8:11 says,

If the Spirit of him who raised Jesus from the dead dwells in you, he who raised Christ Jesus from the dead will also give life to your mortal bodies through his Spirit who dwells in you.

The death of our mortal body is the final deliverance from sin, but also the final transition to the glorified state, thru the firstfruits of the present indwelling of the Holy Spirit (cf. Rom. 8:23). We already have the glory of the Spirit thru our indwelling with the Holy Spirit. The point is when physical death occurs, this body of death is removed, and resurrection being a transition to the heavenly realm, we are transported to heaven in our glorious resurrection body. The humiliation of Christ entailed his putting off his outer glorious state during his time in the flesh on the earth. And upon his death and resurrection, he was transported to heaven by the Glory Cloud to return him to his previous glorious state. (cf. Acts 1:8-9).

The idea of incompleteness or imperfection is antithetical with heaven. The church separates body and soul at death. This is a Greek construct rather than biblical one. In the beginning, Gen. 2:7:

the Lord God formed the man of dust from the ground and breathed into his nostrils the breath of life, and the man became a living creature.

As mankind's original construct was a unified body and soul animated with the life of God, so does his redemptive work retain and return mankind to its original state. As with the mysterious union of man and woman in marriage, so is our union of body and soul with Christ and let not man separate them. The church has separated the Holy Spirit's work and Christ the Lord of all creation's work, in this respect When it teaches the Spirit endowed man needs Christ in heaven to *complete* his redemption by conducting the resurrection of his body on the Last Day. The Holy Spirit does not need further permission to finish his work of building the temple and presenting us complete (soul and body) in heaven. The Holy Spirit is the Spirit of Jesus. We are part of his temple or body now—it is a present reality, only to be brought into the open at death when our inner glorious reality is revealed by our freedom from the pull of our earthly flesh and the removal of its veil. Christ's body was the veil to the Holy of Holies, and although we have access to the heavenly throne now while on earth via his Spirit and are a part of his heavenly kingdom, the death of our mortal body results in our permanent placement in heaven. When the veil representing Christ's fleshly body was torn and removed from the entrance to the Holy of Holies or God's presence, this removal of the body also represented the removal of our mortal body to gain entrance to heaven. This is the same path Christ took upon his death, and then was gloriously transported to his heavenly throne.

Verse three of the 1540 Dutch hymn, "In God, My Faithful God," beautifully expresses this timeless theology:

> *If death my portion be,*
> *It brings great gain to me;*
> *It speeds my life's endeavor*
> *To live with Christ forever.*
> *He gives me joy in sorrow,*
> *Come death now or tomorrow.* [3]

Here is a common doctrinal statement on the resurrection taken from a Christian University.

"We believe in the resurrection of both the saved and the lost; those who are saved to the resurrection of life and those who are lost to the resurrection of damnation."

This statement states two different resurrections and does not identify them as occurring at the same time, on the Last Day. I agree. This view comports with the NT teachings of those who are alive on earth on the Last Day being transformed and resurrected, thus initiating the Last Day judgment. The biblical descriptions of the saint's existence while on earth are in a tent, vessel of clay, home, tabernacle, and body of flesh among others, all representing temporary statuses of the outer housing for the earthly resident. This book will make the case for a further clothing of the saint in glorious robes at death, which is our resurrection body.

PART 1

A FRAMEWORK FOR UNDERSTANDING
THE INAUGURATED VIEW

Because the Inaugurated view differs substantially from the traditional view of the resurrection of the body, it is first necessary to build a broad framework for understanding it. Part 1 explains some foundational topics including the body, Last Days vs. Last Day, the Temple and the comings of Christ. This overview will aid the reader when we deal with the central texts supporting the inaugurated view in Part 2.

CHAPTER 1

THE BODY

The Unity of the Body and Soul

I believe the doctrine of the intermediate state has more in common with gnostic thought than Christian thought as Gnosticism viewed the body and the soul/spirit as consisting of two parts, where the body is evil, and the spirit/soul is good. Because the material part was contrasted with the spiritual, for the Gnostics, separation of the body or material part of man from the spiritual was viewed positively. The Bible, however, does not view mankind as two parts to be separated. Man's original and final state of body/soul unity is maintained, though I acknowledge a change in the body type for its eternal home. The unity of soul and body continues even after the soul/spirit or inner man has been regenerated by God, and the body or outer man retains the corruption of Adam's sin. In intermediate state teaching this unity is not maintained, for it separates soul and body at death until the eschaton. I think this inconsistency is not given the proper regard it deserves, and, as mentioned in the Introduction, has been carried over from Catholic theology.

Defining the type of body a saint has in heaven must be dealt with before delving into the texts concerning the timing of the receipt of the body. I learned this area is fraught with danger when I was rejected as an elder at my home Presbyterian Church of America (PCA) due to my view of the resurrected body. Because I could not conform to the view that the same body that is in the grave upon death is resurrected, nor with the timing of the resurrection, my application was denied. I discovered my view did not conform to their view of the Westminster Confession. We differed on whether or not a flesh and blood body is resurrected, or more specifically the same body that was put in the grave, as I upheld Paul's statement that flesh and blood shall not inherit the kingdom (1 Cor. 15:50, cf. Jesus' statement in Matt. 22:30), whereas the pastor of my Church viewed that it was the same body placed in the grave that is resurrected, and stated, "If you are saying the resurrection body is NOT the same body that was buried, then you are actually denying the resurrection. An entirely different body is not a resurrected body".

In its article on the body, *The New International Dictionary of New Testament Theology* gives an excellent defense of the unity of the body and soul, that man is only represented with a soul and body in scripture.

> Pauls' understanding of soma as "I", as a "person", as distinct from the sarx (flesh) is illustrated by Rom. 7:14 ff. "I am carnal (sarkinos), sold under sin" (v.14). The body is open to the two possibilities of desire and obedience. In this sense there is no difference between "body of sin" (Rom. 6:6) and "sinful flesh" (Rom. 8:3). When Paul cries: "Who shall deliver me from this body of death? (Rom. 7:24), he is thinking of the shattered character of human existence as it finds expression in the body. He sees in his existence the powers of sin, the flesh and spirit which can mean either destruction or life. Man's bodily existence does not in itself desire something good or bad. Rather the body is the concrete sphere of existence in which man's relationship with God is realized. In this light, it is understandable why Paul in 1 Cor. 15 stresses the resurrection of the body as against his Corinthian opponents. Paul's understanding of resurrection is influenced by Jewish anthropology. Man's life is thinkable only in a body. Thus, any division of man into soul and body along the lines of Gk. anthropology is precluded (cf. 2 Cor. 5:1-10). In this discourse on resurrection Paul sets

in opposition an earthly or "physical body" (v.44) and a "spiritual body". These are the two possibilities before man. The former represent his earthly existence and the latter his post-resurrection life.[3]

Likewise, the article on resurrection from the same resource defends the unified or whole person view, making the intermediate state untenable if true.

In the distinctive New Testament usage, resurrection signifies not the animation of corpses but the transformation of the whole person into the image of Christ by the power of the indwelling Spirit, in spite of the intervention of death. . .. The NT does not actually refer to "the resurrection of the body" or "the resurrection of the flesh" but only to "the resurrection of the dead" **or** "resurrection from the dead". The subjects of resurrection are whole persons, *who are transformed outwardly and inwardly in what may be called an acceleration of the process of Christification* (see Rom. 8:29; 1 Cor. 15:49; 2 Cor. 3:18; Col. 3:18; Col. 3:10). (Emphasis mine).[4]

I now refer back to C. F. Keil, who links the new body of saints with the description of "robes," making his case for the bodily resurrection at death.

that white robes were given to the souls...... as the putting on of the white robe involves or presupposes the clothing of the soul with the new body[5]

---

[3] S. Wibbing. "Body." In The New International Dictionary of New Testament Theology, vol. 1 edited by C. Brown, page 236. Grand Rapids: Zondervan, 1986.

[4] C. Brown. "Resurrection." In The New International Dictionary of New Testament Theology, vol. 3 edited by C. Brown, page 302-303. Grand Rapids: Zondervan, 1986.

[5] C.F Keil and F. Delitzsch, *Commentary on the Old Testament*, (Grand Rapids: Eerdmans, 1973), 9: 411.

Adam's Change at the Fall

There are differing views on Adam's original nature before the fall. My position is that Adam was originally part of the invisible heavenly realm and endowed with glory, body and soul, and lost his glory upon his sin.

In Genesis God created the heavens and the earth, two separate and different arenas which are the visible and invisible realms. The Old Testament Tabernacle provides the model for the cosmos[6], but in a horizontal rather than a vertical alignment, in that the outer court represented the earth, the Holy Place heaven, and the Holy of Holies representing the throne or presence of God and its angelic host. Think in terms of a vertical chamber extending from the earth up through the heavens and into the throne room of God. The heavenly and earthly were united and can be seen in Jacob's dream of the ladder extending from heaven to earth in Gen. 28:12-13:

> And Jacob had a dream about a ladder that rested on the earth with its top reaching up to heaven, and God's angels were going up and down the ladder. And there at the top the LORD was standing and saying, "I am the LORD, the God of your father Abraham and the God of Isaac. I will give you and your descendants the land on which you now lie.

Eden, although on earth, was a Temple where God could visit, making it essentially the earthly footstool of the heavenly Temple complex of God, who resides above the cherubim in the Glory Cloud in the Holy of Holies[7]. Eden and thus original Adam were a part of this invisible heavenly realm.

---

[6] For more on the idea of the tabernacle as model for the cosmos see Gregory K. Beale, "Eden, the Temple, and the Church's Mission in the New Creation" Journal of the. Evangelical Theological Society 48, no. 1 (March 2005): 5-31. https://www.etsjets.org/files/JETS-PDFs/48/48-1/48-1-pp005-031_JETS.pdf

[7] Meredith Kline states: "God's theophanic glory is the glory of royal majesty. At the center of the heavens within the veil of the Glory-cloud is found a throne; the Glory is preeminently the place of God's enthronement. It is, therefore, a royal palace, site of the divine council and court of judgment." Meredith G. Kline, "Creation in the Image of the Glory-Spirit" Westminster Theological Journal 39 no.2 (1976/77): 250-272. https://meredithkline.com/klines-works/articles-and-essays/creation-in-the-image-of-the-glory-spirit/

This aligns with both the final nature and destination in heaven of the new mankind Christ, Paul, and the NT describe. Adam was the original Priest-King who was to rule, protect, and expand the kingdom on earth, but his failure made it necessary for Christ to complete the mandate. Adam was to conquer and gain dominion over the entire earth and populate it with sons and daughters made in his righteous and glorious nature which was made in the image of God. We see this original mandate given to Adam fulfilled in Christ as he returns mankind to the original glorious image in heaven throughout the church age, as the elect are taken to heaven.

The fall of Adam resulted in the entire earth becoming a kingdom ruled by Satan, now the god of this world. although not explicitly stated in Genesis, Christ's first advent and subsequent establishing of the kingdom via his Spirit in regenerating his people into his image, finally and ultimately reuniting the heavenly and earthly realms at the eschaton when the heavenly Jerusalem descends back to earth reverses this. The heavenly Temple originally established in Eden will be extended to all the earth, completing both the renewal of the Sons of God, and the cosmos, by the second Adam.

All of this has implications for the body. In 1 Cor. 15:40 Paul makes it clear that there are two types of bodies:

> There are heavenly bodies and earthly bodies, but the glory of the heavenly is of one kind, and the glory of the earthly is of another.

Therefore, the place of residence determines the type of body. An earthly body will not reside in heaven, as both Paul and Christ as recorded in John make clear:

> I tell you this, brothers: flesh and blood cannot inherit the kingdom of God, nor does the perishable inherit the imperishable. (1 Cor. 15:450).

> That which is born of the flesh is flesh, and that which is born of the Spirit is spirit. (Jn. 3:6).

Secondarily, God is a Spirit being and his throne room above the earth in heaven is a spiritual place—part of the invisible realm where creatures, whether angelic or human, bear God's spiritual and invisible nature. Before the fall Adam, while still in Eden, did not have the visible flesh and blood body present in mankind after the fall. The curse resulted in the covering of flesh (skins) given to the pair upon their expulsion from the heavenly realm to the earthly realm in order to fit them for earthly existence. I believe this was the basis for Paul's identification of the two body types, earthly and heavenly, in 1 Cor. 15:40 quoted above. It should not be surprising to us that Eden, while on earth, was part of the heavenly realm as both footstool of God's heavenly temple, where he resides above the earth in his throne room, and a temple on earth. As we have seen, God established a spiritual presence on earth at Mt. Sinai, in the Tabernacle, in the Old Testament Temple, in Christ in his advent, in his people as the temple of God while we are still on earth, and ultimately upon his return on Judgment Day to renew all things. Therefore, the idea of pre-fall Adam in Eden as a spirit being, then recreated anew through Christ's redemption by death in the flesh on the cross and returning mankind to our original state via resurrection at death shows the complete path of the redemption of the sons of Adam into the image of Christ.

Ezekiel 28:12-17 is one of the most misinterpreted sections of the entire Old Testament. It states:

> You were the signet of perfection, full of wisdom and perfect in beauty. You were in Eden, the garden of God; every precious stone was your covering, sardius, topaz, and diamond, beryl, onyx, and jasper, sapphire, emerald, and carbuncle; and crafted in gold were your settings and your engravings. On the day that you were created they were prepared. You were an anointed guardian cherub. I placed you; you were on the holy mountain of God; in the midst of the stones of fire you walked. You were blameless in your ways from the day you were created, till unrighteousness was found in you. In the abundance of your trade you were filled with violence in your midst, and you sinned; so I cast you as a profane thing from

the mountain of God, and I destroyed you, O guardian cherub, from the midst of the stones of fire. Your heart was proud because of your beauty; you corrupted your wisdom for the sake of your splendor. I cast you to the ground.

Most commentators identify the person being described in Eden as Satan, but in fact, this lament over the King of Tyre points back to pre-fall Adam. The Genesis 3 narrative of the fall has two characters: Adam and the serpent. If one were to ask any junior high student with even a rudimentary knowledge of the story which character in the garden was perfect, they would rightly name Adam. Somehow biblical commentators miss the obvious point that Adam was the perfect being in the garden until the fall— Satan never held this distinction in the garden. The description of the covering of precious stones depicts the wardrobe of the High Priest in the OT (cf. Ex. 28, 39), a position Adam held as well. Further, the description of the individual as "an anointed guardian cherub" makes it beyond dispute the reference is to Adam in his role as spirit endowed member of the heavenly council with the mandate to guard and protect the holy place from the serpent's intrusion. This picture of original Adam anointed with the Spirit and residing in an earthly Temple of God, should be familiar to us, and not appear to be a fanciful interpretation of original Adam. For Christ's redemptive work returns the fallen progeny of Adam to endowment with the Spirit residing on a recreated earth, after Christ finishes his mandate to restore what was lost at the fall.

The change to Adam at the fall resulted in the current body of mankind, which should be beyond dispute. We know the result of Christ's work will restore us in heaven in a body of a different type. I believe this body will match Adam's original state. This return to glory and the time which it occurs, is the main thesis of this book. Understanding Ezek. 28:17, quoted above, as describing the transition of Adam from a spiritual body to an earthly body through his casting to the ground, (which was a judgment), matches the original description of Adam's judgment in Gen. 3:17-19:

And to Adam he said, "Because you have listened to the voice of your wife and have eaten of the tree of which I commanded you, 'You shall not eat of it,' cursed is the ground because of you; in pain you shall eat of it all the days of your life; thorns and thistles it shall bring forth for you; and you shall eat the plants of the field. By the sweat of your face you shall eat bread, till you return to the ground, for out of it you were taken; for you are dust, and to dust you shall return.

Adam's fall resulted in God's judgment and Adam being cast out of heaven to the earth, thus the transition point to an earthly body, which would then return to the ground at death. Judgment is a downward movement and salvation (resurrection) a raising up. This judgment and casting to the earth is depicted by the guardian angels with flaming swords standing at the entrance to Eden, thus their path back to heaven was blocked. God declared that death was the penalty, and his body would return to the ground from which he was made.

Adam's glory was original and not something to be received upon his completion of a probationary period. Christ returns us to the original glorious state. An interesting statement is made in Genesis after the fall but prior to the expulsion of Adam and Eve from the garden. First they recognized that they were naked after their sin, so they made fig leaves to cover themselves. Then in Genesis 3:21 God made garments of skins to cover them. I believe this use of a covering (tunic or garment) of skins (flesh) is carried from this point throughout the bible to depict our earthly nature or covering which was given to us by God after our sin. The foremost example of the need to rid ourselves of, rather than remake, our mortal body can be seen in the rite of circumcision in the OT. Here this same skin covering with which God adorned Adam with after his sin is partially cut away. Representing in typical form the inability of Old Testament types and covenants to rid mankind fully from their sin nature, as only a portion of the outer skin is cut away. The New Testament, the sign of baptism, depicting Christ's crucifixion— his entire body—on the cross, reminds us that he fulfilled the promise of complete redemption from Gen. 3:15. Paul uses this same metaphor to explain the same idea, that of a new body upon the death and removal of the old body (cf. Rom. 7:4, 2 Cor. 5:1-5).

On this reading, it appears that the righteous covering God endowed Adam with at creation, has been replaced by a fleshly covering in order to separate us from God and transfer our ownership and nature from a heavenly spiritual one, to an earthly, satanic, or fleshly one. There were two deaths which occurred to the original Adam, a spiritual death to the inner man immediately and physical death to the outer man later upon death to his body. I intend to show that there are also two deaths which occur to bring us to a new resurrected spiritual life in heaven. At regeneration the old inner man is killed and recreated anew through the circumcision of Christ by the Spirit, followed by the death to our outer mortal body, and its recreation into our spiritual body. Paul states:

A man is not a Jew because he is one outwardly, nor is circumcision only outward and physical. No, a man is a Jew because he is one inwardly, and circumcision is a matter of the heart, by the Spirit (Rom. 2:28).

> In him also you were circumcised with a circumcision
> made without hands, by putting off the body of the flesh,
> by the circumcision of Christ, having been buried with
> him in baptism, in which you were also raised with him
> through faith in the powerful working of God, who raised
> him from the dead (Col. 2:11-12.

I propose that the covering Adam and Eve lost was their glorious spiritual body We shall see the links between coverings, robes, homes, and the body later in this discussion. I believe the difference between our earthly and spiritual bodies might be better pictured as being either opaque or translucent respectively, corresponding to their ability to receive or transmit God's glory. The transfiguration of Christ gives insight into the correlation between the earthly body and its ability to veil the outpouring of inner glory. Christ gives the 3 disciples a brief look into the inner glory which was veiled by his human body. And the veil blocking the entrance to the Holy of Holies or throne of God is described as the body of Christ in the New Testament (cf. Mt. 27:51 and Heb. 10:19-20). I believe this symbolizes that our earthly body of sin is the barrier preventing fallen mankind from entering the presence of God. Additionally, upon Christ's death, the veil was torn down and removed but not taken into the Holy of Holies. Both of these points indicate that a new covering or body is required.

Earlier I related how, in the Genesis account of the creation and fall, f man is made of two parts: the dust of the earth, and then God gives him life by breathing in the "breath of life". After the fall God made a covering for the fallen pair indicating that, although they had lost God's covering due to their sin, God saw fit to provide another temporary covering. Ultimately, God, in Christ, would provide a permanent body through which he would redeem mankind. The point of this recap is to highlight that at creation, after the fall, and upon redemption, redeemed mankind was always provided a covering or body in which to dwell. Second, this demonstrates that being without a body or naked is contrary to the creation order and thus abnormal. Third when this separation of body and soul occurs, it is not a part of the redemption plan of God for mankind, but instead a part of the judgment of God. God's judgment removed Adam's glorious covering, however, God did not allow Adam to be "naked" without a body, but immediately proved another. I believe God's provision of new garments of skin for the fallen pair in Gen. 3:21, is really the proto-evangel because it typifies the work of Christ who will provide the ultimate covering, by his death in the flesh and resurrection by the Spirit.

Scripture does provide evidence that this separation of body and soul is not a part of God's original created order. Adam and Eve's recognition of their nakedness after their sin indicates a judgment had already occurred. A second example is seen in the fate of the lost upon death this too is a judgment as scripture teaches after death comes judgment (cf. Heb. 9:27). It is clear upon death that their souls are held in captivity, in my view in the bowels of the earth or more figuratively the depths of the sea. Their bodies return to the grave where the separation is continued until the Final Judgment of the lost and their resurrection on the Last Day. The point I am making is that such a separation for the elect is contrary to the written declaration of scripture Therefore this separation does not apply to the eschatological theology for the saints, as the intermediate state teaches. Fourth, as with the union of a man and woman in marriage where the two become one flesh, and man is not to tear this union apart, so too our own body and soul union. Fifth, in this world we are already part of the Body of Christ and therefore have union with Christ, even before we enter heaven.

Add to this the promises of Christ to never leave nor forsake, and to lead us through the valley of the shadow of death, certainly leaves no sound justification for the separation at death. For certainly if we are united with his body now, this shall not end at death but continue in heaven, for the promise to Christ that God would not abandon his holy one to the grave becomes our promise as well at death.

> Behold, I am coming like a thief! Blessed is the one who stays awake, keeping his garments on, that he may not go about naked and be seen exposed! (Rev. 16:15)

Paul will carry on the descriptions of coverings, robes, and filthy rags as a description of fallen man's body which contains the curse of Adams' sin and wherein lies the seat of rebellion of the saint's carnal or fleshly nature. Paul will contrast the old body with the new spiritual body, and the carnal or fleshly nature with the new spiritual nature made in the image of God. The natures of fleshly and spiritual are in conflict, so that resurrection is not that of a remaking from a part of the sinful original. This body of death will return to the earth, and the saint will put on the new body equipped for heaven and the home Christ has gone before us to prepare. The scripture is full of metaphors which depict the mysterious nature of our transitioning from our earthly body to our heavenly body. These include descriptions of glory, skins, robes, tents, garments, and others. These different metaphors all describe an outer housing in which our soul dwells and further depict the process of changing from unrighteousness to righteousness, earthly to heavenly, or mortal to glorified as removing one covering and replacing it with another.

Body of Flesh-Circumcision-Transfiguration

The Apostle Paul and Christ both make it clear that "flesh and blood", or the earthly body, will not enter heaven, but must be changed into a spiritual body. Although this seems clear in scripture, the issue is resisted— my Pastor and elder both hold to the conviction that it is the same body placed in the grave that is raised. My Pastor went so far as to say that he would be in heaven <u>and</u> in the grave until the second coming when he believes the body is raised and his soul is united with his body. It is a fine point, but my contention is that the heavenly body *is* the body of the soul of the person, but not the same type of body. It is a creation into a new spiritual body and not a remaking of the past mortal body into a suitable condition for heaven. The bodies are in conflict or opposition to each other.

The word "flesh" is used in the New Testament to describe various aspects of man's constitution. It can mean the human body, the whole man, mankind, man's existence apart from God as in his fallen nature, as a contrast between this world and the heavenly world, or between the flesh and the Spirit. Flesh can also be used to identify and differentiate one of the two parts of mankind on earth, the outer covering or the fallen nature. This contrast between these two natures is the focus here. Paul describes this specific contrast between our inner and outer natures or inner and outer man.

> Though our outer self is wasting away, our inner self is being renewed day by day. (2 Cor. 4:16)

> For in my inner being I delight in God's law. But I see another law at work in my body, warring against the law of my mind and holding me captive to the law of sin that dwells within me. (Rom. 8:22-23)

Paul uses the same inner/outer picture to describe the works of the flesh and works of the Spirit as opposing one another.

> For the desires of the flesh are against the Spirit, and the desires of the Spirit are against the flesh, for these are opposed to each other... (Gal. 5:17)

This imagery of outer fleshly and inner spiritual (soul) natures and is connected to the transfer of the saint from an earthly body to a heavenly body at physical death. Other scriptures give additional clarity that the inner man has been created anew, as we are a new creation when the inner man was put to death, and though the outer fleshly man was put to death through Christ's circumcision or death on the cross, our final deliverance will occur at death when our body of sin is laid in the grave. In Gen. 3:17-19 God tells Adam the ground is cursed because of him and that he would return to the ground. Here too we see the idea of the fallen mortal body returning to the ground, thus not rising at death to new life. In fact, God stated this was a curse to the earth as the evil source of mankind's sin was placed in the ground, further separating the redemption of the individual from his or her time of the earth. 1 Thess. 4 shows that the last elect is removed from the earth and united with all those prior resurrected saints before the coming of the Lord of Creation to judgment on the lost and the then recreation of the heaven and earth in 1Thess. 5.

> The point is that the children of the Spirit through Abraham and Sarah—first with Isaac, then the Israelite nation, and ultimately in the single seed of Christ—were all generated from the promise of God via a post-circumcision spiritual generation and not of the fleshly body typified by the foreskin skin prior to circumcision. In fact the curse residing in the mortal body as described in Genesis 3 must be removed from the earth as well in the last act at the eschaton. The sequence of the regeneration of the cosmos is: first the regeneration of the elect who are removed from the earth in resurrections at death culminating in the 1 Thess. 4 rapture of those final believers on earth prior to Judgement Day, followed by the 1 Thess. 5 Day of the Lord with the resurrection to judgment of the evil fallen angels and the lost, and finally culminating in the regeneration of the heaven and earth. there is not a common resurrection day for the elect and the lost. I know that nothing good lives in me, that is, in my flesh... For in my inner being I delight in God's law... What a wretched man I am! Who will rescue me from this body of death? (Rom. 7:18, 22, 24)

Peter describes this process in 1 Pet. 3: 18 in terms of the flesh vs. spirit:

> For Christ also suffered once for sins, the righteous for the
> unrighteous, that he might bring us to God, being put to
> death in the flesh but made alive in the spirit.

This shows how Christ's death and resurrection relate to our redemption. We are made alive by the Spirit at regeneration in the inner man, and our outer man has been crucified with Christ where it no longer has power over our lives, (having been put to death spiritually), and awaits its physical death, the second judgment. Paul ties Christ's resurrection to bringing new spiritual life to our outer body. Paul also ties the Old Testament sign of circumcision in which there was only a partial removal of the outer flesh via the removal of flesh from the reproductive organ of the male to the New Testament sign of baptism in which not just a partial circumcision of the body occurs, but the entire body of flesh is cut off.

> In him also you were circumcised with a circumcision
> made without hands, by putting off the body of the flesh,
> by the circumcision of Christ, having been buried with
> him in baptism, in which you were also raised with him
> through faith in the powerful working of God, who raised
> him from the dead. Col. 2:11-12

The initiation of the sign of circumcision via Abram was not given when God called Abram at age 75 in Genesis 12, nor when God made a covenant with Abram in Genesis 15, as chapter 16 records the birth of Ishmael at age 86 through Hagar prior to Abram's circumcision. Chapter 17 records God's appearance to Abram when both Abram and Sarai were past the age of childbearing and their bodies were dead to the ability to create new life. It is only then, after their bodies were dead to generating new life, that the sign of circumcision is initiated and the promise Abram would be the father of many nations is given. This inability of Abraham's and Sarah's bodies to create new life via the promise is typological for the inability of new spiritual life to be created using the mortal body. This is another marker showing that the new spiritual body of man does not arise from the material or nature of the old body. Rather it arises from the essence of the Spirit as only the Spirit gives new life, just as Christ explained to Nicodemus in John 3.

When God promises that the child of the promise, Isaac, would be born within a year, He also changes Abram and Sarai's names to Abraham and Sarah, the name change signified their new covenant relationship as children of the promise of God. This marks the beginning of the nation of Israel, through which Christ, the promised seed, would arise. After God commands Abraham to keep the covenant, he is recorded as initiating the right of circumcision *"that very same day"* to his entire household, including Ishmael (Gen. 17). The children of the Promise thru Abraham could only be generated after the circumcision of Abraham was completed. As the promise ultimately pointed to Christ, his circumcision by physical death on the cross resulted in progeny who are "sons of God", made in his image. Circumcision then is a typological picture of the old nature having been removed from the reproductive organ via the outer skin, representing the birth of those who would be born of the Spirit, as confirmed in the New Testament.

This brief summary shows that the sign of circumcision with the partial or incomplete cutting away of the outer flesh points to the circumcision of the entire body of Christ. In the New Testament it is signified by baptism which portrays more than the new inner life through regeneration and receipt of the spirit, even though this is the dominant feature taught. Most importantly baptism corresponds with circumcision not primarily as a sign of an inner spiritual transformation which is the dominant feature taught, but also as a sign of the outer body of flesh being removed when it dies and is laid in the ground resulting in immediate resurrection life in the Spirit. Both circumcision and baptism relate to the outer body of flesh which Paul told us in Colossians is the putting off of the body of flesh via the circumcision of Christ (see above). This points to the literal putting off of the outer body of flesh at death, completing the inner spiritual resurrection begun at regeneration. Thus resurrection life occurs at death and not on the Last Day.

When Nicodemus comes at night to speak to Christ in John 3, Jesus tells the Pharisee that he must be born again or of the "spirit" in order to enter the Kingdom because that which is born of "flesh" is flesh, and that which is born of the "Spirit" is spirit. He then proceeds to reference the wind (Spirit) blowing and not knowing where it comes from or where it goes. Jesus is telling him heavenly things which Nicodemus cannot understand without the Spirit, because he has an <u>earthly</u> constitution of body and soul. Christ explains Nicodemus needs to be recreated by the Spirit in order to enter the new Kingdom. This recreation requires a different source, one not of the earth or this present world, but of the Spirit whom Christ would send at Pentecost.

This same concept of regeneration by the Spirit which Christ spoke to Nicodemus about in John 3, is used in two additional places in the New Testament using the transliterated word "paliggenesia"[8], which contains the root words "again" and "genesis". The idea is a second genesis event of creation It is not a changing or transformation of something, but a creating of a new type. The two texts where "paliggenesia" are used are Matt. 19:28 where Christ is speaking of the <u>new world</u> or age <u>in heaven,</u> and in Titus 3:5 where Paul is speaking of the new birth on earth, described as the washing of <u>regeneration</u> and <u>renewal </u>of the Holy Spirit. Both uses tie this new creation to the renewal at the new birth when one receives the Spirit and the soul is made new, and the time when one enters the new kingdom or age in heaven, which occurs at death. In Scripture numbers often have specific meanings (e.g., 3, 7, 40, etc.)., E.W. Bullinger explains that the number two represents either another of a different kind or another of the same kind[9]. We see these two texts are tied together by the purposeful use of paliggenesia which occurs only twice in the NT. This leads to the conclusion that it is intended to reinforce the idea of another genesis of the same kind as the original genesis event via the Spirit, not a regeneration through the flesh. When we take into account the previous arguments on the differences between flesh and spirit, especially in the words of Jesus to Nicodemus, it seems clear that this renewal or regeneration by the Spirit is a new kind of creation altogether.

A second transliterated word used for the same purpose and coincidentally only used twice as well, is "anagennaó"[10] which means to beget again or to be born from on high. Both are from 1 Peter chapter

---

[8] Strong's Concordance. 3824. παλιγγενεσία (paliggenesia) -- regeneration, renewal. biblehub.com. Accessed 9/25/2022.

[9] E.W. Bullinger, *Number in Scripture.* (New York: Cosimo House, 2005), 92-93.

[10] Strong's Concordance: 313. ἀναγεννάω (anagennaó) -- to beget again. biblehub.com. Accessed 9/25/2022.

1. The first is in verse 3 and the second in verse 23. I have added several verses to chow the context below:

> ³ Blessed be the God and Father of our Lord Jesus Christ! According to his great mercy, he has caused us to be *born again* to a living hope through the resurrection of Jesus Christ from the dead, ⁴ to an inheritance that is imperishable, undefiled, and unfading, kept in heaven for you, ⁵ who by God's power are being guarded through faith for a salvation ready to be revealed in the last time.
>
> ....
>
> ²² Having purified your souls by your obedience to the truth for a sincere brotherly love, love one another earnestly from a pure heart, ²³ since you have been *born again*, not of perishable seed but of imperishable, through the living and abiding word of God; ²⁴ for
>
> "All flesh is like grass
>   and all its glory like the flower of grass.
> The grass withers,
>   and the flower falls,
> ²⁵ but the word of the Lord remains forever."
> And this word is the good news that was preached to you.
> (1 Pet.1:3-5, 22-25, emphasis mine).

The first reference (v.3) refers to the future inheritance in heaven awaiting us at death through the resurrection of Christ, and the second (v. 23) refers to regeneration by the Spirit in which we are impregnated with the imperishable seed of God that guarantees our receipt of that future inheritance won by Christ's resurrection. There seems to be a parallel between Christ's death purchasing new life on earth via regeneration and his resurrection guaranteeing future life by resurrection from earth to the heavenly kingdom.

Earlier I mentioned the transfiguration as an example of the eschatological change which occurs in the nature of the elect at resurrection. When the words used for regeneration and the new birth are brought alongside the word used to describe the transfiguration of Christ, we gain additional understanding of the process of recreating the old man into the new man. Paul speaks of the seed of the Spirit implanted in mankind at regeneration, as being the initial cause and also the eventual mechanism for the final redemption of the saint on earth into his spiritual body as we transition into heaven. The idea is one of another genesis creation event birthing the new mankind. I believe this implanted "seed" is the basis for the transformation. In 1 Cor. 15 Paul uses this metaphor to describe the two different seeds. When the old seed of man's fallen body is placed into the ground, it results in the new seed of the Spirit planted inside the believer at regeneration, transforming the saint into the new body.

We know that God not only uses his written word for revelation, but also uses his creation to portray his work. The transfiguration adds the idea of metamorphosis like a butterfly emerging from a caterpillar. Interestingly, this example also shows a transition to an exalted status with the ability of flight from the prior limitation of the caterpillar to the ground. I believe this typifies the new creation saint transforming into a heavenly body, as well as the transition into the heavenly upper realm from an earthly body and existence. The word used for the transfiguration of Christ, "metamorphoó"[11] meaning to transform or transfigure, is the same root word used for the metamorphosis process in nature. It is used in Matt. 17:2 and Mk. 9:2 describing Christ's transformation, in Rom. 12:2 for the renewing of the saint's mind, and in 2 Cor. 3:18 for our transformation into Christ's image of glory.[12]

---

[11] Strong's Concordance: 3339. μεταμορφόω (metamorphoó) -- to transform. biblehub.com. Accessed 9/25/2022.

[12] Interestingly, the word is used two times for Christ's transformation and then twice again for the believer's transformation: first of the renewing the believer's mind such as what happens at regeneration via the new birth, and again in the same context of the believer's further transformation into the image of Christ's glory, which occurs when we are changed into our glorious body. So, we have three words related to regeneration, each of which have only two instances of their use in the scriptures. I believe. the use of numbers and the number of times words are used can lead to further insight as the various uses are reconciled, giving a broader meaning than their singular uses. In this case the repeated pattern of 2 uses signifies their connection.

1 Peter, quoted above, begins with Peter addressing the letter to the dispersed exiles, or heirs to the Promised Land (heaven), living outside the land awaiting the goal of their faith, which is to be with Christ in heaven. He proceeds from the beginning of this hope to its fulfillment by telling them they were born again into a living hope through Christs' resurrection, they have received life from above and now live with faith and hope awaiting the completion of their salvation. For when we are united with Christ in heaven, faith and hope will no longer be needed as the exile has ended and we will have entered the land. Peter says that the current trials will be brought to an end at the revelation of Jesus Christ for although they have not seen him with their earthly eyes, they love him and are filled with an inexpressible glory. Unfortunately, this revelation of Jesus Christ is commonly relegated to the last day or final coming, instead of the moment we see him face to face in heaven which all agree is at death. Peter uses the phrase "manifested in the last times" (v.20), which is plural, clearly indicating the entire interadvent period as the times of the revealing of Christ. Secondly, he described a glory we now have (v.8), which is currently an inner gory thru the indwelling of the Spirit, which will be turned into an outward glory when we enter the land of glory with the glorified Christ to behold face to face. The premise of unglorified bodyless saints in the promised land of glory without their outer glorified body is untenable. The revelation of Christ began with his manifestation in the flesh and he continues to reveal himself throughout the church age culminating in his final revelation to all the world at the end of the age. This is the teaching of the book of Revelation: not a future revelation at the end but Christ as Lord revealing himself throughout the current age. Peter expressly declares when the revelation of Christ occurs by encouraging his readers to live with fear during the time of their exile, clearly teaching the exile ends and the revelation of Jesus Christ begins when we end our exile here on earth and enter the land (heaven/kingdom) at death. Therefore, the revelation of Christ cannot be taken to mean the last day. Peter references Christ and his example of suffering and subsequent glories, to teach and encourage the persecuted church that like Christ, their suffering ends at death and results in glorification. Therefore, we should expect a resurrection like Christ's, not one where our glorification with our body is delayed. Physical death *is* resurrection

life for the one with the guarantee of the Spirit. Peter states God raised Christ from the dead and gave him glory, one follows the other. Peter closes the section by reminding them they were born not of the natural seed of a human or earthly generation but of the imperishable seed of the word of God (Spirit), and that the seed of our fleshly body is like the seed of the flowers and grass that withers and fails. This reinforces the teaching that flesh and blood bodies are not the body we dwell in in heaven, for it shall return to the ground after death to wither in the grave, while we will reside with Christ in bodies like his.

Peter continues his contrasting of the flesh and the Spirit in 1 Peter 3:18:

> For Christ also suffered once for sins, the righteous for the unrighteous, that he might bring us to God, being put to death in the flesh but made alive in the spirit.

It seems clear that Peter is not making the point of Christ's redemptive work being a recreation of the flesh, but rather a death of the flesh which results in a new life (body) in the Spirit, for it states a change from in the flesh to in the Spirit. This distinction of flesh and Spirit is seen clearly in the humiliation and exultation of Christ. Many expositors fail to understand the humiliation of Christ properly, as they understand his coming to earth to take on flesh as not merely a temporary veiling of his eternal glory that was necessary to bear our sin and pay the price of our fallen fleshly nature. But I believe that is not the teaching of the humiliation and exultation. Jesus veiled his glory in human flesh, (though flesh that had not been defiled by sin), in order to redeem and free those in bondage to the carnal devilish nature, thus Christ died in the flesh to pay our curse of death, in order to restore us to spiritual life. The ascension of Christ via the glory cloud was his returning to his previous unveiled glory, as the fleshly body of his descension was transformed into his glorious spiritual body. The apostle John in Jn. 1:13 reiterates the point being made, that the new man is generated from the will of and by the same nature as God. We are children of God rather than children of the flesh, not from the generation of our earthly parents thus born from above. The man born from the first Adam is made in his fallen image and thus destined to die but is remade by the second Adam into his image through new birth via the Spirit.

> But to all who did receive him, who believed in his name, he gave the right to become children of God, who were born, not of blood nor of the will of the flesh nor of the will of man, but of God. (Jn. 1:12-13)

CHAPTER 2

A MATTER OF DAYS

A significant contributor to the confusion around the resurrection of the body lies in the use of phrases like "Last Day", "last days", "Judgment Day", "final judgment" and more. This chapter will attempt to clarify these phrases in order to show that the resurrection for the elect is different than the resurrection of the lost.

Last Day and Judgment Day

The phrase "Last Day" must be framed within a broader context to arrive at a proper understanding of its meaning. The entire period of the Messiah's work (week[13]) which begins at the first advent and continues until his final appearance to judgment, is called the last days (plural). To put this another way, each day during this period is a last day leading up to the final last day. This final day is described in very clear terms: its nature identifies it as being different from all of the preceding days. The two verses below

---

[13] The Messiah's <u>week of work</u> is the 70th week of Dan. 9, which establishes the eternal kingdom or new creation. The week begins with the first advent and extends to the final advent to execute judgment and ends when Christ turns over the restored cosmos to God the Father (1 Cor. 15:28 *when all things are subjected to him, then the Son himself will also be subjected to him who put all things in subjection under him, that God may be all in all.*) The Father's creation week brought perfection. The Son's or Messiah's "week" will restore the fallen cosmos back to the original sinless perfection.

show the difference: the former refers to the full period of time and the latter to the specific "Last Day".

> but in these **last day**s he has spoken to us by his Son, whom he appointed the heir of all things, through whom also he created the world. (Heb. 1:2)

> And there shall be a <u>unique day</u>, which is known to the LORD, neither day nor night, but at evening time there shall be "light." (Zech. 14:17)

The Last Day can refer to physical death, which is a person's final day on earth, or as Judgement Day at the end of time. Judgment Day is described in scripture as the Day of Wrath, Day of Darkness, and Day of the Lord. The resurrection of the dead takes place during this time and this resurrection is traditionally defined as the bodily resurrection of both saints and the lost. In the traditional formulation, all people are understood to be resurrected at the same time on this Last Day at the end of time. If this Last Day really is a combination of blessing for the saints due to their receiving their heavenly body and final judgment for the lost after being resurrected from Sheol, then one would reasonably expect both aspects to be described when it is spoken of in scripture. But we do not find this mixed message. Instead, we only find descriptions of this day as one of judgment, death, and wrath. This point being that Judgment Day should be understood as *primarily* the final judgment of God upon Satan, his angels, and unbelieving mankind. *Secondarily*, this judgment does bring rejoicing to the saints, but only in terms of the final destruction of the curse of death, and the Satanic kingdom, and not a rejoicing due to their receipt of their resurrection body at the same time as the final judgment. This is due to the saints having already passed through a judgement at death, which resulted in their adornment with the new resurrection body and ascension into heaven. Most of the confusion regarding the nature of the Last Day derives from passages where the saints long for this day (cf. Lk. 18:6-8, Rev. 6:10-11), and will see Christ glorified through his destruction of death and sin. What many expositors fail to see is that while the saints rejoice on this day, the events which take place on it, and the recipients of Christ's wrath and judgments are solely the lost—it is their Last Day. Therefore, the traditional understanding of this day as one of the bodily resurrection for both the elect and the lost should not be assumed to be true too hastily.

Understood this way, the unique character of the Last Day as the time of Final Judgment means that we must be careful not to assign general uses of the term last day inappropriately. One must ask when qualifiers such as "day of wrath" or the "Lord's Day" are not used, which "last day" does the text depict? The context always provides the answer. This becomes important as it relates to the resurrection, for if the premise of this book is true that the Last Day or Final Judgment is the day of the judgment of the lost only, then the resurrection associated with that day is only the resurrection of the lost, and not the elect. There is little disagreement that the final judgment of the lost takes place on the Last Day or Judgment Day. The root of the problem is including the elect in the actions of God at the Final Judgment because, as we will see, these actions are clearly descriptions of judgment and the pouring of God's final and full wrath on the ungodly. I agree that the final separation of the lost and the saints is withheld until the Last Day. I agree that this is when the resurrection of the lost occurs. However, as explained in chapter 1, I contend the elect will have already attained their resurrected body at death when they entered heaven.

There is clearly a final separation of the elect and the lost that will occur at the final judgment, for Christ will separate the sheep from the goats,

> When the Son of Man comes in his glory, and all the angels with him, then he will sit on his glorious throne. Before him will be gathered all the nations, and he will separate people one from another as a shepherd separates the sheep from the goats. (Mt. 25:31-32)

I believe this description of Christ sitting on his throne takes place on the earth, as he has descended from his former place in heaven at the right hand of God. Christ has returned to his creation as Lord of all creation after having redeemed his people and the cosmos from both Adam's and their sin. Matthew describes the final act of Christ dividing humanity before casting the lost into hell for eternity. Upon the separation of the sheep and goats, the divided kingdom which was on earth, will cease to exist, because the kingdom of darkness is destroyed forever. But the separation of the sheep and the goats began prior to the final judgment, indeed this separation is central to the entire narrative in the bible and carries through from Genesis to Revelation resulting in this final judgment and separation.

In the creation story of Genesis 1 we see the Spirit of God hovering over the darkness and then a separation occurs between darkness and light. God calls the light day and the darkness night. This *first* day was created perfect as the separation of darkness and light was completed. The first Adam was made perfect, but after his sin, he was changed, and cast out of Eden and God's presence— another separation. Creation was thrown into total darkness again by Adam's sin, whereby this division of light and darkness was temporarily broken, as spiritual darkness again covered the world, until the true light of the world would appear again in Bethlehem. The separation of light and darkness or God's children from the seed of Satan continues throughout the Old and New Testaments. We see this typology in the two kingdoms of Satan and Christ on earth represented by each of their members, described as kingdoms of light and darkness (see. John 1:5 "The light shines in the darkness, and the darkness has not overcome it" and Matthew 4:16 "the people dwelling in darkness have seen a great light, and for those dwelling in the region and shadow of death, on them a light has dawned.") Therefore, the separation and judgment on the Last Day is simply the culmination of the eternal redemption plan whereby God, throughout history, is recreating his people and the cosmos into its original state of glory, and at the same time separating it from sin.

The terms of day and night can refer to more than just a 24-hour earthly time frame. They are also used to describe two kingdoms or two sets of peoples. We will see these terms day/children of light and night/children of darkness depicting a separation of these groups. To walk in the light is to be united with Christ, and to walk in darkness is to be united with Satan. Furthermore, the time of this "day of light" or "day of salvation" extends throughout the two advents of Christ. Christ is the Light of the World, and we are to let our light shine until the "day" ends, and the Day of Darkness and wrath arrives on Judgment Day. The term "day" can describe both individual days, the number of which only God knows, and the period of time from Christ's first advent until his second. This long period of time between the advents is more than a single day, thus called the Last Days, which contrasts it with the singular Last Day of Judgment.

This separation of names into Last Days and Last Day is another clear identification of the separation of these days in purpose and the intended people, further indicating there is not a unification of purpose for the elect and lost on the Last Day. The last days are the Day of Salvation for the lost to come to the savior, which continues until the Last Day. The elect walk in the light and the lost in darkness during this time until the Last Day, both conforming to their respective part of a normal day/night cycle of an earthly day. Therefore, the Last Day is reserved solely for the lost, for it marks the end of the time where the Day of Salvation was available, and Judgment Day, a *"Day of Darkness"* has arrived. Amos 5:18-20 is a good example of the Day of judgment described as one of darkness and no light, because it is speaking of the lost:

> "Woe to you who desire the day of the LORD! Why would you have the day of the LORD? It is darkness, and not light, as if a man fled from a lion, and a bear met him, or went into the house and leaned his hand against the wall, and a serpent bit him. Is not the day of the LORD darkness, and not light, and gloom with no brightness in it?"

The Last Day is described as the Day of the Lord due to the piercing revelation of Christ in light appearing at his descension to the darkened world in order to bring judgment. The term Last Day also takes on the meaning of *final judgment*. This will be seen as occurring at different times for the saint and the lost. The last day or final judgment for the lost is <u>not</u> upon their physical death where the physical body returns to the earth in the grave. Their final judgment still awaits them on Judgement Day, they are held bodyless in sheol, the realm of the death in the earth (cf. Jude 5,6), until that time. When the New Testament uses Last Day for the saint, it refers to their last day on earth or their final judgment at physical death when they are released from their mortal body, transitioned into their spiritual resurrection body, and ascend into heaven. This is their final judgment, as Christ suffered their judgment of death on the cross to justify them before a holy God. We see the difference between the Last Day terminology for the two groups in the following texts:

> Truly, truly, I say to you, whoever hears my word and believes him who sent me has eternal life. He does not come into judgment, but has passed from death to life. John 5:24

> And the free gift is not like the result of that one man's sin. For the judgment following one trespass brought condemnation, but the free gift following many trespasses brought justification. Romans 5:16

The final judgment awaits the lost, but the saints do not come into final judgment because they are already declared righteous— which is their final judgment in God's sight through their faith in Christ's judgment on the cross and resurrection bringing them into the heavenly kingdom. Therefore, the reservation of the Last Day or Judgment Day for the unbelievers. The time of final judgment is not the same day for the two separate groups.

Jn. 6:40 and the context surrounding it is an example of Last Day referring to the time of the saint's death and resulting in resurrection life in heaven. It states:

> For this is the will of my Father, that everyone who looks
> on the Son and believes in him should have eternal life,
> and I will raise him up on the last day. (Jn. 6:40)

The time one needs resurrection life in our new spiritual body is at death when our mortal body perishes. This obvious point is often overlooked, and the promise of new bodily life is deferred for the elect until the eschaton. Christ is not referring to the Last Day of final judgment in these types of texts, rather he is referring to the promise to those who have the deposit of the Spirit, that they will not die but experience bodily resurrection life.

John 6:43-49 provide the context for determining what "Last Day" refers to in John 6:40 (as well as verses 43 and 54). Here Christ responds to the Jews who grumbled at Christ's statement that he was the bread that came down from heaven that would give eternal life. He presents them with the Old Testament typological example of the wilderness generation in order to contrast it with the New Testament reality. The Old Testament references to manna, wilderness, and Promised Land were contrasted with Christ as the bread of life, the saints' earthly journey, and heaven. The faithless who rebelled against Moses and did not combine the understanding of the manna from heaven as pointing towards Christ died and their bodies were buried in the wilderness, thus did not crossover into heaven typified via the Promised Land. This is the same fate unbelievers face at death as they are separated from their earthly body, prohibited entry into heaven, and await the final judgment. It is contrasted with the faithfulness of Joshua and Caleb who did not die and bodily crossed over into the promised land or heaven. The contrast is between the last day on earth of the faithless in the wilderness which resulted in death outside the Promised Land and their bodies returning to the grave, and the faithful who transition into heaven via bodily resurrection life through faith in the true bread of life from heaven. Their bodies did not die and were not buried in the wilderness. Christ is encouraging the faithful to not fear death to our body but understand it as only resulting in continued resurrection life in heaven in our resurrection body. This example of Last Day referring to our final day on earth as a resurrection or raising up, is covered in more detail later in the section on the gospel of John, as well as other examples in part 2.

The pattern of separation begun in the biblical narrative of creation and fall in Genesis continues, separating mankind into generations of either the children of God (light) or of Satan (darkness). We see the separation continue in the birth of Jacob and Esau, the Exodus from Egypt when the Israelites were chosen over the Egyptians, at the entrance into Canaan where only Joshua and Caleb are chosen, and it continues throughout the Old Testament as God establishes in typical form his kingdom in the earthly Jerusalem through David's line. God's presence with his people is finalized through Solomon's construction of the Temple and its filling with the Spirit. The New Testament brings further clarification of this separation. First, the elect are united with Christ and separated from Satan's kingdom. We are a part of Christ's body now, for we have been translated out of the dominion of darkness and into his glorious light. Second, we live as citizens of heaven residing in the midst of a depraved generation while on earth. Third, we groan in the pains of childbirth awaiting our death and union with Christ. Death brings resurrection life for the believer when we become complete sons of God. Although the entire arc of the bible details this separation between the two generations or seeds of Adam, according to the traditional view Judgment Day brings these two classes of mankind before the Judgment seat of Christ or a common judgment. But this is the Day of Wrath, a day of condemnation. Nothing can be more clearly wrong. It is my contention that a wrong understanding of the timing of the resurrection flows from this wrong understanding of Judgment Day as a day of judgment for both the elect and the lost. This comingling of both the purpose and the objects of the Day of Wrath, also commingles the timing of the receipt of resurrection body to Judgment Day as well. But what has been separated for all of time is not brought together for a common judgment at the end. The final judgment on the Last Day of Judgment is the final removal of sin and death via the destruction of the Satanic kingdom and renewal of the cosmos. The elect had been transformed prior to this day.

The Final Judgment is not Judgment Day for the Elect

It is my contention that no error has had more devastating consequences for eschatological theology than the church's misunderstanding of the Final Judgment or Day of God's wrath. The Day of Salvation or the Day of Judgment are the only two final destinations for mankind. One is either a part of the salvation offered by Christ via the gospel during the Day of Salvation, or one is relegated for final judgment on the Last Day.

> Behold, now is the favorable time; behold, now is **the day of salvation.** (2 Cor. 6:2)

Then the Lord knows how to rescue the godly from trials,
and to keep the unrighteous under punishment until the
day of judgment." (2 Pet. 2:9)

These passages clearly mark the distinctive difference between the two "days" and further supports the idea that it is an error to co-mingle the purpose of Judgment Day for both the elect and the lost. By implication it also supports the separation of the "days" of the resurrections of the two groups as well. The confusion lies in that scripture declares the saints are to appear at the throne or judgment seat of Christ on the last day (cf. 2 Cor. 5:10), and it is then assumed they are there for their own trial or judgment. However, as we have seen, the judgment to be rendered is one in their favor, and against those standing before the trial judge, as this judgment eliminates sin and death from all of creation. This day of wrath is for the rebels, but is also a great day for the saints, for it is the day for which they have been longing for, as the kingdom of Satan which has been persecuting them is finally judged, and they bear witness at their trial.

Not everyone who appears before a judge is being judged—indeed most are not. Some are witnesses for the prosecution, others simply to witness the proceedings to ensure justice is granted to the accused. Similarly, on the Day of Judgment the elect appear, not to be judged, but to participate as a witness in the proceedings. We have already been judged and declared righteous or not guilty and our sins have been removed through our faith in the gospel. Indeed, the obvious proof of our previous judgment is that by the Last Day, all of the elect will have already been gathered before the throne, for the temple of his people will be complete prior to the start of the Last Day events. The interadvent period is the Day of Salvation, the light is shining in the world via the availability of the gospel. The commencement of the dark day of judgment ends this period of light, as the elect will have arrived in heaven, removing all remaining light from the earth.

Hebrews 12:11 *"Therefore, since we are surrounded by such a great cloud of witnesses"* makes our purpose on Judgment Day clear, as throughout history saints rise to be with Christ in heaven before his throne, and their exhortations are meant to strengthen the church on earth until the final set of believers is taken into the glory cloud, joining them in the heavenly kingdom. Paul speaks of the final group of saints alive on earth—who have not experienced death—being changed and resurrected to heaven.

> Behold! I tell you a mystery. We shall not all sleep, but we shall all be changed, in a moment, in the twinkling of an eye, at the last trumpet. (1 Cor. 15:51-52)

The heavenly Temple is then complete and all that is left is to judge the unbelievers from all time. One is either a witness or a defendant at the Final Judgment. The separation between the elect and the lost, light and darkness, glorified and inglorious, is maintained per scriptural commands to be separate, but we are then brought together on the Last Day as the lost are then resurrected to judgment. The King then separates these inglorious souls resurrected to judgment, from the glorious holy congregation who were previously resurrected into his glorious presence. Our role as witnesses for Christ does not end when we depart earth for heaven but continues until Judgment Day. As each saint experiences death, they appear with Christ, awaiting the final day to be witnesses and judges at the final judgment of the lost.

> 1 Cor. 6:2 Or do you not know that the saints will judge the world?

Three texts in particular are commonly cited as indicating both the elect and the lost appearing before the judgment seat of Christ on the Last Day: 2 Cor. 5:10, 1 Cor. 3:12-13, and Rev. 20:11-15. The first is, 2 Cor. 5:10:

> For we must all appear before the judgment seat of Christ, so that each one may receive what is due for what he has done in the body, whether good or evil.

Paul is encouraging the church not to lose heart because of their afflictions, and to look forward to their reward in heaven. However, as we all agree, for the elect appearing before Christ in heaven happens at death. Therefore, it is at their death that saints are with Christ in heaven at his judgment seat (throne) at the right hand of the Father not on the

Last Day as is normally assumed. In fact, the saints had been with Christ in the throne room since their entry into heaven. Secondly, the text does not state that the saints are on trial or will be judged, only that they receive what was due them for what was done while in the body (i.e., before death). So, if one does not assume that glorification and resurrection of the body occurs for the saint at the Final Judgment, then receiving heavenly rewards in this text at the judgment seat is easily explained as cotemporaneous with resurrection to bodily life at death. In other words, this text is compatible with the view that saints receive their reward prior to the Last Day and upon their entry to heaven at death. Further, the text does not say both the elect and the lost arrive on the Last Day, it only identifies two rewards, good or evil, corresponding directly to the two people types, elect and lost. In terms of rewards, it should be noted that scripture is dominated by the doctrine of Christ as the goal in heaven, meaning Christ himself is the reward for the saint (cf. Phil. 3:14, Heb. 12;1-2). Being in heaven is the receipt of the reward or crowns. This text does not require judgment to occur on the Last Day for the elect, it only states they appear at the judgment seat of Christ. Simply put, the saints will have been at the throne (judgment seat) of Christ prior to the Last Day, for they reside in heaven since death and therefore have received their reward already.

2 Corinthians 5:10 does not stand alone, it must be combined with Rom. 2:6-8 to gain the full meaning;

> He will render to each one according to his works: to those
> who by patience in well-doing seek for glory and honor
> and immortality, he will give eternal life; but for those
> who are self-seeking and do not obey the truth, but obey
> unrighteousness, there will be wrath and fury.

Because of the doctrine of the intermediate state, and especially Paul's use of the word "glory", many assume that this passage must be referring to the Last Day. This text refers to the rewards for both the elect and the lost, for works done on earth, but notice that like in 2 Cor. 5:10 the text does not say their rewards are given on the same day. The phrase "render to each one according to his works", refers to works performed in life, however,

Paul connects this reward of glory and the giving of eternal life. We have eternal life now! It is not a gift to be granted to saints on the Last Day.

I grant the final evidence of our faith and entrance into eternal life is realized when we die and cross over the Jordan river into Christ's heaven, but the fact of that life is already a reality for the saint who is still awaiting the completion of our work here on earth. The consummation of our eternal life occurs at death when faith becomes sight. Hebrews 2:7 says that Christ was "crowned with glory and honor" after his ascension. Both Perter and Paul indicate that we too are crowned with glory (cf. 1 Pet. 5:4, 2 Tim. 2:5-10). Our future outer glory is guaranteed by the Holy Spirit's indwelling, as the lamp shade of our mortal body is removed at death. John expresses the link between faith and eternal life in regeneration in Jn. 17:3:

> Now this is eternal life: that they know you, the only true
> God, and Jesus Christ, whom you have sent.

Matthew 25:31-34 gives further information about our appearing before the judgment seat,

> When the Son of Man comes in his glory, and all the
> angels with him, then he will sit on his glorious throne.
> Before him will be gathered all the nations, and he will
> separate people one from another as a shepherd separates
> the sheep from the goats. And he will place the sheep on
> his right, but the goats on the left. Then the King will say
> to those on his right, 'Come, you who are blessed by my
> Father, inherit the kingdom prepared for you from the
> foundation of the world.

The saints appear with the lost for the purpose of the final separation of the sheep and the goats, the final judgment of Satan and death. But what is the means Christ uses to distinguish the sheep from the goats? Perhaps the parable of the wedding banquet in Matthew 22 explains it.

> But when the king came in to look at the guests, he saw
> there a man who had no wedding garment. And he said to
> him, 'Friend, how did you get in here without a wedding

garment?' And he was speechless. Then the king said to
the attendants, 'Bind him hand and foot and cast him into
the outer darkness. (Matt. 22:11-13)

Those without the outer covering or garment of glory (wedding
garment) are easily separated from the glorious robes of the saints who
received their "white robes" or glorious body at death and resurrection
into heaven. There are several texts which I believe identify the white
robes as representing the outer glory of the resurrected saints in heaven
after their death. These saints become the "great cloud of witnesses" of
Heb. 12:1. They are not awaiting a Last Day glorification, but only a Last
Day avenging of the blood of the saints. Notice the parable identifies
the wearing of the wedding garment or "white robe as a requirement
for getting *into* the wedding (heaven), not a garment to be given on the
Last Day. Many believe this wedding event occurs on the Last Day,
however, it I believe it should be understood somewhat differently. Verse
10 indicates that the wedding hall was already filled with guests—past
tense. This is an allusion to the completed filling of the Temple, that the
number of the elect in heaven at Christ's feast, had been reached. The
guest without a wedding garment, or wearing an inglorious garment is
removed and cast into "outer darkness" (v.13) This is the resurrection of
the lost to judgment and their removal from heaven. Revelation 7 offers
a similar picture:

I said to him, "Sir, you know." And he said to me, "These
are the ones coming out of the great tribulation. They
have washed their robes and made them white in the
blood of the Lamb. Therefore, they are before the throne
of God, and serve him day and night in his temple; and he
who sits on the throne will shelter them with his presence.
(Rev. 7:14-15)

Those wearing "white robes" had come out of the "great tribulation" or
period of suffering on earth for the saints which ends when they arrive in
heaven at death. This passage also confirms their location before the throne
of God, in the Temple, after removal from earthly persecution and trials.

The second text commonly used to define Judgment Day as a day of judgment for the elect as well as the lost is 1 Cor. 3:12-13

> Now if anyone builds on the foundation with gold, silver, precious stones, wood, hay, straw— each one's work will become manifest, for the Day will disclose it, because it will be revealed by fire, and the fire will test what sort of work each one has done. If the work that anyone has built on the foundation survives, he will receive a reward.

The most obvious indication that this may not be referring to the final Judgment Day is the terminology used. The final judgment is the "Last Day", yet in this passage we read "the Day", not "the Last Day". Thus "the Day", easily falls within the Last Days (plural) or "Day of Salvation" which could be any day prior to the Last Day. As discussed earlier, "last days" is simply referring to each day within the entire "Day of Salvation" or gospel dispensation which culminates in the ultimate Last Day of judgment. There is a judgment given at death, in which all mankind know their future destiny or judgment. I believe this is "the Day" being and the judgment in view in this passage. We already know that the elect enter heaven at death, therefore a positive judgment was rendered at death. The context of the chapter speaks of both the work that a person does and the foundation which is being built during our sojourn on earth. This work will determine the reward to be given. Thus, if entrance to heaven is granted, the judgment was rendered at that time, not deferred until the Last Day. It is appropriate and conforms to the analogy of scripture that after a person has finished their work or time on earth, they receive their reward at the same time.

> And just as it is appointed for man to die once, and after that comes judgment, so Christ, having been offered once to bear the sins of many, will appear a second time, not to deal with sin but to save those who are eagerly waiting for him. (Heb. 9:27-28)

This passage clearly speaks of judgment at death, it does not contain any language deferring this judgment at death for the elect. The context of Hebrews 9 is of Christ's death opening the way into heaven for all mankind. Therefore our death mimics Christ's and provides an entrance into heaven. Additionally, Heb. 9:15 states

> so that those called may receive the promised eternal inheritance, since a death has occurred that redeems them.

This is speaking of Christ's atoning death which is the basis of our eternal inheritance at death. There is no support for deferring our judgment at death until the Last Day.

Paul, in his final letter, encourages Timothy, by speaking of his imminent death and future reward with the crown of glory, which he describes as being rewarded to him, "on that day" which can only mean his impending death.

> For I am already being poured out as a drink offering, and the time of my departure has come. I have fought the good fight, I have finished the race, I have kept the faith. Henceforth there is laid up for me the crown of righteousness, which the Lord, the righteous judge, will award to me on that day, and not only to me but also to all who have loved his appearing. (2 Timothy 4:6-8)

Paul describes his death as a departure from this world and into the spiritual heavenly realm. The final result of his earthly time is described here as "the crown of righteousness". Other times this same crown awarded upon a completion of a race is described as one of glory, of life, or as golden crowns. These crowns all represent the completion of the race on earth and receipt of resurrection life in heaven upon death. Paul speaks of his death, his good fight (work), the finished race, that he kept the faith, and the final reward of the crown of righteousness that will await him on that Day. Again, there is no reference to "Last Day" or "Day of Wrath", and the clear context of the entire letter and this text in particular refers to his day of death as being "that Day". He encourages Timothy and thus the church to be confident that death will only bring resurrection life.

In the texts below we notice a couple further points: First, they mention those who have loved (past tense) his appearing, which is a reference to Christ's first appearance as the lamb to be slain. Second, they speak of "when the chief shepherd appears" (future tense) you will receive the "unfading crown of glory". This future appearance occurs when we arrive in his presence in heaven after death. It is combined with the "unfading crown of glory" awarded when we reach heaven. This unfading crown of glory is in contrast to the "fading" glory of Moses which could only typify the future eternal crown of glory which Christ was awarded and awards to his faithful servants. Third, in Rev. 5:4 we have the combined reference to both white robes and golden crowns. As previously discussed, the robes refer to outer resurrected life in glory. Finally, the crown of life means resurrected life via the new body of glory.

> Blessed is the man who remains steadfast under trial, for when he has stood the test he will receive the crown of life, which God has promised to those who love him. (James 1:12)

> Henceforth there is laid up for me the crown of righteousness, which the Lord, the righteous judge, will award to me on that day, and not only to me but also to all who have loved his appearing. (2 Tim. 4:8)

> And when the chief Shepherd appears, you will receive the unfading crown of glory. (1 Pet. 5:4)

> Around the throne were twenty-four thrones, and seated on the thrones were twenty-four elders, clothed in white garments, with golden crowns on their heads. (Rev. 5:4)

The third text commonly used to declare a judgment for the elect on the Last Day is Rev. 20:11-15:

> Then I saw a great white throne and him who was seated on it. From his presence earth and sky fled away, and no place was found for them. And I saw the dead, great and

small, standing before the throne, and books were opened. Then another book was opened, which is the book of life. And the dead were judged by what was written in the books, according to what they had done. And the sea gave up the dead who were in it, Death and Hades gave up the dead who were in them, and they were judged, each one of them, according to what they had done. Then Death and Hades were thrown into the lake of fire. This is the second death, the lake of fire. And if anyone's name was not found written in the book of life, he was thrown into the lake of fire.

This verse is often misconstrued to portray a picture of judgment before the throne for everyone who has ever died, a compilation of both the elect and the lost for "final judgment" but, in fact, it is only a description of the lost before Christ being judged. There is only an indirect reference to the elect through the use of the Book of Life, in which all the elect are enrolled. Revelation in particular, and scripture in general uses the terms dead, earth dwellers, and naked to describe the lost. This passage is full of references which only pertain to the lost. Again, we come across a text where it would make sense to state clearly or explicitly what the intermediate state assumes to be true: this passage could state that all mankind are resurrected to their earthly bodies to stand before Christ for final judgment on the Last Day. Perhaps it does not say this because it is not true. This text only refers to the "resurrection of the dead". The error is in construing "the dead" to mean everyone's dead bodies which went to the earth in the grave, thus the mistaken interpretation of everyone receiving their resurrection bodies at this time. But given our previous arguments and the language used in Revelation for the lost, it is more than plausible that "the dead" here refers to only those without eternal life, those "dead" in trespasses and sins, because that is who awaits this judgment of wrath ending in the second death. The locations these souls are raised from, "the sea" and "Death and Hades," refer to the realms where the "dead" were held pending judgment. If this judgment was to include the elect, we should expect that an attributing reference to their location would have been included too. The "dead" are also judged *according to what they had done"* vs. the elect having been prejudged by what Christ has done for them.

In this passage, we notice a reference to "books" and a singular book called "the Book of Life", which I believe is the only reference to the elect. The text clearly states only those people identified with "the books" were judged. On my reading, this implies that those in the Book of Life are not judged at this time. Finally, the only judgment rendered is the *"second death in the lake of fire"*. There is not a positive judgment mentioned at all. If this were to be construed as two judgments for two different classes of people, we would expect some kind of positive judgment. All of these indicators lead to the conclusion that this is a resurrection of the lost to their final judgment of the *"second death"* in the lake of fire, as fire is representative of God's judgment. Their first death resulted in the judgment of awaiting this final judgment in Hades. That leaves another time for the resurrection of the elect, which I am believe occurs at death and entrance to heaven.

One final note on the context of Revelation 20:11-15. In the immediately preceding text, we read:

> And when the thousand years are ended, Satan will be released from his prison and will come out to deceive the nations that are at the four corners of the earth, Gog and Magog, to gather them for battle; their number is like the sand of the sea. And they marched up over the broad plain of the earth and surrounded the camp of the saints and the beloved city, but fire came down from heaven and consumed them (Rev. 20:7-10)

Here we have the final battle in which Satan comes out to *"deceive the nations"*. The nations are the earthly nations comprised of the lost, which is in contrast to the singular "holy nation" of God. The location of these nations is described as *"at the four corners of the earth"* which is to be contrasted with the "holy nation" of God in the heavenly realm. Therefore, the judgment of verses 11-15 is of these earthly apostate nations of unbelievers left on earth at the Final Judgment. Secondly, these *"nations"* surround the *"beloved city"* of the earthly Jerusalem to be destroyed, which is in contrast to the actual eternal city of God, the "*heavenly Jerusalem*". The final result is presented next in Rev. 21:1-2

Then I saw a new heaven and a new earth, for the first heaven and earth had passed away, and the sea was no more. I saw the holy city, the new Jerusalem, coming down out of heaven from God, prepared as a bride adorned for her husband. Here the heavenly city comes to earth after the destruction of the earthly typological city.

CHAPTER 3

BUILDING THE KINGDOM'S TEMPLE

We must separate the eschatological path and the timing for the <u>individual</u> from that of the earthly <u>Kingdom's</u> final restoration or renewing by Christ. As the previous chapters argue, I do not concede the traditional view's belief in a common judgment on the Last Day. My belief is that when the last elect person is brought to heaven, the Temple is complete. This sets the stage for the soon to follow judgment of the earthly kingdom and its rulers, resulting in the completion of the new heavens and earth. This chapter shows that the Temple is progressively building during the gospel age.

A Progressively Building Temple

In the Old Testament, the completion of the journey of the people of God was achieved upon entrance into the Promised Land. The Promised Land typified heaven and the Temple for Christ. Israel was not given another destination or further escalation or replacement for the kingdom after David and Solomon's reigns, Such a destination or escalation could correspond to the two-stage model of the intermediate state, where entrance into the Promised Land/Davidic kingdom is analogous to heaven as a partial redemption of the traveler in which a bodyless soul enters heaven and is awaiting completion of the glorious image bearing of

Christ until a bodily resurrection at the Last Day at the Final Judgment at the end of the age, however, such a correspondence does not exist. The Temple which Christ is building began at his first advent and will be completed before his final appearing to judgment on the Last Day, per Paul's instruction in 1 Cor. 15:50-56 and 1 Thess. 4:13-18, where Christ's first act upon the sounding of the last trumpet announcing the arrival of Judgment Day is the removal of the saints still on earth to the glory cloud in heaven.

The completed temple must therefore include all the works Christ won at the cross and resurrection to heaven of the elect, including the possession of their heavenly or resurrection body. The Kingdom (Temple) is therefore complete prior to the events of Judgment Day. Because the Temple is constructed from all the elect, the resurrection to the glorious bodies of the elect must precede the resurrection of the lost on Judgment Day. Our understanding of the nature of the Kingdom of God determines our interpretation of the status of the saints currently residing in heaven. Is entry into heaven a partial completion of Christ's work that is awaiting a future completion on the Last Day, or is enrollment in heaven the completed promise and entry into eternal rest for the saint?

The Kingdom: Complete Yet Growing

Daniel prophecies the establishing of the eternal Kingdom with the coming of the fourth beast,

> And in the days of those kings the God of heaven will set up a kingdom that shall never be destroyed, nor shall the kingdom be left to another people. It shall break in pieces all these kingdoms and bring them to an end, and it shall stand forever, just as you saw that a stone was cut from a mountain by no human hand, and that it broke in pieces the iron, the bronze, the clay, the silver, and the gold. A great God has made known to the king what shall be after this. The dream is certain, and its interpretation sure. (Dan 2:44-45)

Daniel 7 foretells the return of the Son of Man to his exalted status once his work on earth had been completed, and the establishment of the indestructible heavenly kingdom described in chapter 2:

> In my vision in the night I continued to watch, and I saw One like the Son of Man coming with the clouds of heaven. He approached the Ancient of Days and was led into His presence. And He was given dominion, glory, and kingship, that the people of every nation and language should serve Him. His dominion is an everlasting dominion that will not pass away, and His kingdom is one that will never be destroyed. (Dan. 7:13-14)

Here Christ establishes his Kingdom upon his ascension to heaven. He is led into the presence of the Ancient of Days, and he receives authority and power from God the Father. Daniel informs us that the coming of the fourth beast's earthly kingdom (Ch. 2) coincides with the establishment of another kingdom — the heavenly Kingdom of Christ (Ch. 7). Christ's ascension back to heaven ushered in his Kingdom in heaven, a Kingdom which will then be in conflict with the earthly kingdom until its destruction forever on the Last Day. Christ's first advent and ascension ushered in the Messianic Age or the last days which are synonymous with the coming of Christ Kingdom in heaven. Christ's final advent to judgment will destroy the earthly kingdom resulting in the uniting of heaven and earth in the heavenly rule under Christ's reign when the city of God comes down from heaven to earth in Revelation 21:2. Daniel's prophecy does not describe a partial kingdom awaiting fullness in power and authority, nor a partial possession of the kingdom by the saints. The Kingdom that was established will not pass away, nor decrease, and the picture is that of a kingdom already possessing all of its glory, kingship, and dominion, as proven by the restoration of the dominion and glory to the Son of Man.

Therefore, all the members present in the heavenly kingdom possess these traits through the King's victory, and his distribution of these gifts to his saints when they are translated to the heavenly kingdom. We have no other glory or further dominion to be given us after our entry into heaven when we receive our crown of glory. The partial dominion our Messiah had over our actions while we were in exile on earth was due to our possession of our mortal body of death. This will be eliminated once this nature is left behind at death and we receive our glorious crown of our heavenly body. The kingdom is complete because the King is ruling with complete authority and dominion and those residing in the completed heavenly kingdom possess all the fruits gained through his victory. Those still on earth but members of the kingdom are described as members in exile, awaiting their final reward in heaven. Understanding the Kingdom in this way allows us to see that the Kingdom is both complete and growing: it is complete because Christ's dominion in heaven is complete because the saints residing there have obtained perfection in their heavenly bodies. It is growing as individual saints die and are no longer in exile but home with Christ. This is a very different understanding from the traditional view which posits an incomplete redemption until final completion on the Last Day, a teaching which I believe is irreconcilable with the passages from Daniel above, with Paul and with the Kingdom parables.

John the Baptist testified to the nearness of the Kingdom being at the appearance of Christ.

> Matt. 3:1 "In those days John the Baptist came, preaching in the wilderness of Judea and saying, "Repent, for the kingdom of heaven is near."

Jesus declared the Kingdom of God was in their midst or at hand, not a future event. Luke records this interaction of Jesus with the Pharisees:

> When asked by the Pharisees when the kingdom of God would come, Jesus replied, "The kingdom of God will not come with observable signs. Nor will people say, 'Look, here it is,' or 'There it is.' For you see, the kingdom of God is in your midst. (Lk. 17:20-21)

This was because he had descended and his presence with them while on earth was synonymous with the Kingdom being present. The kingdom was inaugurated as a present reality upon his arrival and reached fulfillment with his exaltation and the sending of his Spirit. Similarly, fulfillment of the Kingdom for the individual saint is accomplished upon their exaltation into heaven at death. The final fulfillment of the Kingdom for the entire cosmos takes place with the revelation of his personal presence at the final judgment on the Last Day. At each stage in the Kingdom progression the picture is of growth and expansion by the initiation of the new creation in the lives of reborn saints. Those saints are now translated into the Kingdom, bringing heaven to earth through their new life while they remain for a short time as ambassadors with the ministry of reconciliation to a lost and apostate world.

If the Kingdom was present for his people when Christ was on earth with his disciples, how much more is it present and complete, when we are with him, in a redeemed state in heaven—a state in which our mortal body has been taken away from us at death and therefore all the residual vestige of our fallen nature is gone. For the Christian death means resurrection life, a life more abundant or escalated than our earthly life. As we have seen, Paul makes it clear that the new birth is a transfer into the Kingdom, our redemption is accomplished as evidenced by the present reality of the forgiveness of our sins.

> Col. 1:13-14 "He has rescued us from the dominion of darkness <u>and brought us into the kingdom</u> of His beloved Son, in whom we have redemption, the forgiveness of sins."

This redemption includes our continued cleansing through the sanctifying work of the Holy Spirit while we reside on earth. The Kingdom inside the saint is now united with the heavenly perfected Kingdom, the final redemptive act is the removal of the outer man as we pass through death into heaven.

Jesus describes the Kingdom in terms of a seed which grows larger and larger until it is a fully mature tree, but we need to recognize that throughout the growing process it was always fully a tree.

> Then Jesus asked, "What is the kingdom of God like? To what can I compare it? It is like a mustard seed that a man tossed into his garden. <u>It grew and became a tree</u>, and the birds of the air nested in its branches. (Lk. 13:18-19)

Paul describes the process from regeneration via the implanting of the imperishable seed of the Holy Spirit, to our final transformation into our glorious bodies using basically the same metaphor in 1 Cor. 15:35-49. The kingdom was presented to all for rejection or acceptance. The unshakable kingdom in heaven with our King is our ultimate prize.

> But you have come to Mount Zion and to the city of the living God, the heavenly Jerusalem, and to innumerable angels in festal gathering, and to the assembly of the firstborn who are enrolled in heaven, and to God, the judge of all, and to the spirits of the righteous made perfect, and to Jesus, the mediator of a new covenant, and to the sprinkled blood that speaks a better word than the blood of Abel. (Heb. 12:22-24)

I cannot wait to reach heaven, to hear the angelic choir and to be united with all the saints who have been made perfect. But most of all I want to be united with Christ who died for my sins and remade me into his image through the new birth via the Holy Spirit.

The Comings of Christ: Invisible and Visible

As has been noted, there are multiple comings of Christ to execute his judgments, whether positive or negative, upon mankind. He has come and will come at the end of time for the last judgment, but these two comings are not the only ones. I believe the clearest way to understand the comings of Christ is to describe them as either visible or invisible. Both his first and final coming are visible to the world. There are times when we get a glimpse of the invisible world through a manifestation of the Spirit including, light, wind, fire, among others. For example, the coming of Christ via his Spirit at Pentecost was accompanied by visible manifestations of tongues of fire. An example of an invisible coming is regeneration in which the Spirit comes to indwell an individual but cannot be seen. Christ also comes to us at death to take us to our heavenly home in our new body. Christ is at work in both of our deaths: first, when our old nature is put to death at our regeneration and our mortal body is crucified though we still reside in it on earth, and second when we physically die and we are resurrected into new glorious bodies in heaven. As we will see in chapter 4, this mirrors the OT type of Red Sea and Jordan River crossings culminating in the glorious land.

Christ teaches his disciples in the upper room that it is better for him to leave so that he may send his Spirit. The Spirit's coming was necessary to renew the creation and build his Temple. Therefore, whenever a person comes to faith this is a coming of Christ into the believer in which his rule is established. At the same time, this coming also necessarily includes a judgment—but the judgment is "not guilty". This is in contrast to the Final Judgment of the lost who are then judged guilty. This is how the eternal kingdom grows, one soul at a time, as sons and daughters of God are reconciled to God by the Spirit. The great tree of Daniel that will reach its foreordained height, (the height of which only the Father knows), is being continually growing until the Final (Last) Day. There will not be another judgment for the elect on the Last Day because Christ has already come to us and we have already been declared righteous and endowed with his Spirit as our guarantee of his promise. The lost, already under a judgment of death because of their sin nature remain faithless await their judgment on the last day in Sheol because Christ has not come invisibly to Them. At a time set by the Father Christ will be Revealed visibly as King of Kings and Lord of Creation. This Last Day, the Day of God's wrath upon all the kingdom of darkness and its citizens and their kingdom will be destroyed.

This idea of Christ's coming can be further seen in several places in the New Testament:

> And if I go and prepare a place for you, I will come back and welcome you into My presence, so that you also may be where I am. (Jn. 14:3)

> Truly, I say to you, there are some standing here who will not taste death until they see the Son of Man coming in his kingdom. (Matt. 16: 28)

Jesus answered him, "If anyone loves me, he will keep my word, and my Father will love him, and we will come to him and make our home with him." (John 14:23)

in order that all may come under judgment who have refused to believe the truth and have taken pleasure in unrighteousness. ... (2 Thess. 2:12)

Louis Berkhoff uses two terms to describe the coming of Christ.

Several terms are used to designate the future coming of Jesus Christ. The term "*parousia*" is the most common of these. It means in the first place simple "presence" but also serves to designate *a coming before a presence*. . . . A second term is "*apocalupsis*" which stresses the fact that the return will be a *revealing* of Jesus Christ. It points to the uncovering of something that was previously hidden from view, in this case, of the concealed glory and majesty of Jesus Christ.[14]

Berkhof's definition of parousia, as "*a coming before a presence*" describes what I have identified as the "invisible" comings of Christ before Judgment Day. His use of apocalupsis as a revealing of what was previously hidden corresponds to what I am calling the visible manifestation of Christ's coming for final judgment, a coming which all the world will see. These visible comings in the flesh at the first advent and his last visible coming to judgment mark the starting and end points of the Day of Salvation.

C. F. Keil added needed insight to both meaning of the "comings" of Christ and the timing of the resurrection in his Old Testament commentary on Ezekiel. In a section exploring the relation of Ezekiel to the differences between the millenarian (dispensational) view and the amillennial view of Revelation 20, he states:

According to the statements made by the Apostle Paul in 1 Cor. 15, everyone will be raised "in his own order:

---

[14] Louis Berkhof, *Systematic Theology*, 4th ed., (Grand Rapids, MI: Eerdmans, 1991), 353-4.

Christ the firstfruits, afterward they that are Christ's at His coming;" then the end, i.e., the resurrection of all the dead, the last judgment, the destruction of the world, and the new creation of heaven and earth. Consequently, the first resurrection takes place along with the coming of Christ. But, according to the teaching of the New Testament, the parusia of Christ is not to be deferred till the last day of the present world, but commences, as the Lord Himself has said, not long after His ascension, so that some of His own contemporaries will not taste of death till they see the Son of man come in His kingdom (Matt. 16:28). The Lord repeats this in Matt. 24:34, in the elaborate discourse concerning His parusia to judgment, with the solemn asseveration: "Verily I say unto you, this generation (ἡ γενεὰ ὕτη) will not pass till all these things be fulfilled." We therefore understand that the contemporaries of Christ would live to see the things of which He says, "that they will be the heralding tokens of His second appearance;" and, still further (p. 641): "We have already seen, from Matt. 16:28, that the Lord has solemnly affirmed that His own contemporaries will live to see His royal coming." Concerning this royal coming of the Son of man in the glory of His Father with His angels, which some of His contemporaries live to see (Matt. 16:27 and 28), Paul writes, in 1 Thess. 4:15, 16: "We which are alive and remain unto the coming of the Lord shall not anticipate them which are asleep; for the Lord Himself shall descend from heaven with a shout, etc., and the dead in Christ will rise first," etc. Consequently, the New Testament teaches quite clearly that the first resurrection commences with the coming of Christ, which began with the judgment executed through the Romans upon the ancient Jerusalem. This was preceded only by the resurrection of Christ as "the first-fruits," and the resurrection of the "many bodies of the saints which slept," that arose from the graves at the resurrection of Christ, and appeared to many in the holy city (Matt. 27:52, 53), as a practical testimony that through the resurrection of Christ, death is deprived of its power, and a resurrection from the grave secured for all believers.[15]

There is not simply a singular coming of Christ or rapture of all the saints prior to Christ's coming in judgment, as described in Dispensational Eschatology, but rather a continuing coming or presence throughout this age culminating in the final coming of Christ on Judgment Day. I will briefly summarize Keil's points as they relate to this book.

First, Christ is coming throughout this age in judgment and salvation, therefore every mention of a coming must not be assigned to the final coming to judgment. Second, Rev. 20 1-10 describes the new age (Kingdom) which Christ's victory at the cross initiated and which accomplished two tasks: (1) broke Satan's absolute rule over the nations' elect members, wounding that kingdom; (2) Christ's first resurrection initiated the elect's resurrection to heaven during the age of the gospel proclamation (the time for accepting the offer of salvation from God's wrath), which terminates on Judgment Day. Therefore, the bodily resurrection begins with Christ's resurrection and ascension and continues throughout this age for believers. Keil ties the binding of Satan and the destruction of the penalty of death for believers because they occur in the same time period of time, the "thousand years", which is the church age. This leaves the resurrection day of the lost for the final judgment. Third, the first resurrection is indicated in Rev. 20: 4-5 as being for those who did not have the mark of the beast. They came to life and reigned with Christ for a thousand years. These are the elect. It is again called the first resurrection in v.6, which states, "Blessed and holy is the one who shares in the first resurrection!" This is all within inside the 1000-year time frame. Peter exhorts the saints in 2 Pet. 3:8, is to not fear for the Lord will fulfill his promise of destroying the evil kingdom, saying:

> But do not forget this one thing, dear friends: With the Lord a day is like a thousand years, and a thousand years are like a day.

---

[15] C.F Keil and F. Delitzsch, *Commentary on the Old Testament*, (Grand Rapids: Eerdmans, 1973), 9: 409-410.

This is more than a general statement that God does not mark time as we do. Instead it ties this period to the same 1,000-year period in Revelation. Both these references to the 1,000 years refer to the church age in which patient endurance is needed by the saints as they endure persecution and death at the hands of God's enemies. All agree that physical death results in resurrection life with Christ, however, everyone does not acknowledge that bodily resurrection occurs at death. Professor David Engelsma disagrees with the idea that the first resurrection of Revelation 20 is the resurrection of the body:

> The taking up to heaven of the soul of the believer at death is, indeed, resurrection. There is an act of the risen Christ upon the soul at the instant of death purifying it from all sin and transforming it from a soul adapted to earthly life into a soul adapted to heavenly life. There must be this resurrection of the soul by Christ if the soul is to be with Christ in heaven. Souls do not automatically fly away to heaven at death. Souls of believers do not naturally fly to heaven. The Heidelberg Catechism indicates Christ's raising of the soul of the believer at death in Question 57: "my soul after this life shall be ... taken up to Christ its head." `The saint goes to heaven by resurrection, and only by resurrection. There are two stages. The first is the resurrection of the soul. This is the resurrection of Revelation 20:5. The second is the resurrection of the body. This is the second resurrection, implied by the first resurrection of Revelation 20:5. Accordingly, the first death of the reprobate ungodly is the suffering of God's wrath in his soul at the moment of physical death. The second death will be his suffering of God's wrath in hell in soul and body after the final judgment (see Rev. 20:6, 14).[16]

Professor Engelsma correctly states that "[t]he saint goes to heaven by resurrection, and only by resurrection," however, he only applies this to

---

[16] David J. Engelsma, "A defense of (Reformed) Amillenialism (2): Revelation 20", www. prca.org/articles/amillennialism.html#No2. Accessed 10/11/2022.

the soul. He then articulates a process whereby the soul must be further purified from sin, in the following sentence. But there is no warrant in scripture for this process of further purifying the soul from sin at death. 1 Pet. 1:21-22 states:

> you who through him are believers in God, who raised him from the dead and gave him glory, so that your faith and hope are in God. Having purified your souls by your obedience to the truth for a sincere brotherly love, love one another earnestly from a pure heart.

This passage clearly states our souls were purified by Christ by our obedience to the truth through faith and is not to be improved upon at death. If this was true, we could not be the righteousness of God now. Similarly, in Rom. 7:20 Paul states:

> now if I do what I do not want, it is no longer I who do it, but sin that dwells in me.

Finally, 1 Jn 1:9

> If we confess our sins, he is faithful and just to forgive us our sins and to cleanse us from all unrighteousness.

Granted, the sanctification process is worked by the Spirit of Christ upon believers in which the heart and mind are renewed in thought and actions according to the new nature (life) given by the Spirit at regeneration. But this further purifying from sin at death does not relate primarily to the soul. Instead, the focal point of the purifying effect is the release of the saint from the body of death which is where our battle has been waged. We are already seated in heavenly places in Christ. We are already declared righteous and justified. Arguing that there is another point when the risen Christ must purify the soul reduces the completed work of Christ on the cross that was wrought in or imparted to the believer at the new birth or new creation. We have been united with Christ; we are in Christ. Can Christ be united with sin? Can the Holy Spirit dwell in darkness? We already have access to the throne of Christ because the dividing wall or barrier to the most holy place was broken down by the body (flesh) of Christ. We are already seated with Christ. I am resurrected and have eternal life with the Spirit *now*. Christ is my own *now*. He mediates and cleanses us from all sin during the time we walk the earth and await the final stage of our glorification and adoption as sons. This glorification is the redemption of our bodies. All is well with my soul now for I have been brought from death to life, a resurrection of the soul whereby I see my savior by faith, and I await the day when my faith turns to sight. I am not saying that we do not sin in this life and or are not in need of repentance during our earthly journey. Rather, as Romans 4:5 says, our faith is counted as righteousness:

> And to the one who does not work but believes in him who
> justifies the ungodly, his faith is counted as righteousness.

Louis Berkhof dismisses Keil's connection of the believers' resurrection during the present age with the use of the 1000-year period of Rev. 20(the "first resurrection"). Berkhof calls Rev. 20:4-6 *"extremely dubious"* to be speaking of a bodily resurrection.[17] He sees this scene occurring in heaven not on earth, and speaking not of bodies that were raised up, but of souls which "lived" and "reigned". For these reasons he rejects the implication of bodily resurrection. However, the scene's location in heaven and the description of saints as "souls" certainly does not disqualify a completed man as being described, as "soul" is frequently used to describe the entire man or individual. Because heaven is the ultimate residence of mankind with his body, whether at death or at the eschaton, in cannot be a disqualifier because whichever view one holds, we obtain our body for eternity either a) upon entry, or b) after a delay, which means that the scene is the same for both views. Therefore, the idea that this passage refers to a complete man cannot be dismissed for any of these reasons.

The second significant passage describing the time frame for obtaining our resurrection body during this present age is 1 Cor. 15: 22-24:

> For as in Adam all die, so also in Christ shall all be made
> alive. But each in his own order: Christ the firstfruits,

---

[17] Louis Berkhof, *Systematic Theology*, 4th ed., (Grand Rapids, MI: Eerdmans, 1991), 726.

then at his coming those who belong to Christ. Then comes the end, when he delivers the kingdom to God the Father after destroying every rule and every authority and power.

Berkhof rejects the idea that this passage refers to the three sequential stages of resurrections set out above (1) Christ's, 2) believers, 3) and of the wicked at the end). Although he is not directly commenting on Keil's exegesis, but is instead refuting Premillennial thought, he takes issue with the word "then" in verse 23 representing a separation in time from then in verse 24.[18] This is a poor argument because Paul declares an order of events from which the clear designation of a sequence is described. Additionally, "firstfruits" further identifies the language as beginning from first and then proceeding to the end or harvest of the completed crop. The crop references three crops which are harvested out of the earth, identifies these with the death of our mortal body when it is laid into the grave, and that these three resurrections occur in a sequence of time.

When one considers and then examines that the doctrine on a singular resurrection of both the elect and the lost occur at the same time on Judgment Day is in error, then it is easy to see that this text clearly supports the separate resurrection times for the elect prior to Judgment Day and the lost at the final judgment. This leaves no other description of the middle resurrection other than as occurring in the interim period of time after Christ's resurrection and before the final resurrection of the lost on the Last Day. The first/last or beginning/end terminology ties this work to Christ as the Lord of Creation, the alpha and omega, in which the middle period is the time when he performs his redemptive work for the elect. He who began it will bring it to completion. The final act for the elect is returning them to himself and placing them into his body of which he is the head. This act is completed during this middle period. Therefore, upon the body's (temple) completion, the Last Day judgment commences. It is not consistent with scripture to have the Temple completed (all the elect in heaven) yet our bodies are not completed but awaiting the Final Day when the lost are resurrected. All of scripture declares a Day of Salvation and a Day of Wrath. These are not the same day. The inaugurated view

---

[18] Louis Berkhof, *Systematic Theology*, 4th ed., (Grand Rapids, MI: Eerdmans, 1991), 725-6.

matches the Rev. 20 period of the 1000 years, forming two clear time markers for the resurrection of believers during the interadvent period. It is only "dubious" when one brings a prejudice of resurrection occurring at the end for all on the Last Day of judgment.

Peter adds insight in 2 Peter 3:4-8 referring to the present Day of Salvation and the final Day of Judgment.

> They will say, "Where is the promise of his coming? For ever since the fathers fell asleep, all things are continuing as they were from the beginning of creation." For they deliberately overlook this fact, that the heavens existed long ago, and the earth was formed out of water and through water by the word of God, and that by means of these the world that then existed was deluged with water and perished. But by the same word the heavens and earth that now exist are stored up for fire, being kept until the day of judgment and destruction of the ungodly. But do not overlook this one fact, beloved, that with the Lord one day is as a thousand years, and a thousand years as one day."

As I will further explain in a later chapter, Peter is contrasting the interadvent period or the Day of the Lord with the final Day of Judgment. Peter is describing scoffers appearing during the last days who mock the promise of Christ's coming to judgment and is giving encouragement to the believers that he will keep his promise to judge. Again, the two days are set for two different sets of people, the elect and the lost. These are not 24-hour days but markers of different items of the same kind, one of redemption, the other of death. The Day of the Lord (salvation) continues on until the final Day of Judgment. Both days are seen as one day by God as both are hastening the coming of the final day, but for different reasons. One day is to gather the elect, the other to judge the lost. The elect hasten the coming of the Last Day by calling for the Lord to quicken this day and avenge their death, while the lost quicken their Day of Judgment through their sin and escalating hardness of heart. Th Day of Salvation is also called the day of light, for the light has come, in contrast to the day of darkness which none will escape.

As Christ is the firstfruits of the resurrection, so we are partakers of the first resurrection which returns us to our original perfection. In Revelation 20, the rest of the dead (those without eternal life) did not come to life until after the 1,000 years (v.5), which is the second resurrection. They suffer the second death (v.6) which has no power over the elect, for whatever is first is restored to the original state of perfection in Eden, and whatever is second remains in the state of sin via Adam's fall and is reserved for destruction on the Last Day.

Hebrews reinforces the link between firstfruits, firstborn, and first resurrection, especially as it relates to the thesis of this book.

> But you have come to Mount Zion and to the city of the living God, the heavenly Jerusalem, and to innumerable angels in festal gathering, <u>and to the assembly of the firstborn</u> who are enrolled in heaven, and to God, the judge of all, <u>and to the spirits of the righteous made perfect</u>, and to Jesus, the mediator of a new covenant, and to the sprinkled blood that speaks a better word than the blood of Abel. (Heb. 12:22-24)

Here the writer of Hebrews clearly connects those saints already in heaven, "the assembly of the firstborn", and "the spirits of the righteous made perfect". The point cannot be escaped that whatever is "first" relates to the Kingdom of God and therefore means "restored to initial perfection", or redemption completed for the saints. Therefore, the assembly of saints already in heaven are called the assembly of the firstborn. While the word translated "spirits" is sometimes used by those defending the intermediate state to mean "bodyless souls", as we have seen above, we cannot conclusively determine whether this refers to the soul only or refers to a complete person. However, the term "perfected" clarifies what is going on here. I submit perfected means complete, body and soul. Perfect is the completed stage of any progression, for it cannot be improved upon and therefore the perfected saints in heaven cannot be awaiting the further grace of their bodies because they are perfect in heaven watching us. How can bodyless souls be declared perfect? They cannot because they are not complete. I believe the text provides the answer, as "the spirts of the righteous made perfect" perfectly describes what happens in the saint's life as we are declared righteous upon new birth, as our spirit/soul is given new life and recreated in Christ's image, but remain entombed in a spiritually dead body, awaiting perfection in our resurrection to our eternal spiritual body.

Part 1 has provided an overview of my defense of the bodily resurrection of the saint upon death and the resurrection to God's wrath on Judgment Day for the unbeliever. We now proceed to the texts supporting this view. Part 2 begins by analyzing the Old Testament typology, from Moses leading the exodus of the Israelites from Egypt through Joshua leading the nation into the Promised Land. (Egypt typifying bondage to sin and the Promised Land entrance into heaven for the saint). We will then begin the New Testament exposition with the clearest and most complete description of the bodily resurrection by Paul in 1 Corinthians 15 and then move to other texts. Mankind needs another body when our mortal bodies perish. I encourage the reader, when they read Part 2 and during their personal bible studies, to consider if the goal of the Christian's life on earth is to be freed from our body of sin, transformed into our glorious heavenly body, and resurrected to heaven to be united body and soul with our Lord. Part 2 will defend this rather than the common teaching of an intermediate state looking forward to the Day of Judgment. May God give us wisdom by his Spirit.

PART 2

EXEGETICAL BASIS FOR THE
INAUGURATED VIEW

Part 2 takes the framework laid out in Part 1 and explores key biblical texts supporting the Inaugurated view. We begin with several Old Testament typologies and then move to John's Gospel, central passages in both of Paul's letters to the Corinthians and 1 Thessalonians and then review other New Testament texts looking for overall congruence. The central focus of Part 2 being whether these texts better support the traditional view or the Inaugurated view.

CHAPTER 4

OLD TESTAMENT TYPOLOGY

It is imperative that any exegetical work for this kind of study first look at the Old Testament to make sure that our views, based in the New Testament, align with what was written there. Christ stated that everything written in the Old Testament testified of him. Therefore, any New Testament exegesis that departs from the timeline for judgment in Old Testament bears the burden of proof. Further, because everything points to Christ, typologies are the first place we must look.

The Old Testament provides clear examples of the work Christ was to perform. This work is the salvation of his people and is prefigured in the building of the Kingdom of God on earth through the nation of Israel. My goal in this section is to reinforce that understanding that the Promised Land in the Old Testament is a type of heaven and that, applied to our resurrection, the completion of the redemption of mankind is upon entry into the Promised Land or heaven where the true Temple of Christ dwells.

Moses / Joshua, and Red Sea /Jordan River Types

We can trace the future work of Christ using of two sets of figures from the Old Testament: David and Solomon and Moses and Joshua[19]. The Old Testament often produces a pattern in which the successor of one person receives the promises made by God. David was a man of war battling the earthly enemies, but Solomon was allowed to build the temple. Typologically, we see David leading the church (nation) into battle on earth, and in Solomon we see the church in its eschatological fruition in heaven. We see this motif predecessor and successor in Moses and Joshua as well. Moses led the nation during the wilderness journey typifying the saint's journey while exiled and still on earth with enemies to battle, and Joshua who led the nation into the Promise Land typifies heaven where rest from the previous battles was obtained. Similarly, we see a relationship between Moses crossing the Red Sea and Joshua crossing the Jordan River.

I will focus on the Old Testament examples of Moses and Joshua to establish a clear typological basis for NT resurrection life using the Red Sea and Jordan River crossings as the primary focus because these OT water crossings have a clear New Testament antitype. Our questions are then should be 1) what do the water crossings of Moses and Joshua tell New Testament readers about Christ's redemption plan? and 2) does our theology match this Old Testament type? These are the important questions because these crossings were much more than just geographical obstacles to overcome. These were the dangerous waters which provided the entry point or boundary into the Kingdom of God while still on the earth, first at the Red Sea then via the Tabernacle with God's presence guided the nation in their wilderness wanderings though exiled from their future home in the Promised Land. Second, when they entered the Promised Land at the Jordan River crossing an earthly kingdom where Jerusalem and the permanent Temple would become the centerpieces. After the trials and battles in the wilderness were over, they had entered into God's rest in the secure city with the Temple mount.

These Old Testament water crossings typified death experiences that resulted in new spiritual life in Christ: the Red Sea crossing typifying death to the old Adamic nature resulting in new inner spiritual life (regeneration)

---

[19] Other examples such as Elijah and Elisha can also be seen.

while still residing on the earth in their mortal bodies as they made their way to the Promised Land. Moses was prohibited from entering the Promised Land by God in Deut. 32:51-52, but the task would be taken up by Joshua at the Jordan River, who is also a type of Christ. The crossing of the Jordan River typified death to their mortal body as they obtained their resurrection life via an escalated or glorified outer covering as they were resurrected from earth to heaven and entered the Promised Land where they lived in Jerusalem where the Temple resided. These two death-to-life experiences through a watery grave represented the realm of the dead. The first death at the Red Sea brought new resurrection life to the soul or inner man, the second death at the Jordan River brought resurrection life to the outer man or body as the saint rises to its heavenly home. A saint has a body fit for either an earthly or a heavenly residence and is not ever found "naked" as Paul will make clear later in 2 Corinthians 5. Nakedness is not a characteristic of the child of God, but rather a characteristic of the lost: at death as they lose their mortal body, but no resurrection life awaits them, thus are "naked".

The task of taking the Israelites into the Promised Land was given to Joshua, therefore he typifies Christ in his exultation providing the way for the saint at death to enter heaven. Even more importantly, Joshua's entrance to the Promised Land through the Jordan River depicts Christ's presence with his people as they make this transition from death to life or from the earthly to the heavenly realm. This is represented by the Ark being borne by the priests as the nation makes the crossing. Christ is active in the lives of his people throughout the church age and is with us in our darkest hour of death to safely bring us into his heavenly kingdom. I believe the singular event of Christ's death and resurrection initiated a two-fold realization of death-to-resurrection life experiences for his people as seen in the Old Testament types of the Red Sea new life and Jordan River resurrection life to heaven.

We see this two-part life and death timing in Adam's fall and our redemption. This short synopsis of the Moses / Joshua / Christ typology details the relationship between the Red Sea and Jordan River passages to the timing of the resurrection for the believer. Water is regularly depicted in the Old Testament as a death experience. Satan is the agent of death as thru his deception man lost his life and suffered the penalty of death in the garden. The great sea monster Leviathan resides in the deep waters. The seas depict chaos[20]. God uses the sea to drown his enemies in both Noah's flood and the Exodus, thus it represents a depository for the dead and the lost. I make the case that the Exodus through the Red Sea and the entrance to the Promised Land through the Jordan River correspond to two life-through-death experiences for the New Testament saint. GK Beale identifies these two exodus water crossings as exiting the chaos of oppression in Egypt and chaos of exile in the wilderness, resulting in new creation through both the Red Sea and the small red sea (Jordan River)[21] . These new creation through death experiences identified by Beale match my identification of the crossing of the Red Sea as new life through regeneration and the crossing of the Jordan as new resurrection bodily life at our death on earth.

The Exodus corresponds to our participation in the death of Christ on the cross and the crucifying of our old carnal nature which at the same time bringing new life by our regeneration via the Holy Spirit. The Israelites were saved by God, through his Spirit, holding back the waters of the sea while walking through on dry ground while the same sea drowns and thus brings death to the Egyptians.

> Was it not you who dried up the sea, the waters of the great deep, who made the depths of the sea a way for the redeemed to pass over? (Isa. 51:10)

> Therefore, if anyone is in Christ, he is a <u>new creation</u>. The old has passed away; behold, the new has come. (2 Cor. 5:17)

Likewise, the Jorden River crossing and Joshua's leadership presents another life through death experience as they pass through the river at flood stage on dry ground, mimicking the Exodus from Egypt. God did wonders at their crossing.

---

[20] The beasts of Revelation also rise from the sea.

[21] G.K. Beale, *A New Testament Biblical Theology*, (Grand Rapids, Baker Academic, 2011), 60.

> Then Joshua told the people, "Consecrate yourselves, for tomorrow the LORD will do wonders among you. (Josh. 3:5)

> For if we have been united with him in a death like his, we shall certainly be united with him in a <u>resurrection</u> (life) like his. (Rom. 6:5)

The closing verses of Joshua tie this land to the end times or heavenly reality to be cleansed and opened by Christ, where rest and security were secured, and all the promises of God were either fulfilled or will be fulfilled.

> Thus the LORD gave to Israel all the land that he swore to give to their fathers. And they took possession of it, and they settled there. And the LORD gave them rest on every side just as he had sworn to their fathers. Not one of all their enemies had withstood them, for the LORD had given all their enemies into their hands. Not one word of all the good promises that the LORD had made to the house of Israel had failed; all came to pass. (Josh 21:43-45)

The complete victory over God's enemies which began with Joshua and was typologically fulfilled with the reign of David and Solomon is prophesied to include the perfect rest and completion of this Old Testament example by the Messiah.

E. De Pressense in his sermon, "The Passage of Jordan the Symbol of Death", gives his thoughts on the Jordan passage as a symbol of death,

> The passage of Jordan as the necessary way of entrance into the land of promise has always been regarded as symbolic of the death of the Christian. The same causes which allowed the children of Israel to cross the stream without being buried in its waters, operate in the case of the believing soul, to enable him also to pass through the deep-water floods without being overflowed by them.[22]

---

[22] https://biblehub.com/sermons/auth/pressense/the_passage_of_jordan_the_symbol_of_death.htm

The procession which began at the Red Sea ends upon crossing the Jordan River and entering the Promised Land. We who had already been united in life and resurrection with our Lord, enter heaven as the outer sinful nature housed in the mortal body is removed, as nothing unclean may enter heaven. But imagine the procession into heaven without the full victory Christ wrought on the cross—for this is what is taught in the intermediate state because it is not a victory over death for the body. The body has no part in the parade into heaven because it is not included in the entrance into heaven in the doctrine of the intermediate state. It is an enigma for me how the Church recognizes the spiritual death of the old man (mortal body) at the cross but refuses to understand that the mortal body's physical death is the final victory over death for the body and does not see the transition which takes place at death into a new spiritual body, allowing the spiritual body to take part of this procession into heaven. This process is a mirror image of the two stages of death for Adam in Genesis, where he experienced spiritual death immediately, and his mortal body experienced physical death later. In redemption the process of Adams fall is reversed: first the inner soul is given new life when the old nature is circumcised by Christ's death, followed by the new resurrection life in heaven when the mortal body is removed at death.

The only conclusion to be drawn from the doctrine of the intermediate state is that the power of the cross and the resurrection—the gospel—has been morphed into only a partial victory for just the spirit at death, thus Christ becomes only the "life" and "resurrection" for the soul at death and the body's resurrection waits till the eschaton. As with the problem of Dispensationalism creating a millennial reign on earth with unglorified saints on earth at the same time a glorified Christ has returned to earth, creating an amalgamation of different states of mankind on earth, so too the doctrine of the intermediate state creates the same issue but in reverse: a glorified Christ in heaven with saints who have not experienced complete glorification, for their glorified bodies are still in the future. The Old Testament typology in which the death experience of the Exodus through the Red Sea resulting in new life to the wilderness journey with the Spirit, and through the death experience of the Jordan River, typifying physical death and resulting in entrance into the Promised Land, refutes the intermediate state model.

More importantly, the important point is that physical death of the mortal body at the end of the earthly existence results in two clear but different patterns. Saints and the lost do not share the same pattern, but they do share the fact that the end of their time on earth results in the conclusion of their work done in the body, either for good or evil. Paul describes the saint as going from "life to life" and the lost as from "death to death". This describes a continuing state for both, either in life or death. But as the resurrection was a present and continuing reality for the saint, it results in the transition into the new body fit for heaven. Immediate transition at death is the saints' pattern. The patten for the lost is the removal of the mortal body into a condition of nakedness or without the outer bodies covering. It is in this state that they await Final Judgment on the Last Day, when the lost are resurrected to heaven only to experience the second death. These differing time frames for the elect and the lost, as opposed to a common resurrection day, will be a continuing focus and detailed in later sections.

> Isaiah 43:2 "When you pass through the waters, I will be
> with you;
> and through the rivers, they shall not overwhelm you;
> when you walk through fire you shall not be burned,
> and the flame shall not consume you."

Here in Isaiah, we see echoes of the deep waters of the Red Sea and the stream of the Jordan River where the elect escaped death, combined with a final walk through fire, a judgment, but a judgment in which they escape death as they did through the water passages. I believe the final walk through fire is the judgment at death. Instead of death, the saint passes into resurrection life for the new body, as the flames will not set them ablaze. It is the final acquittal of Adam's curse as we enter past the flaming sword placed to guard the reentrance by Adam or his progeny, to heaven after his sin in Genesis 3. The lost, however, will not escape this judgment of fire after death.

The obvious difference between the Old Testament typology and the intermediate state, is that the former has only one Jordan River crossing representing a death to life transition resulting in perfect rest in the

Promised Land. For the intermediate state, the Jordan River crossing into the Promised Land results in only a transition of the soul into the Promised Land, requiring another Jordan River crossing to correspond to the entrance of the glorious body of the saint into heaven on judgement day. There is no such Old Testament type representing the additional Jordan River crossing required for the transition of the body into the Promised Land. This is the fatal flaw. The entire person of the Old Testament saint walked through on dry ground through both the Red Sea and the Jordan River, unlike the wilderness example of the faithless OT generation whose bodies died, and whose bodies were buried in the wilderness, prior to the Exodus. The intermediate state presents a death to the body at the Jordan River crossing, as the saint's mortal body perishes and does not enter the Promised Land, but no resurrection life at death for the saint via a glorious heavenly body is awarded to the saint. This is not the gospel.

Jordan River and Christ as the Second Adam

At the crossing of Jordon God exalted Joshua (Josh. 3:7), pointing to the future exaltation of Christ in heaven after his death. Heaven is an exultation or raising to the invisible realm, and not to be confused with a resurrection to new life while still on earth: the difference is in where we are located and our state of perfection and rest. The beginning of Jesus ministry at his baptism in the Jordan River would certainly have brought the OT figure of Joshua who led the nation into the Promised Land or heaven to the minds of the Jewish people. John the Baptist informs them that the one whom the Holy Spirit descends upon was "the Son of God". In this brief section I will attempt to explain how Christ, as the ultimate fulfillment of the example of Joshua, fulfills his role as the second Adam as the "Son of God" who then leads his people through the same path he takes on earth to return to his preincarnate glory. I will make the case that Christ's death and resurrection correspond to the Red Sea crossing and his ascension into heaven corresponds to the Jordan River crossing. I believe current theology does not properly distinguish between Christ's resurrection to new life upon his time in the tomb, and his resurrection to heaven and return to his preincarnate glory. The ultimate goal of the

Messiah's work is to restore us to the glorious image of Christ, body and soul, and not to simply restore new life to the soul via inner glory on earth through regeneration. Rather it is to restore the entire man to outer glory which is accomplished upon arrival via resurrection when our mortal body is changed into our glorious, immortal, spiritual, and heavenly body when we are resurrected to heaven. The goal is the completion of the glorious inner/outer image which is only accomplished upon entrance to the heavenly kingdom. Resurrection must be understood not as a return to life on the earth, but more than that, a resurrection to heaven. The church celebrates Easter Sunday, or Christ's work to animate the mortal body and recreating the soul for work on earth. There is virtually no focus, teaching, or celebration of Christ's ascension to heaven after 40- days and return to his glory. This is our eschatological goal as well, but it is not properly taught because it is not properly understood, due to a misunderstanding of what resurrection is and when it takes place. Resurrection to new life, yes, but resurrection to heaven via death and new life to the body is the goal, per Christ's example and the Old Testament typology of Joshua's entrance into the eternal Promised Land. The wilderness was temporary. The following chart shows the same path for the Old Testament type, Christ, and the elect. The three distinctives to notice are 1) the combining of the cross and third day resurrection to new life on earth via the Old Testament Red Sea example, 2) the Old Testament Jordan crossing by Joshua type of the ascension of Christ resulting in heavenly glory in the Promised Land, and 3) the parallels between Christ's 40-day witness on earth upon new life and the wilderness Old Testament type, which is also our pattern after regeneration while remaining on earth until our resurrection to heaven at death. But it is a resurrection to glory, not an inglorious existence awaiting an end time completion.

Old Testament Type	Red Sea	Wilderness	Jordan River	Promised Land
Christ	Death/Life/Cross	40 DAYS	Ascension	Heaven
Elect	Death/Life/Cross	Earthly Life	Death/Life	Heaven

The topics of Old Testament circumcision and its New Testament counterpart of baptism play and important role. I will also make the case that the body in which Christ rose from the tomb and continued to testify for 40 days while on earth was the earthly body, and that upon his ascension, the transformation into his glorious spiritual body was completed. The glory cloud is the transport vehicle to the invisible heavenly realm. I base this claim upon four scriptural points: 1) the immortal body is part of the invisible realm yet based on the characteristics Paul lists in 1Cor. 15, the body of the resurrected Christ was visible and inglorious to all who witnessed it while on earth for 40 days; 2) the transfiguration demonstrated both the veiling of the outer glory of Christ while in the earthly body and the future outer glorious body; 3) the depiction of Christ when Paul was on the road to Damascus (Acts 9) and the vision of John in Rev. 1:12-18 describe the resurrected Christ in his glorious heavenly body post ascension, and; 4) Paul in 1 Cor. 15:37, 40 states:

> And what you sow is not the body that is to be . . . There are heavenly bodies and earthly bodies, but the glory of the heavenly is of one kind, and the glory of the earthly is of another.

Thus, the type of body corresponds to either an earthly or heavenly form depending on the location of the saint or in this point Christ.

As we retrace Christ's path from his death on the cross, to resurrection life three days later, to the 40-day witness on earth, and ultimately his resurrection to glorified life in heaven at his ascension, we will see this follows the Old Testament typology. The new life in Christ's body, which he received upon his resurrection from the dead, ultimately resulted in a glorified resurrection body and completed his return to his preincarnate state of outer glorification in heaven. As is true for Christ, so it must be true for his people as we follow him. Christ at his baptism and receipt of the endowment of the Spirit, begins his work as the new Joshua or second Adam, who will lead his people into the Promised Land which the first Adam had failed to accomplish, due to his sin. Christ's next act upon exiting the Jordan River after his baptism was his entrance into the wilderness to be tempted. Jesus succeeded in defeating Satan where Adam had failed because he did not yield to the temptations. In short by his victory in the wilderness over Satan, Christ was now the victorious second

Adam who would redeem his people from the tyranny of Satan through his death and subsequent resurrection. He would ultimately defeat Satan, destroying his entire kingdom, and restore heaven and earth to its intended sinless and glorious state on the Last Day. Upon his wilderness victory over Satan, Christ began the same journey Israel took in the Old Testament typology. His death and resurrection would provide the atonement to allow his people to receive new life as the people of Israel received new life when they passed through the Red Sea. His ascension would provide new resurrection life for the body as the crossing of the Jordan brought rest in the Promised Land.

Christ, the new Adam, experienced his Red Sea circumcision or baptism of death experience on the cross. Unlike the Old Testament rite of circumcision, in which the partial cutting away of only the foreskin represented an incomplete killing of the entire old nature of man, Christ underwent a complete circumcision of death to his entire body. This entirely destroyed Satan's claims on his people, as he died for his people in their stead. Here Christ, through this Red Sea death experience on the cross, becomes the new Moses, who led his people out of slavery in Egypt and through the Red Sea to begin their wilderness journey. This wilderness journey depicts the Old Testament saint's journey on earth led by the Spirit's overshadowing protection in the barren and waterless desert. Christ's wilderness journey of earthly witness was the 40-day period after his resurrection where he presented himself as alive to the world. For the New Testament saint, this 40-day witness of Christ's is analogous to our indwelling via our baptism (circumcision) by the Spirit, and our recreation from Adam's image and into Christ's image internally still veiled by our mortal body as we reside on earth until physical death. Following our earthly witness as in the Old Testament Joshua type, death to the body will lead us to resurrection life for our body in heaven. Paul states:

> For I do not want you to be unaware, brothers, a that our fathers were all under the cloud, and all passed through the sea, and all were baptized into Moses in the cloud and in the sea, and all ate the same spiritual food, and all drank the same spiritual drink. (1 Cor. 10:1-3)

> By no means! How can we who died to sin still live in it? Do you not know that all of us who have been baptized into Christ Jesus were baptized into his death? We were buried therefore with him by baptism into death, in order that, just as Christ was raised from the dead by the glory of the Father, we too might walk in newness of life. For if we have been united with him in a death like his, we shall certainly be united with him in a resurrection like his. (Rom. 6:2-5)

Interestingly, here in Romans, Paul describes Christ as raised from the dead as in "the restoration of his life", but our life is described as newness of life (spiritual), as in "not the life (actually spiritual death) we had before as Satan's progeny", but rather recreated anew and a part of the new creation with the life of Christ in our inner man. It follows then, that after the death of the body resurrection life for the outer body will likewise follow as immediately, just as when we were changed from a state of death to a state of life in Christ at regeneration and death to the old spiritual nature. Both are death to life events which happen at the time of death of either the inner man or outer man as Paul describes in Rom. 7:22 and 2 Cor. 4:16. This understanding negates the possibility of a period nakedness, or time without a body, for the elect. As Paul declares in 2 Cor. 5:1-5:

> For we know that if the tent that is our earthly home is destroyed, we have a building from God, a house not made with hands, eternal in the heavens. For in this tent we groan, longing to put on our heavenly dwelling, if indeed by putting it on we may not be found naked. For while we are still in this tent, we groan, being burdened— not that we would be unclothed, but that we would be further clothed, so that what is mortal may be swallowed up by life. He who has prepared us for this very thing is God, who has given us the Spirit as a guarantee.

This understanding of a difference in new inner life at regeneration and resurrection life to the outer body at our death gives a greater appreciation of

Christ stating he was "the life" and "the resurrection" where new life begins on earth but is completed upon the resurrection to heaven and receipt of the glorious body which had been veiled previously by the mortal body.

> For in him the whole fullness of deity dwells bodily, and you have been filled in him, who is the head of all rule and authority. In him also you were circumcised with a circumcision made without hands, by putting off the body of the flesh, by the circumcision of Christ, having been buried with him in baptism, in which you were also raised with him through faith in the powerful working of God, who raised him from the dead. And you, who were dead in your trespasses and the uncircumcision of your flesh, God made alive together with him, having forgiven us all our trespasses, by canceling the record of debt that stood against us with its legal demands. This he set aside, nailing it to the cross. He disarmed the rulers and authorities and put them to open shame, by triumphing over them in him. (Col. 2:9-15)

> I have a baptism to be baptized with, and how great is my distress until it is accomplished! (Luke 12:50)

> For as many of you as were baptized into Christ have put on Christ. (Gal. 3:27)

The circumcision of Christ, or baptism of death, would not in itself bring new life to his people, only upon his resurrection back to life on the third day would the two events combine to destroy the claims Satan had over those who had been taken captive and assumed his fallen nature. Christ's death killed our old nature, and his resurrection life would now recreate our nature into his image, but still awaiting its future release from the mortal body of death, and elevation to heaven and transformation into our glorious heavenly body at our death.

The next event after Christ's Red Sea death experience was his resurrection to life on the third day. The water passages combined a death to life experience in which the Egyptians died in the water, but the Israelites exited the sea into new life in the wilderness. Likewise, in the gospel Christ's death and resurrection to life provide our entrance into our life of witness to the world. The same is true for Christ's transition from resurrection to his 40-day period of witness on earth, described earlier as the resurrection of his earthly body. The resurrection of his earthly body was the final visible sign Christ gave to the world that no one could deny and follows the narrative in John's gospel where Christ performed visible signs no one could deny that testified that he was the promised Messiah.

> He presented himself alive to them after his suffering by many proofs, appearing to them during forty days and speaking about the kingdom of God. (Acts 1:3)

He presented himself alive in the same body for 40 days as proof of his return to life.

> As they were talking about these things, Jesus himself stood among them, and said to them, "Peace to you!" But they were startled and frightened and thought they saw a spirit. And he said to them, "Why are you troubled, and why do doubts arise in your hearts? See my hands and my feet, that it is I myself. Touch me, and see. For a spirit does not have flesh and bones as you see that I have." And when he had said this, he showed them his hands and his feet. And while they still disbelieved for joy and were marveling, he said to them, "Have you anything here to eat?" They gave him a piece of broiled fish, and he took it and ate before them. (Lk. 24:36-42)

Here Christ makes it clear he was not yet glorified and in his spiritual body, as Paul describes the body which has been exalted or resurrected to heaven. He corrects the disciples who "*thought they saw a spirit*" or that he was in his future spiritual form by: 1) instructing them to look with their eyes and touch him, for the invisible world cannot be touched or seen; 2) instructs them that a spiritual being (*spirit*) does not have flesh and bones "that I have" making it beyond dispute his earthly form is presented alive to them, and; 3) as they "*still disbelieved*" due to their marveling at his resurrection, he gave another proof by taking boiled fish and eating it in their presence.

This 40-day earthly witness by Christ corresponds to the 40-year wilderness journey for the nation of Israel before they entered the Promised Land, as well as the period of time on earth between regeneration and physical death for the individual saint. Upon death they are taken to heaven because their time to witness for Christ had ended.

The final stage of Christ's pilgrimage to heaven after the 40-day witness on earth was his exaltation and transition into his glorious state upon his ascension to heaven via the glory cloud. Below are two examples where the glory cloud is identified with the heavenly realm, the transfiguration and ascension. The transfiguration prefigured what would soon take place as Christ warned them not to speak of it until after his resurrection, when apparently, they would understand the event more fully.

> And when he had said these things, as they were looking on, he was lifted up, and a cloud took him out of their sight. (Acts 1:9)

> And as the men were parting from him, Peter said to Jesus, "Master, it is good that we are here. Let us make three tents, one for you and one for Moses and one for Elijah"— not knowing what he said. As he was saying these things, a cloud came and overshadowed them, and they were afraid as they entered the cloud. And a voice came out of the cloud, saying, "This is my Son, my Chosen One; listen to him!" (Lk. 9: 33-35)

The ascension to heaven via the glory cloud is the point at which Christ transitioned from his earthly body to his glorious spiritual body as he enters the heavenly realm. Until this point, the characteristics of his body must then meet all the characteristics Paul lists in 1 Cor. 15. This will be covered in greater detail in a following chapter. The theology of Christ entering heaven in the same body he rose from the grave and walked the earth for the 40 days following his resurrection to life is incorrect. The point of this short synopsis of Christ's journey after his baptism in the Spirit is that his path is the same path his people will take, and after their time of suffering on earth they too will proceed at death to heavenly glory and transition into their heavenly glorious body. This transition is the Jordan River death to life experience of the Old Testament, in which passage the Israelites entered into the Promised Land.

Joshua's Jordan River Crossing in Chapters 3-5: A Death to Life Event

The final stage of Christ's work was his exodus, departure, or ascension into heaven. Like the Jordan crossing, this was a death to life event to an escalated or exalted status for Christ and therefore for his people—a second baptism or circumcision resulting in the final victory over death for the saint in the heavenly kingdom after the journey of suffering and trials of the earthly pilgrimage typified by the Old Testament 40-year wilderness journey and Christ's 40-day witness. In Joshua 3:7, 13 a comparison to Moses Red Sea exodus is made,

> The LORD said to Joshua, "Today I will begin to exalt you in the sight of all Israel, that they may know that, as I was with Moses, so I will be with you." … And when the soles of the feet of the priests bearing the ark of the LORD, the Lord of all the earth, shall rest in the waters of the Jordan, the waters of the Jordan shall be cut off from flowing, and the waters coming down from above shall stand in one heap.

Here in verse 13, as well as in 3:16 and 4:7 the phrase "cut off" is used. This is the Hebrew word *karath*. *Karath* is used in the rite of making a covenant where the dual sanctions of either blessing or death (curse) are sworn to by the covenant parties. The cutting of the sacrifices represents the death sanction for breaking the covenant. Circumcision and baptism are the Old Testament and New Testament signs respectively, of this inward and ultimately outward manifestation of the death and cutting away of the fallen nature. It is a death resulting in new life, and as the Israelites pass through the Jordan this reality is typologically enacted, a baptism to death and a circumcision of the flesh. What is portrayed in two stages in the Old Testament via the Red Sea and Jordan River crossings for the nation, was initiated through the singular circumcision of death and resurrection of Christ. In this way, the Jordan crossing is the final removal of the outer body of death and endowment with the outer spiritual and glorified body for the saint. According to John and Paul, we have inner glory while still on this earth:

> The glory that you have given me I have given to them, that they may be one even as we are one, I in them and you in me, that they may become perfectly one, so that the world may know that you sent me and loved them even as you loved me. (Jn. 17:22-23)

> And we all, with unveiled face, beholding the glory of the Lord, are being transformed into the same image from one degree of glory to another. For this comes from the Lord who is the Spirit. (2 Cor. 3:18)

The indwelling of the Spirit is the proof of our possession and the guarantee of this future endowment of glory at death. It is not a future endowment with glory, after having resided in heaven, at the end time resurrection of the dead. The "dead" are all those who rejected his first appearance or the Old Testament revelation in prophecy, as contrasted with those with life in Christ. The final appearance of Christ does result in the glorification of the cosmos and final judgment.

> On that day the LORD exalted Joshua in the sight of all Israel, and they stood in awe of him just as they had stood in awe of Moses, all the days of his life. (Josh. 4:14)

The greater work than Moses is the exaltation of Joshua, the successor after Moses. Moses was not allowed to lead the Israelites into the Promised Land, but only into the wilderness.

then you shall let your children know, 'Israel passed over this Jordan on dry ground.' For the LORD your God dried up the waters of the Jordan for you until you passed over, as the LORD your God did to the Red Sea, which he dried up for us until we passed over. (Joshua 4:22-23)

This passage uses the same imagery of waters passing over the nation while they walked through the dry riverbed as when they walked on the bed of the Red Sea. As the Angel of the Lord passed over the Israelites and destroyed the Egyptians, here death to our outer body passes over the saint to new life in the midst of the Jordan. A further point can be deduced from the depth of the Red Sea and the relative shallowness of the river crossing. I believe this indicates that this final journey is the finishing of a prior work. Christ made a similar comment to Peter when he washed of the disciple's feet, stating their bodies were already clean and only needed their feet to be washed, meaning the tie of our feet to this present earth was the only further cleansing required.

Now before the Feast of the Passover, when Jesus knew that his hour had come to depart out of this world to the Father, having loved his own who were in the world, he loved them to the end. During supper, when the devil had already put it into the heart of Judas Iscariot, Simon's son, to betray him, Jesus, knowing that the Father had given all things into his hands, and that he had come from God and was going back to God, rose from supper. He laid aside his outer garments, and taking a towel, tied it around his waist. Then he poured water into a basin and began to wash the disciples' feet and to wipe them with the towel that was wrapped around him. He came to Simon Peter, who said to him, "Lord, do you wash my feet?" Jesus answered him, "What I am doing you do not understand now, but afterward you will understand." Peter said to him, "You shall never wash my feet." Jesus answered him, "If I do not wash you, you have no share with me." Simon Peter said to him, "Lord, not my feet only but also my hands and my head!" Jesus said to him, "The one who has bathed does not need to wash, except for his feet, but is completely clean". (Jn. 13:1-9)

The baptism via the Red Sea or new life in Christ had made them "clean"—this is regeneration. Here we see unmistakable parallels between baptism and exodus with renewal of the inner man, and between the Jordan crossing with the outer garment (body) being put aside, and transition to heaven with both an Old Testament and New Testament context as the event takes place during the Passover. Notably, however, the text ties the event not to the cross but to his coming departure and return to the Father, or his ascension, which is described as the end of his time here on earth. He then lays aside his outer garment foretelling our laying aside our outer garment, our mortal body, which needs this final cleansing or passage through the Jordan River to remove any curse from Adam as we transition to heavenly outer glory and our eternal rest.

CHAPTER 5

GOSPELS

Gospels: The Final Sign was Christ's 40-day Earthly Witness

John's gospel is characterized as a book of "signs"—the miraculous signs performed by Christ—which were visible proofs to the witnesses, that he was the promised Messiah. Each of these signs depicted a deeper spiritual transformation that the Messiah came to accomplish through a physical and visible miracle (e.g., the healing of the blind man in Jn. 9 which showed Christ's ability to open eyes of those formerly blinded by Satan to the revelation of God in him. The 40-days Christ remained on the earth after his resurrection to life was the final visible sign given to his followers, that he was alive and had risen from the dead. Luke records this in Lk. 24: 46-49:

> Thus it is written, that the Christ should suffer and on the third day rise from the dead, and that repentance for the forgiveness of sins should be proclaimed in his name to all nations, beginning from Jerusalem. You are witnesses of these things. And behold, I am sending the promise of my Father upon you. But stay in the city until you are clothed with power from on high.

As with my contention that this resurrection back to life was in the same mortal body placed in the grave, here Luke documents Christ expressing this same idea. Luke describes the visible events the disciples testified had occurred—his death, bodily resurrection, and the proclamation of the gospel both prior to his death and now after his restoration to life while he remained on the earth. The things of this world, in this case what the disciples had seen (including the body of Christ they could see was risen and standing before them), were all visible to them. But the things of the Spirit in heaven are invisible. Christ tells them to await the promise of the Spirit which he could only give after he ascends into the invisible heavenly realm. Only after Christ's ascension into the spiritual realm and return to his former glory, could he then send them the Spirit. For this witness to visible or earthly events then cannot be a witness of his resurrection to heaven which was veiled in the cloud and is an invisible realm to them while on earth. They only saw the cloud into which he entered, and then he was gone from their sight, so they did not see his ascension with their eyes, so the resurrection to life on earth they did see was the earthly body. The future sending of the Spirit at Pentecost was their validation he had arrived in heaven at the right hand of God. So, this event clearly occurs prior to his ascension and therefore the body is the earthly body. Luke begins the book of Acts with the same thought in, Acts 1:1-5:

> In the first book, O Theophilus, I have dealt with all that Jesus began to do and teach, until the day when he was taken up, after he had given commands through the Holy Spirit to the apostles whom he had chosen. He presented himself alive to them after his suffering by many proofs, appearing to them during forty days and speaking about the kingdom of God. And while staying with them he ordered them not to depart from Jerusalem, but to wait for the promise of the Father, which, he said, "you heard from me; for John baptized with water, but you will be baptized with the Holy Spirit not many days from now."

Here Luke describes the 40-day time period after Jesus' resurrection as the occasion for him to provide "many proofs" of his resurrection. This identified his body as his mortal body, not a glorious body. This is most clearly seen in Lk.24:37-40:

> But they were startled and frightened and thought they saw a spirit. And he said to them, "Why are you troubled, and why do doubts arise in your hearts? See my hands and my feet, that it is I myself. Touch me, and see. For a spirit does not have flesh and bones as you see that I have." And when he had said this, he showed them his hands and his feet.

Here Christ is making it clear he is mortal and not a Spiritual man at this time, confirming this bodily resurrection as the final sign as prophesied by Christ, in Lk. 11:29-30:

> "This is a wicked generation. It demands a sign, but none will be given it except the sign of Jonah. For as Jonah was a sign to the Ninevites, so the Son of Man will be a sign to this generation."

Christ states his resurrection from the dead will be the only sign given to that wicked generation at his first advent. To summarize: Christ during the 40-day period, witnessed to his resurrection to life in his mortal body on earth, and this period corresponds to our regeneration and our earthly exile or wilderness journey prior to resurrection to new life for the body in heaven. The wilderness journey was 40 years, providing another textual reference to these two events.

The point of this section is to show that Christ's resurrection to new life after his death by crucifixion corresponds to the saint's regeneration to life. This new life bears witness on earth in the earthly flesh and blood body, as seen both in Christ's 40-day witness and the saint's life on earth prior to ascending to heaven. Upon the completion of this period of visible witness on earth, our resurrection into heaven and transition into our spiritual body results in glorification and the completion of both Christ's redemption of his church, and for the individual saint, their return to the image of Christ, body and soul. Our resurrection to bodily glory is not a Last Day of judgment event at the final return of Christ.

Gospel of John-The Last Day as our death or Judgment Day

The phrase "last day" is used to describe both the day a person dies and the "Last Day" or the time of final judgment in the New Testament. A simple way to understand the difference is that "last day" refers to an individual human at death, and a "Last Day" refers to the end current age at Christ's coming to judgment for all mankind. Individuals experience either a positive or negative judgment at death in which their eternal fate has been determined. The earthly or Satanic Kingdom awaits its judgment along with the lost who await a second judgment resulting in the "second" death on their "Last Day" which is synonymous with Judgment Day. John's gospel in particular highlights that our bodily death is in view when we read the phrase "last day". The truth and simplicity of resurrection life at death for the believer has been morphed into the fallacies of the intermediate state doctrine and the common resurrection of all mankind on Judgment Day, by the assigning of "last ay" to only the final Judgment Day.

The resurrection of Lazarus in John 11 is central for understanding when the resurrection to life occurs. Martha's and Mary clearly only have Last Day resurrection at the end of time in view. This view will be corrected by Christ. He never denied their view of a Last Day resurrection— leaving in place the final resurrection of the lost at the end—but he did supplement their understanding, showing the reality of resurrection life he would soon initiate for his people. This teaching mirrors Paul's 3-part order of resurrection in 1 Corinthians 15 in which Christ is the first resurrection, next his people, and third the lost at the end of time.

> But each in his own order: Christ the firstfruits, then at his coming those who belong to Christ. Then comes the end, when he delivers the kingdom to God the Father after destroying every rule and every authority and power. (1 Cor. 15:23-24)

The themes of death of our mortal body being our "last day", and Christ as the true bread of resurrection life in which brings life at our death are common threads both leading up to the Lazarus section and continuing to the completion of John's gospel. Because of this, I believe the resurrection life at death can only be understood as a glorious new bodily resurrection. The curse to the lost is the loss of their body at death, resulting in "nakedness" and awaiting resurrection to the second death. Chapter 6 is a case study tying the idea of death described as "last day" leading to immediate resurrection with the Lazarus text in chapter 11:

John 6 begins with the feeding of the 5000 verses 1-15. It is full of allusions of Christ as the Shepherd leading his sheep to rest in heaven. The setting—a mountain during the Passover—links to his future death and resurrection which will lead to death passing over us and to the receipt of resurrection life and eternal rest in heaven as we transition to the true mountain of God in heaven. The 5,000 sat down, typifying our rest in heaven with Christ as described by Paul in Ephesians 2:6 where the believer is seated with him in the heavenly realms. Eating the bread that only the Son of God can provide can be understood as our current status on earth, represented in communion in which we feed by faith in the life-giving bread while awaiting the fullness of life at our death. The 12 baskets point to the full number of the elect to be redeemed, represented by the 12 tribes of Israel. Verse 14 identifies this miracle as a "sign" which, for John, is a visible miracle representing a deeper spiritual reality.

Immediately following, in 6:16-21, the disciples' journey by boat at night over the water of the Sea of Galilee, at first without Christ, resulted in fear. The night and sea can easily be seen as picturing the realm of the dead which all mankind must pass through. Immediately upon Christ's arrival via walking on the water, however, the disciples took him into the boat and they safely reached the land (Promised Land) on the other side of the sea. This is a picture of Christ "coming to us" in our hour of death and providing safe entry to heaven instead of a watery grave in the realm of the dead. Death passed over the disciples as it did for Noah and the nation at the Exodus, as both were protected from the waters of death. Death holds no fear for his people. Death means resurrection life.

The "Bread of Life" discourse in 6:22-59 begins at the other side of the sea which is more than just a good place to have this discussion: it sets the picture that this land on the other side of the watery trial at death is to be understood as heaven and the realization of resurrection life. The feeding of the "bread of Life" prior to the transition across the water was the promise that resulted in the reality of this resurrection life.

It is interesting that only the disciples entered the boat which Christ brought safely to the other side, as there is only one "boat" that offers salvation—an allusion to Noah and ultimately Christ. The crowd left behind entered other boats to arrive at the other side. Christ makes the point that those arriving were only interested in the physical bread and not the "bread of life" he provides:

> When they found him on the other side of the sea, they said to him, "Rabbi, when did you come here?" Jesus answered them, "Truly, truly, I say to you, you are seeking me, **not** because you saw signs, but because you ate your fill of the loaves. Do not work for the food that perishes, but for the food that endures to eternal life, which the Son of Man will give to you. For on him God the Father has set his seal. (Jn. 6:25-27)

Christ the true "bread of life" is contrasted with both the Old Testament manna from the wilderness and the earthly bread Christ had previously fed them. It describes the bread of this world as working for what perishes, an allusion to an end resulting in death, whereas the true "bread of life" results in eternal life, which refers to our death not resulting in perishing but rather more abundant resurrection life in heaven.

The next section, 6:30-51, clearly shows the "last day" is the day of death for the individual, not the "Last Day". Either resurrection (raising) to life occurs or a judgment (lowering) to the realm of the dead awaits one's death. This section contrasts Christ as the true bread of life, with the typical bread supplied by God to the wilderness generation. That bread did not result in resurrection life at death for that generation: they died and their bodies were buried in the desert due to their lack of faith. They only perceived the manna as normal food rather than pointing to Christ. Recall the wilderness is typifies life on earth which should have resulted in entrance to the Promised Land for the nation upon the Jordan River crossing. But entrance into the land was conditioned on faith in the manna pointing to the true bread of life which was the coming messiah. As with the wilderness generation, the lost will experience death without new life at their "last day".

A closer look at verses 37-40, will confirm whether "last day" in this context is at death or end time judgment for the elect.

> All that the Father gives me will come to me, and whoever comes to me I will never cast out. For I have come down from heaven, not to do my own will but the will of him who sent me. And this is the will of him who sent me, that I should lose nothing of all that he has given me, but raise it up on the last day. For this is the will of my Father, that everyone who looks on the Son and believes in him should have eternal life, and I will raise him up on the last day. (Jn. 6:37-40)

"All that the Father gives me" are the elect, who's coming to Christ will result in a resurrection. Jesus identifies two stages for the elect corresponding to regeneration and resurrection to heavenly life. Verses 37-38 identify this work of Christ as a "coming down" to bring salvation (regeneration) to the elect who would remain on earth. In verse 39, the only resurrection or ascension to heaven identified occurs on the Last Day. The statement *"but raise them up on the last day"* refers to one's death or last day on earth, for we remained on earth upon our regeneration.

Noticeably absent from this (as all other) texts is a clear description of differing times for the resurrection of the soul and the body. There is no identification of two resurrections in this text for the elect, only a resurrection to life on their last day (death) on earth. If the "last day" here is taken to mean a resurrection of the body on the Last Day of Judgment via the intermediate state, then this example does not account for the saint's resurrection to heaven as a soul at death. It is utterly implausible for this important aspect of the intermediate state doctrine to have been ignored by Christ. Therefore, it is my contention that these two differing resurrections derive from a false understanding. There is only one resurrection to life at death for the elect. Verse 40 repeats for emphasis, the same point I made about verses 37-39,

> For this is the will of my Father, that everyone who looks
> on the Son and believes in him should have eternal life,
> and I will raise him up on the last day.

Christ states a singular "last day" again. If there were two "last days" such as the resurrection of the soul at death and a future raising of the body on Judgment Day, Christ would not have only mentioned one. John summarizes the gospel in verse 40 which is the death and singular resurrection of Christ, where belief in him results in being "raised on the last day". Last day cannot be referring to Judgment Day if the Old Testament typology of the wilderness journey holds. There, bodily death resulted for those without faith but new bodily life in the "Promised Land" to Joshua and the nation. Second, this view accurately describes only one resurrection for the elect. Third, this section deals with the term "comings" or appearances which only refer to his advent to bring salvation, and our coming to Christ in heaven, not his final coming to earth for judgment. To insert in this section a reference to Final Judgment for the lost is inconsistent and contextually untenable. The "comings" are:

1. Christ *coming down* to earth to give life (v. 33)
2. Whoever *comes to Christ* shall never hunger (v.35)
3. All that the Father gives me will *come to me*, and whoever comes to me I will never cast out (v.37)
4. For I have *come down* from heaven, not to do my own will but the will of him who sent me. And this is the will of him who sent me, that I should lose nothing of all that he has given me, but raise it up on the last day. For this is the will of my Father, that everyone who looks on the Son and believes in him should have eternal life, and I will raise him up on the last day." (v. 38-40)
5. So the Jews grumbled about him, because he said, "I am the bread *that came down from heaven*." (v.41)
6. No one can *come to me* unless the Father who sent me draws him. And I will raise him up on the last day. (v.44)
7. Everyone who has heard and learned from the Father *comes to me* (v.45)

8. This is the bread that *comes down from heaven*, so that one may eat of it and not die. I am the living bread that *came down from heaven*. If anyone eats of this bread, he will live forever. And the bread that I will give for the life of the world is my flesh." (v, 50-51)

The last day here is <u>not</u> referring to the coming of Christ to judgment because the comings in this text all refer to Christ's coming down to earth for the salvation of his people. The Final Judgment is also a coming down of Christ to earth. The only two visible manifestations of Christ's "comings" to earth are at the first advent in the flesh, and the final coming to Judgment where all the lost world will see him. The assignment of "last day" here as being synonymous with the Judgment Day derives from the wrong assumption of a common resurrection day for all.

The result of this "coming" is the giving to his people these promises: life, will never hunger, never be cast out, have eternal life, and will not die. Notice the possession of eternal life is associated with not dying, thus instead of dying when our mortal body extinguishes, the result is resurrection life in the new body because we are free from the punishment of death through Christ's sacrifice in "the flesh". The future result of these promises for the elect is then being resurrected to life on their last day. As stated previously, the resurrection of the lost on Judgment Day does not result in eternal life but eternal death. This, it seems to me, unmistakably refutes the "last day" referred to here which brings eternal life is the same "Last Day" which brings death. Christ came to bring salvation (life) which is followed by his coming to bring judgment (death).

The final point of this section is in verse 51, "And the bread that I will give for the life of the world is my flesh." Here Christ speaks of the central and simple gospel message that death to our flesh means resurrection life in heaven, not an intermediate state. The death of Jesus body (*in the flesh*) on the cross purchased new life in our resurrection body when the mortal body perishes, for we receive the benefit of continued life at death. The substitutionary death of Christ is transferred to his people at their death, which is not death but more abundant life. The simplicity of the gospel message of his death resulting in our life instead of our death has been corrupted.

Christ connects the bread he offers with the wilderness example we explored in the last chapter. The death and burial of unfaithful Israelites in the wilderness, did not result in continued life in the Promised Land. Jesus contrasts this death to our mortal bodies to the eternal resurrection life he offers twice in verses 47-50, and again in verse 58.

> Truly, truly, I say to you, whoever believes has eternal life. I am the bread of life. Your fathers ate the manna in the wilderness, and they died. This is the bread that comes down from heaven, so that one may eat of it and not die. . .. This is the bread that came down from heaven, not like the bread the fathers ate, and died. Whoever feeds on this bread will live forever.

The account of Lazarus's resurrection in chapter 11 builds on this teaching, making the point that Christ initiated the resurrection from death to life for the elect upon his first advent and ensured the future resurrection of the dead (lost) on Judgment Day. Christ makes the point that he is the resurrection life now and not on the last day in John 11:1-44, correcting the first century Jewish belief that his coming would result in a singular restoration of all things on the Last Day, referring to the end time. Several verses in chapter 11 stand out:

> So the sisters sent to him, saying, "Lord, he whom you love is ill." But when Jesus heard it he said, "This illness does not lead to death. It is for the glory of God, so that the Son of God may be glorified through it. (3-4)

> Martha said to Jesus, "Lord, if you had been here, my brother would not have died. But even now I know that whatever you ask from God, God will give you." Jesus said to her, "Your brother will rise again." Martha said to him, "I know that he will rise again in the resurrection on the last day." Jesus said to her, "I am the resurrection and the life. Whoever believes in me, though he die, yet shall he

live and everyone who lives and believes in me shall never die. Do you believe this?" (21-26)

Now when Mary came to where Jesus was and saw him, she fell at his feet, saying to him, "Lord, if you had been here, my brother would not have died." (32)

Then Jesus, deeply moved again, came to the tomb. It was a cave, and a stone lay against it. Jesus said, "Take away the stone." (38-39)

Jesus said to her, "Did I not tell you that if you believed you would see the glory of God?" (40)

"Lazarus, come out." The man who had died came out. (43-44)

In verse 24 Martha tells Christ that she believed in a future resurrection at the end of time. Christ does not refute the truth of a resurrection at that time but corrects Martha and Mary's belief in the resurrection on the Last Day (a future event) and proves that he is the resurrection and life now for those who believe in him. He equates faith in him to resurrection life even in death and declares that what they see with Lazarus' resurrection is evidence of the glory of God being displayed (v.40). The resurrection of Lazarus and the future bodily resurrection of Christ must both be interpreted through the broader context of the entire book of John to arrive at the point Jesus is making to Mary and Martha. The spiritual sign he performed thru Lazarus was not merely an earthly resurrection but of a heavenly resurrection at death. This sign testified to the future resurrection of Christ and his subsequent ascension into heaven, thus proving for the apostles, that generation, and all future believers that physical death results in bodily resurrection

The signs which Jesus performed testified to the nation of Israel, that he was the Messiah. They could not deny the miracles or the fact that only one anointed by God could perform such breathtaking miracles. The resurrection of Lazarus was the sign that he was the bodily resurrection life at death, and corrected the sister's theology which was still looking for a final common resurrection day in the distant future for both believers and the lost. Christ did not deny the Final Judgment for the lost. The resurrection was standing before them. Granted, Lazarus would die again, but this sign would provide evidence that Christ was the resurrection life at death and would commence the resurrection of his saints upon his ascension and restoration to his previous glorious state in heaven. Lazarus's resurrection, Christ's resurrection, and ultimately the destruction of the Temple and the city of Jerusalem which would be the final sign he was the Messiah who had come to bring salvation to those who would believe, but also the final covenant curses upon the apostate nation of Israel and bring to end the old age. Finally, verses 40-44 connect Christ's proclamation that they will see the "glory" of God with the statement "the man who had died came out", thus connecting forever that our death to our body in the grave results in our "coming out" in glory.

CHAPTER 6

RESURRECTION OF THE BODY IN 1 CORINTHIANS 15

I will summarize what I believe are the critical errors of the intermediate state doctrine for clarity so that one can analyze the series of texts highlighted in the next several chapters, starting with 1 Corinthians 15, to see to which resurrection doctrine they support. The first error is of the belief in a common resurrection of the body for all mankind on Judgment Day. There is a second part of this same error: the belief that the lost will be resurrected in the body laid in the grave. The New Testament only speaks of a resurrection to new life by Christ for the elect in which they receive a new glorious body at death and are incorporated into the heavenly temple, which is Christ (see 2 Pt. 2:4-6, 1 Cor. 3:16, Eph. 2:19-22). The lost are resurrected bodyless to Judgment and eternal death, as there is no resurrection body other than that of to life. This is the second death for them after the first death of their body. The lost truly are bodyless souls awaiting final judgment on the Last Day. This curse must not be ascribed to the elect.

The second error is not distinguishing the prior completion of the heavenly Temple, (composed of all the elect with their outer glorious bodies), from the Judgment Day events resulting in the destruction of Satan, his kingdom, and unbelievers. There are two great days: the "Day of Salvation", followed by the "Day of Judgment". Along with this is a failure to understand the removal of the last elect on earth, (who will not experience death, but are taken up to heaven at Christ's final appearing to Judgment), as the final act of the "Day of Salvation", and these believers must be rescued from earth prior to the destruction of the old world.

Third, the resurrection of Christ is properly understood as his bodily resurrection on the third day. However, this is not the entirety of his resurrection. He was resurrected to his glorious body at the ascension to heaven. Because of this, the traditional view makes the error of believing that the resurrection of the body for the elect must be of our physical, mortal body.

The teaching regarding the resurrection in both First and Second Corinthians (chapters 6 and 7 respectively) concerns the resurrection of the body and cannot be read as only a spiritual resurrection of the soul or spirit. It is imperative to understand this so that one does not truncate resurrection to a partial resurrection of only the soul into heaven at death.

Chapter 15 is the central passage concerning the resurrection in 1 Corinthians. In it, Paul breaks down the resurrection into four sections:

1. The resurrection of Christ (1-11)
2. The resurrection of those who have or will die in Christ (12-34)
3. The type of the resurrection body (35-49)
4. The resurrection of those who do not experience death due to being alive at the Final Coming of Christ on Judgment Day (50-58)

This four-part instruction on the resurrection is further divided into two further subdivisions:

1. 3 resurrection types-
    •   Christ's (1-11)
    •   those who die in faith in Christ in this age (12-34)
    •   those in Christ who do not experience death (50-58)
2. The resurrection body type (35-49)

This second subdivision is important because Paul will use these same 3 resurrection examples (types) later in his expositions on resurrection.

Section 1: verses 1-11 Christ's resurrection

Now I would remind you, brothers, of the gospel I preached to you, which you received, in which you stand, and by which you are being saved, if you hold fast to the word I preached to you—unless you believed in vain. For I delivered to you as of first importance what I also received: that Christ died for our sins in accordance with the Scriptures, that he was buried, that he was raised on the third day in accordance with the Scriptures, and that he appeared to Cephas, then to the twelve. Then he appeared to more than five hundred brothers at one time, most of whom are still alive, though some have fallen asleep. Then he appeared to James, then to all the apostles. Last of all, as to one untimely born, he appeared also to me. For I am the least of the apostles, unworthy to be called an apostle, because I persecuted the church of God. But by the grace of God I am what I am, and his grace toward me was not in vain. On the contrary, I worked harder than any of them, though it was not I, but the grace of God that is with me. Whether then it was I or they, so we preach and so you believed.

The gospel is death to resurrection life. We need new life in our resurrection body that is fit for heaven when our mortal body perishes. I believe that the example of Christ's bodily resurrection must match our bodily resurrection at death, and that this is the heart of the gospel. The intermediate state doctrine severs the connection of the body and the soul, and denies that our entire man, body and soul, is resurrected at death. Protestant doctrine never addresses what I believe to be the glaring inconsistency of the bodily resurrection of Christ after his death, and our bodily resurrection not occurring at our death and entrance into heaven.

1 Corinthians 15 is the clearest exposition of the resurrection and the resurrection body in scripture. Notice that Paul does not separate and describe a first resurrection of the soul to heaven at the death of our body and then further explain that the soul would be united with the body during a common resurrection of all mankind on Judgement Day. We must ask "why not?" as this would be the perfect location to instruct us in this important aspect of the gospel. There is no clear teaching of differing resurrections for the soul and body in the gospels and there isn't one here. Is it plausible that Christ himself, the gospel narratives, and Paul left this important aspect of the gospel to us to weave together an amalgamation

of other verses? I believe the answer is no. Paul describes the "different" timings of three resurrections to heaven, and all of them refer to the complete man, body and soul. This teaching includes details regarding the manner in which the new glorious resurrection body differs from the mortal body. There is never a description of a gap in the resurrection of soul and body. In fact, the resurrection is described as a transition from one into the other.

Paul begins by reminding the readers of the gospel, and their need to "hold fast" to it, but until what point? The common understanding of the end of our walk of faith is when we die and reach our home with Christ in heaven. The gospel is no longer required for those who have entered heaven and are seated with Christ. Heaven is the end point for the Christian as our union with Christ in his heavenly Temple has been achieved. We have been resurrected out of the dangers of the evil kingdom on earth and released from the corruption which resided in our mortal bodies as we receive our immortal ones. Faith has become sight. The gospel and faith are left behind as they were gifts of grace to achieve our recreation into Christ's image as we transform into our glorious body, as faith becomes sight as we enter the presence of Christ in heaven. In 2 Cor. 5:6-7, Paul states this:

> So we are always of good courage. We know that while
> we are at home in the body we are away from the Lord,
> for we walk by faith, not by sight.

Here Paul contrasts being at home in our mortal body and walking by faith, with sight and the glorious body in heaven. These are the only two conditions of the saint, and both are with a body.

The process of salvation begins with faith at regeneration and ends with "sight" upon our entrance to heaven. The latter is seen in the 2 Corinthians passage cited above. The former is seen throughout the first section of 1 Corinthians 15. Paul's statements regarding the gospel: "which you received", "in which you stand", and "by which you are being saved, if you hold fast to the word I preached to you—unless you believe in vain", mirror the stages of Christian life on earth and provide the parameters for the recreation of the saint. The end parameter is not the Last Day.

The three points are: 1) regeneration (*which you received*), 2) the Christian life on earth or the wilderness journey (*in which you stand*), and 3) bodily death (*by which you are being saved, if you hold fast to the word I preached to you—unless you believed in vain*). The third marker is death as this is when faith is no longer required and is Paul's point here. For one's death is a judgment and results in either an exalted status in heaven, or if their faith did not hold fast, thus was only temporary faith, it would have been in vain.

The description of bodily death being the completion of the salvation experience can be easily seen from other texts from the Apostle Paul in which he encourages the saints to persevere through earthly trials which end at death. Resurrection life is continued life at death. Paul's clearest example of death being the culmination of one's work for Christ on earth and the receipt of resurrection life in heaven is 2 Tim. 4:6-8:

> For I am already being poured out as a drink offering, and the time of my departure has come. I have fought the good fight, I have finished the race, I have kept the faith. Henceforth there is laid up for me the crown of righteousness, which the Lord, the righteous judge, will award to me on that day, and not only to me but also to all who have loved his appearing.

Paul states all who loved Christ's work (gospel) accomplished at his first advent will receive crowns at the end of their life. Paul expresses his confidence in his heavenly reward due to his having kept the faith during his earthly trials, and where faith ends, fullness of salvation is consummated. The day of the awarding of the crown is the day of his death and cannot be taken to indicate the Last Day of Judgment. The entirety of 2 Timothy concerns Paul's awareness of his impending death. He describes his departure to heaven in the same terms as Christ's departure after death. Furthermore, Christ recognized his imminent departure and warned his followers beforehand, the same way as Paul does here in 2 Timothy. Paul ties the receipt of his heavenly award of his crown to his death, after having kept the faith and finished his race. There is no more for him to gain after his departure and crowning in heaven because as he enters heaven and can see the risen Lord.

Because of these facts, faith in a glorified body at a time after arrival in heaven is untenable. Paul tells them this promise is their hope and promise as well upon death it is not therefore a future Last Day realization. Our hope is always in the gospel and is defined as death, burial, and resurrection, it is a serious mistake to alter the gospel and morph its hope and meaning by extending it to the Last Day. Theologians conflate the end of the saint's journey upon reaching the Promised Land which is heaven with the end of the evil kingdom on the Last Day, which then unites the heavenly and earthly kingdoms. Paul's gospel is Christ's gospel which is our gospel, therefore Christ's departure and receipt of his heavenly crown of glory, is Paul's death and crown, and is ours: a resurrection like Christ's.

Some additional texts concerning death and the end of the old man and the endowment with the new man.

> Hebrews 3:14 "For we have come to share in Christ, if indeed we hold our original confidence firm to the end"

> Hebrews 10:36 "For you have need of endurance, so that when you have done the will of God you may receive what is promised"

In 1 Corinthians 15:3, Paul summarizes what "is of first importance": the gospel he preached. Christ died, was buried, and was raised on the third day per the scriptures. This sequence without a break as in the intermediate state, is the gospel. The gospel uses Christ as our example, so Paul had repeated the sequence of Christ's death and resurrection to the readers. Paul is making the point that our resurrection must mimic Christ's. Next, he connects the three aspects of the gospel in time without a break, like Christ who was the forerunner and our earthly example. Christ died, was buried, and was resurrected on the third day. He then details all the witnesses to the resurrection of Christ including Paul himself and many who were still alive and could be questioned... But Paul also mentions those "who have fallen asleep" or have died who were also witnesses. He does this to lay the foundation for what is his central point in the next section and throughout 1 and 2 Corinthians, namely that if Christ is raised then those who have died such as those in v. 6, are currently raised (glorified in body) as well and in the same manner and timing as their Lord. Those who died were glorified upon entrance to heaven as Christ was upon his ascension. The writer of Hebrews (whom I believe is Paul) makes this same point regarding deceased believers who are currently witnesses of Christ and their own completed resurrections in heaven in Heb. 12:1-2:

> Therefore, since we are surrounded by so great a cloud of witnesses, let us also lay aside every weight, and sin which clings so closely, and let us run with endurance the race that is set before us, looking to Jesus, the founder and perfecter of our faith, who for the joy that was set before him endured the cross, despising the shame, and is seated at the right hand of the throne of God".

The text states "let us also lay aside every weight, and sin which clings so closely", which is the perfect description of our mortal body described in terms of "flesh" clinging so closely to us now. The description of that which is a weight and cause of sin is another description of the body of death that contains the old nature that we are released from at death. Again, the race is our earthly existence, its faithful completion is rewarded with heavenly union with Christ. The recipients of Hebrews are instructed to be encouraged in their trials by Christ's perfect example whose trials resulted in enthronement and glorification. The end of a life of faith (life) is death, which results in a heavenly resurrection into the Glory Cloud of heaven.

Section 2: verses 12-34: Those who have died in Christ

Now if Christ is proclaimed as raised from the dead, how can some of you say that there is no resurrection of the dead? But if there is no resurrection of the dead, then not even Christ has been raised. And if Christ has not been raised, then our preaching is in vain and your faith is in vain. We are even found to be misrepresenting God, because we testified about God that he raised Christ, whom he did not raise if it is true that the dead are not raised. For if the dead are not raised, not even Christ has been raised.

And if Christ has not been raised, your faith is futile and you are still in your sins. Then those also who have fallen asleep in Christ have perished. If in Christ we have hope in this life only, we are of all people most to be pitied.

Section 2: verses 12-19

As stated above, the resurrections spoken of in this entire chapter are bodily resurrections and that must be kept at the forefront so to not transfer the meaning of resurrection here to that of the soul. Here Paul speaks first of Christ being raised from the dead, secondly of those who had already died in faith (v. 6), as he questions them on their belief that those who had already died are not raised from the dead. Paul presents the case that all of their faith would be in vain if their understanding that those who had died were not currently resurrected was true. What does Paul present in the text that would potentially prove their faith be in vain? The unlinking of the resurrection of Christ and the dead saint's resurrection at death. Paul directly connects the two: if Christ is presently raised, then those who have died are presently raised as well. No identification of a two-part or partial resurrection without the body is mentioned. He assumes the audience knows and believes Christ has been raised, so answers those saying there has not already been a resurrection of those who died by asking a rhetorical question in v12: "How can you say there is no resurrection of the dead?". He then supplies the answer: if Christ is currently raised, then the dead are raised as well. The present reality of the resurrection for both Christ and those who have died are tied together. The negation of either resurrection negates both resurrection truths for Christ and his people. These people had lived through the time of Christ's resurrection, it was well established, and there were still some alive who had witnessed it, as Paul stated in verse 5 "some of which are still alive ". Thus, the invalid basis of the rhetorical question, for how could they doubt the resurrection having already taken place for the saints who have already died, but then be able to affirm Christ's resurrection? The belief in Jesus' resurrection but not of those saints who died in faith are mutually exclusive: the resurrections are tied together or denied together. A singular resurrection of Christ alone or a complete resurrection of Christ and an incomplete resurrection of the saints is inconsistent with his position as head of the church, and our shepherd. Conversely, Paul provides the consequences of the belief that those who had died had not been resurrected, namely, if the dead are not currently raised, then not even Christ is raised. If either the dead in Christ or Christ himself are not currently raised, then their faith and the apostles preaching of this truth being in vain. I believe the point of this section is that if one is true the other is true as well, for the two resurrections are connected to Christ's example, in logic, in practice, fullness of man image (body and soul), and most importantly in timing, which is upon death and entry into heaven.

Paul expresses this same thought in Romans 6:3-5:

> Do you not know that all of us who have been baptized into Christ Jesus were baptized into his death? We were buried therefore with him by baptism into death, in order that, just as Christ was raised from the dead by the glory of the Father, we too might walk in newness of life. For if we have been united with him in a death like his, we shall certainly be united with him in a resurrection like his.

Using the phrases "just as" and "certainly be united with him in a resurrection like his". (These phrases were instrumental in forming the basis of this book's title). Here Paul is clearly tying the death and resurrection of Christ and his people together. Our death takes place on earth which results in a raising or lifting up into heaven, which is our resurrection. A similar resurrection or a resurrection after eons of time as portrayed in the intermediate state is never mentioned and whose absence speaks harshly for those advocating it.

So, Paul in verses 15-19 states two present, and not future realities: either Christ and the dead in Christ are resurrected now, or if those who have died are not resurrected now then Christ is not resurrected, and the gospel is not true.

> We are even found to be misrepresenting God, because we testified about God that he raised Christ, whom he

did not raise if it is true that the dead are not raised. For if the dead are not raised, not even Christ has been raised. And if Christ has not been raised, your faith is futile and you are still in your sins. Then those also who have fallen asleep in Christ have perished. If in Christ we have hope in this life only, we are of all people most to be pitied.

These verses clearly lay out the danger in teaching that those who have died in faith are not resurrected bodily now, for the gospel is his death and resurrection. If we change the resurrection body doctrine to a Last Day resurrection, I believe we have misrepresented the critical doctrine of redemption from Adam's curse. Paul continues by stating if Christ is not raised, we are still in our sins, and those who have died did not receive resurrection life at death but have perished. He had an opportunity here to make a case for an intermediate state of a resurrection life in heaven without a resurrection of the body, but he does not. He could have stated what current doctrine teaches, that only the mortal body has perished, the soul lives on in a resurrected state, and the body will be reunited again with the soul on the Last Day, but he did not, stating instead that this would result in perishing or death, and not more life, even of a partial type of the soul. If either Christ or those who died in Christ were not resurrected means death. Period. Paul gave only two options either death or a resurrection in the manner or order of Christ. Man is not to be separated in this manner into a separate soul and body via an intermediate state. Instead, Paul reinforces the previous statements by stating they have perished if not resurrected.

To repeat, the context is resurrection of the body because they already have resurrection life via the Spirit. Paul has in other texts such as Romans clearly laid out new life through regeneration at the beginning of the Christian life, so this chapter can only be describing a life via the new body after death. To take this chapter and artificially insert a type of resurrection which is not a bodily or of whole man, is altering scripture, and assigning a meaning outside of the text. Then Paul clearly links our bodily death with resurrection life for the body when he states, "If in Christ we have hope in this life only, we are of all people most to be pitied". He offers no hope to a future resurrection at the end time apart from the time of our death and supplies the reason by using the examples of those past saints already resurrected and their union with his resurrection, matching Hebrews 12:1-2 as discussed in chapter 4, in which the Old Testament saints are in the glory cloud of heaven witnessing through their completed resurrection and offering encouragement to those still residing where Satan rules.

Section 2: verses 20-28: the status of those who have died continues

> But in fact Christ has been raised from the dead, the firstfruits of those who have fallen asleep. For as by a man came death, by a man has come also the resurrection of the dead. For as in Adam all die, so also in Christ shall all be made alive. But each in his own order: Christ the firstfruits, then at his coming those who belong to Christ. Then comes the end, when he delivers the kingdom to God the Father after destroying every rule and every authority and power. For he must reign until he has put all his enemies under his feet. The last enemy to be destroyed is death. For "God has put all things in subjection under his feet." But when it says, "all things are put in subjection," it is plain that he is excepted who put all things in subjection under him. When all things are subjected to him, then the Son himself will also be subjected to him who put all things in subjection under him, that God may be all in all.

Paul continues his doctrine that because Christ has already risen we have hope in the life to come at death through resurrection life (v.20). He ties this resurrection hope possessed by the Corinthian believer with those who have already died and to their completed resurrection which is a present reality. This present reality was based on Christ's present resurrection life. Firstfruits is an agrarian term in which farmers plant wheat in the fall to have a harvest in early springtime. In the Old Testament, the Israelites would celebrate the initial early spring harvest called "firstfruits" and present a portion of this harvest unto the Lord as they trusted him to provide the full harvest of the later crop. The word translated firstfruits in verse 20 is singular in the original, firstfruit, and refers to Christ alone. Therefore, his "first" resurrection initiates the full harvest of resurrections of his saints at death. Christ as firstfruit in his resurrection at death is the guarantee of our being the future crop resurrected at our death. We are tied to his resurrection at death.

Paul conspicuously does not connect the bodily resurrection of those in Christ with the Last Day, a continuing and glaring absence in texts where we would clearly expect it to be included if true. There is no Last Day terminology or context present. In fact, we will see the opposite of a tie to the Last Day with the resurrections of those in Christ. Further, we will see a separation between the timing of the resurrections of those belonging to Christ from those resurrected at the end time judgment in verses 20-28 below. My position is that resurrection occurs at physical death for everyone in Christ until the salvation period or Day of Salvation ends. Both the elect and the lost are subject to this death to the body as the application of the curse in Genesis. The curse of death was described in Genesis as when the body returns to the earth from which it was formed. The cure of resurrection life at death must match the curse of bodily death given to Adam and a continuing spiritual life of the soul alone at physical death does not fit this. the doctrine of the intermediate state assigns a resurrection life to heaven to the soul only at physical death to the body which I believe is inconsistent with these texts, because physical death does not result in resurrection life to the body but only in a hope for life to the body on the Last Day.

As previously argued, this Day of Salvation period or the church age of continuing resurrections for the elect, is directly followed by the Last Day Trumpet, announcing the resurrection only a resurrection or raising from earth to heaven for judgment and the second or eternal death for the lost, not life. Physical death or "first death" results in either further resurrection life at physical death for the elect, or a "second death" at the final judgment for the lost. The first resurrection for the saint occurs at the first or bodily death during the church age. It results in a new spiritual body along with union with Christ due to our union with Christ's first resurrection. This first resurrection must be properly defined as resurrection life to the body and transferring of residence from earth to heaven, and not simply the new inner life of regeneration. Christ was the resurrection and the life, which I believe equate to continued resurrection life for both the body at death and new life through regeneration at new birth. Thus, the new life of a Christian begins with a birth (regeneration) and ends at the death of the body resulting in resurrection life to the body. This pattern is the same pattern seen in normal life patterns of a humanity on earth: from birth to bodily death. Absent the first resurrection life of Christ at death, the lost experience the second resurrection to judgment on the Last Day culminating in the second death or eternal death in the lake of fire. The times when the resurrections take place after physical death are different for the elect and the saint: the resurrection to heaven of the elect occurs at each individual's death throughout the church age, and the lost are resurrected at one time on the Last Day.

Christ identifies the nature of resurrection to life for the believer in John 5:24, saying:

> Truly, truly, I say to you, whoever hears my word and believes him who sent me has eternal life. He does not come into judgment, but has passed from death to life.

This is where Paul derives his theology in which it is by faith in Christ and the indwelling of the Holy Spirit that the saint has possession of the firstfruits of eternal life which then guarantees the resurrection life to the body at death. Christ states that he who believes has eternal life but secondly and most important for our topic, is that he then states that the believer does not come into judgment but has already passed from death to life. He has already or is presently abiding in the eternal life through the new creation and death's hold on him is already broken. Resurrection life for the elect and resurrection to judgment which awaits the lost on the Last Day are separate events in time. The believer has eternal life now and transitions into his heavenly body for his heavenly home throughout the church age because, as Christ stated, they have passed from death to life. The heavenly kingdom has been brought to earth via the new creation at regeneration. The believer's inner man is recreated and is being reformed into the image of Christ while on earth. Death to the believer's mortal body is actually the transition point to resurrection life in the new heavenly body. This resurrection life is clearly different than the experience of the lost who experience judgment at death. When their mortal body is placed in the ground, they wait bodyless in the abyss until resurrection to judgment.

Christ identifies the two different resurrections a few verses later in John 5:28-29:

> Do not marvel at this, for an hour is coming when all who are in the tombs will hear his voice and come out, those who have done good to the resurrection of life, and those who have done evil to the resurrection of judgment.

Here Jesus identifies not a common resurrection of all mankind, but either one of resurrection life at death to the mortal body into the spiritual and glorious body for the elect or a judgment at death and a waiting in the abyss until the resurrection to judgment resulting in the second death via the lake of fire for the unbeliever. I believe this "hour" representing a short duration of time refers to the releasing of the Old Testament saints to their resurrection life in heaven after Christ's resurrection as Christ was the first to enter heaven after death. This hour identified the start of the new creation for the elect in the graves and any future saint going forward at death. This victory hour of the death and resurrection of Christ also sealed the end time resurrection of the lost on the final day of judgment.

Here are short definitions for the first/second death and first/second resurrections reference above:

First death: bodily death for the earthly body of all mankind

First resurrection: -New resurrection life at first death for the elect as we receive our new spiritual or heavenly bodies. The old body is returned to the dust.

Second resurrection: resurrection to judgment on the Last Day for the lost, as they were not part of the first resurrection.

Second death: eternal fire for the lost as they were not part of the first resurrection.

Notice there is no second death for the elect. Additionally, the curse to Adam and his progeny of the return of the mortal body to the dust is rendered to all mankind through the first death to the mortal body. No one escapes this curse. Christ redeems the elect from the curse not by removing the curse from the old body, but rather through a new creation of our spiritual and glorious body. A different body or not the same body as Paul declares later in v. 37, when describing the type of body resurrected.

Returning to 1 Corinthians 15, Paul continues: *"For as in Adam all die, so also in Christ shall all be made alive" (v.22).* The obvious question arises: when did those in Adam die? Was it upon their initial sin or upon bodily death? This appears at first to be a silly question but determining when the curse of death given to Adam was executed in turn tells us when the antidote of resurrection life is needed. When God breathed into Adam the breath of Life and he became a living being, so also when one stops breathing, death, occurs. So, resurrection life and physical death of the body are tied together via the curse and the remedy. Adam did not experience the curse of death to his body immediately upon his sin, therefore resurrection life is needed at the point of death. If one is to ascend to heaven as a man then a resurrection of the soul and body is required but the intermediate state does not assign a resurrection of life to the body at death, which does not therefore assign the full power of the gospel which Christ won at his resurrection after death to his people at their death.

Paul says, "so also in Christ, shall all be made alive". The preceding text made the point that Adam brought death to all and it is clear that meant in death to the body, so it follows that those in Christ shall be made alive refers to the resurrection life to the new body at death to the old body in order to dress the saint for his heavenly home. Those *"in Christ*—a present position— "shall all be made alive"—a future position which is resurrection life. Paul has clearly defined "in Christ" elsewhere. For example, Romans 6:3 says,

Do you not know that all of us who have been baptized into Christ Jesus were baptized into his death?

Clearly this means regeneration and possession of the Holy Spirit resulting in the elect entering into the new creation. So those in Christ are awaiting their future resurrection life in heaven which Paul stated as, "shall all be made alive" which cannot mean the new life of regeneration, for those in Christ already possess eternal life. Verse 22 clearly ties the new life via the Spirit through regeneration— "in Christ"—with the future resurrection life to the mortal body at death— "shall be made alive". The same thought is seen in in Romans 8:9-11:

> You, however, are not in the flesh but in the Spirit, if in fact the Spirit of God dwells in you. Anyone who does not have the Spirit of Christ does not belong to him. But if Christ is in you, although the body is dead because of sin, the Spirit is life because of righteousness. If the Spirit of him who raised Jesus from the dead dwells in you, he who raised Christ Jesus from the dead will also give life to your mortal bodies through his Spirit who dwells in you.

What is truly remarkable about this tie between the life of the Spirit and the resurrection life to be given to the mortal body at death, is that Paul describes the life of the Christian in terms of life through the Spirit even now: "You, however, are not in the flesh but in the Spirit" (v. 9). Here the meaning of "in Christ" in Paul's thought is laid out in clear terms, defining the relationship between the life via the Spirit in the "inner man" and the death residing in the "outer man" or mortal body of the saint while on earth. The outer man or body of the Christian has been crucified and is already dead and condemned to its eventual grave in the earth. Paul further states "But if Christ is in you, although the body is dead because of sin" (v. 10), and "will also give life to your mortal bodies through his Spirit who dwells in you" (v. 11). What is the point to be made here for those in Christ as it relates to death and resurrection? It is that currently, although the body still has physical life due to the breath of life, Christ killed its ability to have sin dominate our actions thru his death on the cross and our baptism into his death. Our earthly body has already been judged and condemned by God. And that the body of death (sin) we carry now will, at the time of cessation of our breathing or our physical death, be transformed into our glorious body of resurrection life thru the Spirit of Christ already present in our 'inner man". Our "outer man" will receive its heavenly body or be further clothed, and not be found naked or ever without a body or covering as Paul will explain in 2 Corinthians 5:1-5:

> For we know that if the tent that is our earthly home is destroyed, we have a building from God, a house not made with hands, eternal in the heavens. For in this tent we groan, longing to put on our heavenly dwelling, if indeed by putting it on we may not be found naked. For while we are still in this tent, we groan, being burdened— not that we would be unclothed, but that we would be further clothed, so that what is mortal may be swallowed up by life. He who has prepared us for this very thing is God, who has given us the Spirit as a guarantee.

This will be discussed in detail in the 2 Cor. exposition but the "naked" is clearly a reference by Paul to the Genesis fall, when after Adam and Eve had sinned, they discovered they were "naked" which refers to their loss of their outer glorious covering by their sin. The soul without the body is the curse of sin resulting in eternal judgment which is what happened to Adam and why God provided an immediate covering for the pair. Likewise, the lost do experience this curse upon death as their mortal body is laid in the grave, and they await the final judgment and are brought to the judgment without a body. There is no resurrection body for the lost as the resurrection body of the elect is "spiritual" or part of the "spiritual nature of God" as Paul teaches in 1 Cor. 15. Therefore, the mortal body's death is resurrection life for the body for the elect. The down payment of the present indwelling of the Spirit is the guarantee of the future resurrection life at death as made clear in Romans 8:9-11 below. It clearly states death results in new resurrection life to the body, and this new resurrection body is a consequence of the previous indwelling of the Spirit. Therefore, the saint on earth, already in possession of life via the Spirit, would not gain any benefit upon death to the body via the indwelling Spirit at death if they are not awarded the new resurrection body at that time. This is a perversion of the gospel as taught in an immediate state.

You, however, are not in the flesh but in the Spirit, if in fact the Spirit of God dwells in you. Anyone who does not have the Spirit of Christ does not belong to him. But if Christ is in you, although the body is dead because of sin, the Spirit is life because of righteousness. If the Spirit of him who raised Jesus from the dead dwells in you, he who raised Christ Jesus from the dead will also give life to your mortal bodies through his Spirit who dwells in you.

This is the Gospel. The Gospel is not a future life to be gained on the last day, it has begun at regeneration and is consummated upon physical death and the resurrection to heaven. The difference between new life while on earth and resurrection life in heaven is primarily one of position: either on earth and a part of the heavenly kingdom but still residing in the sphere of Satan's kingdom, or resurrection life in which the entire saint has been transferred upward to the unshakable heavenly kingdom of Christ. Resurrection is not to be taken as merely a new spiritual life even though we are in a sense united with Christ and can enter heavens throne room to obtain grace. Resurrection is a raising up or a transferring of position from the earthly to the heavenly realm. The idea of the intermediate state resulting in a resurrection life without the body and thus all of man is not to be found in this passage. As I will state in other places, the guarantee of resurrection life at death is the indwelling presence of the Holy Spirit, a guarantee and promise already given. It is the blessed hope for the individual saint at death not the command of Christ on the Last Day. We do not await a future hope after death, in which the final defeat of death and its kingdom and the new creation resulting in the uniting again of heaven and earth forever happen in a single event.

We now continue with verse 23 in 1 Cor. 15. Here Paul identifies three separate and sequential time periods along with the members of each group of resurrections by describing a series of events. He presents the order of the three resurrections in its *"own order"*:

1. Christ the firstfruit
2. next, those who belong to Christ at his coming.

3. finally, when he delivers the kingdom to God the Father after destroying every rule and every authority and power".

Paul begins by clarifying that each resurrection group has its own order. This rules out the intermediate state position which posits a common resurrection of the elect and the lost on the Last Day. The statement "then comes the end" (v. 24) is after the raising of those in Christ (v. 23) Interestingly, the 3 resurrection groups also coincide with the entire reign of the Messiah, (the 70th Old Testament Messianic week prophesied in Daniel chapter 9). This is apparent in the compacted descriptions of the 3 periods: his first advent ("resurrection of Christ"), followed by the church age or the period of salvation, a time when light is available, (""), and culminating in the Day of Darkness and gloom when the light has been taken away and the End Time Judgment has arrived ("Then comes the end, when he delivers the kingdom to God the Father after destroying every rule and every authority and power").

The entire first advent of Christ is summarized by the singular event of his first resurrection ("Christ the firstfruits"), because this event initiated the new creation. The gospel has no power absent the resurrection, likewise resurrection life has no power absent a full resurrection of the saint at death. The two remaining orders or resurrection groups are also separated in time from each other. The second group is the building of the Temple or the gospel age ("then at his coming those who belong to Christ"), which is comprised of the resurrection of the saints to heaven throughout the interadvent period. This is followed by the third group or period (" Then comes the end"). Who is getting resurrected at the end? It can be none other than the lost from all of time who now are brought to the throne of Christ for judgment. Why them alone? The previous period dealt entirely with the elect. When is the end (time)? After the coming to heaven or resurrection to life of the saints ("then comes the end"). The initiation of the Final judgment occurs at the Last Trumpet, signaling the Day of Judgment has arrived ("when he delivers the kingdom to God the Father after destroying every rule and every authority and power"). The end includes all end time events from bringing the lost to the judgment seat through the destruction of the earthly kingdom and evil spiritual powers ruled by Satan.

The phrase the latter days and last days (plural) are used in various biblical texts to describe the Messianic period (cf. Is. 2:2, Micah 4:1, Heb. 1:2, Acts 2:17). It confirms my analysis that the second period as a longer period than the end time designated as a singular Last Day. This phrase is identified with the Day of Salvation or the church age versus the singular Day of Judgment or Last Day. This latter days and Last Day terminology also argues for different times and thus different resurrection periods for the elect and the lost, matching the sequential order Paul has clearly outlined here in 1 Corinthians 15.

If Paul was intending to communicate a common resurrection of the lost and the elect on the Last Day, he would not separate the resurrections of those who belong to Christ in the second order by stating, "then comes the end". The End time judgment is described after Christ's coming(s) for his people:

> Then at his coming those who belong to Christ. Then comes the end, when he delivers the kingdom to God the Father after destroying every rule and every authority and power. For he must reign until he has put all his enemies under his feet. The last enemy to be destroyed is death. (1 Cor. 15:24-26)

Therefore, the resurrections of his people occur before Judgment Day's Last Trumpet signals the beginning of the end. This does not align with the Last Day per intermediate state doctrine. I confess this is a difficult section, but these three clear markers of time cannot be dismissed because of Paul's preface "each in his own order".

Christ "coming" for his people is a continual "coming" thru his Spirit throughout the church age, as he regenerates and resurrects his people into heaven, building his heavenly Temple, which when completed ushers in the Last Day or Judgment. This coming of Christ to build the Temple in heaven can then be easily understood as the coming of the Spirit at Pentecost, as characterized by him in John 16:7:

> Nevertheless, I tell you the truth: it is to your advantage that I go away, for if I do not go away, the Helper will not come to you. But if I go, I will send him to you.

The Holy Spirit is the Spirit of Jesus, so the coming of Christ Paul speaks of in Corinthians verse 23, is more than likely his Spirit.

In his final coming—the coming to judgment—Christ is not alone. The elect, including those last saints on earth who are resurrected without experiencing death, are with him as Judgment Day commences. These continuing "comings" of Christ before the final coming to judgment will be discussed in greater detail later. The third group referenced by Paul in 1 Cor. 15:20-28 is a coming or resurrection within the context of the events of the Last Day. Both the second and third groups can be described as comings of Christ, for although "coming" is not specifically the wording used in this passage in relation to the end, it is understood that the end time judgment is a coming of Christ as judge and conquering King of Kings. The Last Day events include the resurrection of the lost to face the final or white throne judgment, so the 3 resurrection peoples and time frames are identified.

There are only two groups of people on earth, the elect and the lost, and both are identified here along with the Lord of Creation as a singular head in separate resurrections.

I believe Paul did not identify in the third group of events on the Last Day as a resurrection because of the common view among the Jews, including his audience at the time, of a singular resurrection on the "Last Day" associated with the final coming of the messiah. In other words, this Last Day resurrection was already a part of their eschatology and the point of this entire exposition in 1 Corinthians is to highlight that the resurrection is not just an event occurring at the end time judgment for the lost, but that Christ's death and resurrection initiated the new creation of his eternal kingdom now. Resurrection for his people is a present reality to be differentiated from the truth of a final resurrection of the lost on the Last Day. The kingdom has come, is coming, and will come in fullness on the Last Day when Christ will finally destroy the Kingdom of Satan and the heavenly city comes down to the new earth in John's revelation.

Section 2: verses 29-34

> Otherwise, what do people mean by being baptized on behalf of the dead? If the dead are not raised at all, why are people baptized on their behalf? Why are we in danger every hour? I protest, brothers, by my pride in you, which I have in Christ Jesus our Lord, I die every day! What do I gain if, humanly speaking, I fought with beasts at Ephesus? If the dead are not raised, "Let us eat and drink, for tomorrow we die." Do not be deceived: "Bad company ruins good morals." Wake up from your drunken stupor, as is right, and do not go on sinning. For some have no knowledge of God. I say this to your shame.

Paul continues the topic that Christ has already risen and therefore those who have died have risen and links the purpose of baptism with this truth. He does this by indicating in the first two sentences above that baptism would lose any value if the resurrection were not true, saying, "If the dead are not raised at all, why are people baptized on their behalf?" My position on baptism as primarily being the sign pointing towards resurrection life for the body at death is supported by Paul in this section. Paul links physical or bodily death to baptism through rhetorical questions. The first is, "Why are we in danger every hour?", and the second, "What do I gain if, humanly speaking, I fought with beasts at Ephesus?". He is building on the point of the entire discourse on resurrection—that it occurs at death or not at all for the saint.

Paul's answer clearly ties resurrection with the day of death as he concludes that, if resurrection is not awaiting them on the day of death, why should they not conduct themselves as the gentiles do: "Let us eat and drink, for tomorrow we die." This links bodily death with either resurrection or death (no eternal life) on that day by using "tomorrow" as the time marker. That is Paul's argument—death to the body without Christ's transforming resurrection life on that day results in a continuing state of sin and eternal damnation. The intermediate state is incompatible with this section. Once again, another perfect opportunity was presented for teaching this doctrine if it were true, but it was not. If Paul meant life would continue after the death without resurrection of the body at death, he would not have stated "for tomorrow we die", because it would not be true if the intermediate state is true, for it teaches a continuing of eternal life without life for the body in heaven upon death. Paul saw only two options at a saint's death, either eternal resurrection life if the gospel is true, or eternal death if the gospel is not true. He does not allow for an intermediate state with no life for the body at death. Therefore, the intermediate state it is not taught here, and is refuted by the text. Can a theology continue to teach a resurrection nowhere found in Paul's most detailed exposition? He concludes this section with a stern warning to those altering the gospel via the intermediate state,

> "Do not be deceived: "Bad company ruins good morals."
> Wake up from your drunken stupor, as is right, and do
> not go on sinning. For some have no knowledge of God.
> I say this to your shame."

Section 3: verses 35-49 The type of the resurrection body

> But someone will ask, "How are the dead raised? With
> what kind of body do they come?" You foolish person!
> What you sow does not come to life unless it dies. And
> what you sow is not the body that is to be, but a bare
> kernel, perhaps of wheat or of some other grain. But God
> gives it a body as he has chosen, and to each kind of seed
> its own body. For not all flesh is the same, but there is
> one kind for humans, another for animals, another for
> birds, and another for fish. There are heavenly bodies
> and earthly bodies, but the glory of the heavenly is of one
> kind, and the glory of the earthly is of another. There is
> one glory of the sun, and another glory of the moon, and
> another glory of the stars; for star differs from star in glory.
> So is it with the resurrection of the dead. What is sown
> is perishable; what is raised is imperishable. It is sown in
> dishonor; it is raised in glory. It is sown in weakness; it

is raised in power. It is sown a natural body; it is raised a spiritual body. If there is a natural body, there is also a spiritual body. Thus, it is written, "The first man Adam became a living being", the last Adam became a life-giving spirit. But it is not the spiritual that is first but the natural, and then the spiritual. The first man was from the earth, a man of dust; the second man is from heaven. As was the man of dust, so also are those who are of the dust, and as is the man of heaven, so also are those who are of heaven. Just as we have borne the image of the man of dust, we shall also bear the image of the man of heaven.

Paul now changes his focus on the resurrection times and the types of people to an exposition on the difference between earthly and heavenly bodies. "Do they come" (v. 35) refers to the type of body that the saints coming to Christ in heaven at death possess. It ties to the second set of resurrections referred to above, in which Christ via the Holy Spirit came to the elect and here the saint coming to Christ at death in his new body. Once again, we see the connection between death and bodily resurrection, as the context of this entire topic in 1 and 2 Corinthians is a resurrection of the body, as man is body and soul. Therefore, there is no justification for using this section to describe this as happening on the Last Day. The apostle asks, "With what kind of body do they come?". Where do the bodies come to? Heaven. The question concerns the status of those who had already died, as some were teaching the resurrection had already happened. This entire section corrects and further explains the resurrection of man. This language brings to mind four specific "comings" related to our topic.:

1. Christ's (Spirit) coming to earth via Mary to take the form of mankind
2. Christ's (Spirit) coming to heaven upon his death
3. Christ sending his Spirit back to earth to indwell mankind on Pentecost and including a continuing coming of the Spirit at each subsequent moment of regeneration during this age.
4. Our (Spiritual) body coming to heaven at death.

Here again Paul ties the coming to heaven with the death of the body. The question is, "in what kind of body will the saint come to heaven?" it is not a discourse on how they come to heaven without a body. If that were the case, the obvious implications would need to be discussed in detail in this passage, but they are not. Paul then proceeds to explain to the Corinthian believers the type of body in which they will come to heaven. He does not explain that they go bodyless to heaven and the body will then reattach on the Last Day. There is only one coming to heaven for each man or woman and it is body and soul. Remember this exposition began with the question of whether those who had already died were already resurrected, which they are, therefore the believers who are currently alive are assured of the same resurrection at death. Thus, the comings of Christ via the Spirit at regeneration match his people's comings via resurrection by the Spirit to resurrection life in the new body in heaven. The Spirit (Jesus) comes to earth, performs the work God the Father ordained for the saint through the power of the Spirit, and finally at death the Spirit transports them into heaven. This is the same sequence for both our Lord and his sheep. A resurrection like Christ's.

These questioners are foolish according to Paul: "You foolish person! What you sow does not come to life unless it dies" (v. 36). The mortal body must die before the new spiritual body is raised. Protestant doctrine of a resurrection of the mortal body is unscriptural, it is a new body in the same way the old spiritual nature or man was killed and we become a new creation in Christ. Paul described this new inner man in these terms in Galatians 2:20:

> I have been crucified with Christ. It is no longer I who live, but Christ who lives in me. And the life I now live in the flesh I live by faith in the Son of God, who loved me and gave himself for me.

Immediately the connection between the death of the old body and the resurrection life of the new body at the same time is reinforced through the metaphor of a seed planted in the ground. The seed is planted like our earthly body is interred at death, and the coming to life of the plant is like our spiritual body, which requires the death of the earthly body first. Verse

37 continues: "<u>And </u>what you sow is not the body that is to be, but a bare kernel, perhaps of wheat or of some other grain". This clearly states that the mortal body is not the body to be raised, thus refuting the resurrection of the mortal body. I believe at least part of the basis of his calling them foolish was that they believed the earthly body would be the body that is to be raised, and the bodies of their loved ones who had died were still in the tombs, unlike Christ's body which rose from the grave. The new creation which Christ's death and resurrection brought is founded upon this notion of a new body.

Christ corrected the Sadducees concerning the resurrection in Matt. 22:29-32,

> Jesus answered, "You are mistaken because you do not know the Scriptures or the power of God. In the resurrection, people will neither marry nor be given in marriage. Instead, they will be like the angels in heaven. But concerning the resurrection of the dead, have you not read what God said to you: 'I am the God of Abraham, the God of Isaac, and the God of Jacob'? He is not the God of the dead, but of the living."

Christ clearly differentiates the resurrection of the elect from the resurrection of the lost and does not comingle the two resurrections into one event and purpose, as in the intermediate state. In this passage, Christ first deals with the resurrection of life for the elect then transitions to a different type of resurrection via the word "but". He contrasts our resurrection to life with the resurrection of the lost or dead stating that God is not their God, for he is the God of the living. Thus, although God is Lord of all creation, he is not the covenant God of the dead or unbeliever, as Christ foretold the apostate Jewish nation. He gave the final sign of the end of the first covenant by completing the final curses of their covenant apostasy with God in 70 AD when he destroyed the Temple and the people suffered horribly under the Roman siege and destruction of the city. As the angelic host in heaven does not have an earthly body, so Christ explains to the Sadducees, neither do we in the resurrection to heaven. Christ is giving the basis for Paul to call the Corinthians foolish when he states

God is not the God of the dead, but the living. The dead body is not part of the new creation or resurrection. Again, the dead without Christ are resurrected not to life but only to judgment. The resurrection of the dead without Christ is not a resurrection of their mortal body but only a rising to heaven as bodyless souls to be judged and cast into the lake of fire. This is what is so destructive to the gospel in the intermediate state doctrine. It changes the resurrection to life to the body that Christ wrought for his people into a resurrection of the soul only, which is in fact the fate of the lost, in effect transferring the curse to Adam which resulted in his being found "naked" to the elect as they enter heaven. That is not a blessing but a curse. Only the new body with resurrection life created in God's image enters the Kingdom.

In this Matthew quote Christ also affirms a point which will be explored later, namely that Adam was initially created in the spiritual order and part of the heavenly council, and therefore the recreation returns mankind to the order of spiritual beings in heaven. This is seen in Christ's statement, "instead they will be like the angels in heaven". This false idea that the literal mortal body will be raised is still present in Reformed thinking. My Presbyterian Church of America Pastor will consider himself in the grave and in heaven at the same time, while he awaits his resurrection body from the earth, all the while residing in heaven. I lost an eldership because of this understanding. The new creation is not a reconditioning of the old but a glorious transformation into the image of Christ, the man from heaven.

There is a mysterious way in which Paul expresses the old body in 1 Cor. 15, as being liken to a bare kernel of seed that is planted at death in the earth. This seed contains everything needed to produce the mature man. It might refer to the dust from earth from which Adam was made and represent the humanity of man in the new body. But surely Paul's main point is that the earthly body must die before the transformation occurs, "it does not come to life unless it dies"." It is the old body that dies per the curse in the garden. The point must be made again that in this most detailed description of the transfer from our mortal to our spiritual body, there is no indication of any time gap between the mortal body to the resurrected spiritual body. The comparison is one of transition from one to another in which no separation in time between the two bodies is indicated, as seen in the seed to maturity metaphor. Why is there not a gap in time in Paul's text or in the metaphor for this transition? Because one does not exist. If there is a gap in time between death to the physical body and when saints receive their resurrected bodies at the Last or Judgment Day as taught by the intermediate state, certainly this would have been the ideal place to make it known to the church.

Paul will describe this same transformation process from death to life or mortality to immortality in 1 Corinthians 15:50-55 again, but first he moves from the topic of what happens when our body dies while we are still on this earth to tan explanation of the mystery of what will happen to the bodies of those who are still alive on earth at the second advent. How will this transition then take place as they never experience death? Paul states,

> But God gives it a body as he has chosen . . . "There are heavenly bodies and earthly bodies, but the glory of the heavenly is of one kind, and the glory of the earthly is of another. (vv.38, 40)

These verses clarify that the type of body corresponds to its location, either earthly and mortal or heavenly and spiritual. Verses 42-49 show the difference in glory between the two locations and that the entrance into heaven results in an exceedingly greater glorious body:

> What is sown is perishable; what is raised is imperishable. It is sown in dishonor; it is raised in glory. It is sown in weakness; it is raised in power. It is sown a natural body; it is raised a spiritual body. If there is a natural body, there is also a spiritual body. Thus, it is written, "The first man Adam became a living being", the last Adam became a life-giving spirit. But it is not the spiritual that is first but the natural, and then the spiritual. The first man was from the earth, a man of dust; the second man is from heaven. As was the man of dust, so also are those who are of the dust, and as is the man of heaven, so also are those who are of heaven. Just as we have borne the image of the man of dust, we shall also bear the image of the man of heaven.

Here, as Paul continues the comparison of the two different bodies, there is never a reference to a time where the soul is identified as separated from the body, nor is any indication given that the resurrection is segmented into a resurrection of the soul at one time and the body at a later time. Instead there is one resurrection or transition to heaven. A separation in time violates the original point Paul began with—that the resurrection of those dead at the time of his writing were tied to Christ's resurrection, (either they both were or were not resurrected). It also violates the order of resurrections previously discussed and violates the metaphor of the seed springing to life upon death and being planted in the ground. If the correct representation of the resurrection of the body had been at the Last Trumpet on Judgment Day as taught in the intermediate state, then that would have been incorporated here, but it was not. Why? Because the correct doctrine is that only the resurrection of the Lost occurs on the Last Day. This is signaled by the Last Trumpet, the same Trumpet Paul will later refer to when answering the mysterious question of what happens to those saints alive, and who do not experience death on earth. The Last Trumpet initiates the first requirement to allow for the judgment and destruction of the earthly evil kingdom, namely the final removal of the elect to heaven and resurrection life in their glorious bodies. Therefore, the Last Trumpet on the start of the Last Day is a time marker to the resurrection of life for those still on earth at its sounding, and also the soon resurrection of all the dead in sin from throughout eternity to the White Throne Judgment. Here are the respective pairs of bodies described by Paul.

Perishable	Imperishable
Dishonorable	Glorious
Weak	Powerful
Natural	Spiritual
Earthly	Heavenly
Adam's image	Christ's image

Paul completes the section in verses 48-49, stating:

> As was the man of dust, so also are those who are of the dust, and as is the man of heaven, so also are those who are of heaven. Just as we have borne the image of the man of dust, we shall also bear the image of the man of heaven.

There are only two kinds of man (mankind), there is not a hybrid bodyless man, which does not comprise either of these two image bearers. Mankind bears an image of either Adam or the New Adam.

Section 4: verses 50-58 Those alive on earth at Christ's Final Coming

We now turn to the last section of chapter 15, the resurrection of those who did not experience death on earth because they are alive at the Final Coming of Christ on Judgment Day.

> I tell you this, brothers: flesh and blood cannot inherit the kingdom of God, nor does the perishable inherit the imperishable. Behold! I tell you a mystery. We shall not all sleep, but we shall all be changed, in a moment, in the twinkling of an eye, at the last trumpet. For the trumpet will sound, and the dead will be raised imperishable, and we shall be changed. For this perishable body must put on the imperishable, and this mortal body must put on immortality. When the perishable puts on the imperishable, and the mortal puts on immortality, then shall come to pass the saying that is written:
>
> "Death is swallowed up in victory."
> "O death, where is your victory?
> O death, where is your sting?"
>
> The sting of death is sin, and the power of sin is the law. But thanks be to God, who gives us the victory through our Lord Jesus Christ.

Therefore, my beloved brothers, be steadfast, immovable,
always abounding in the work of the Lord, knowing that
in the Lord your labor is not in vain.

Paul begins this last section by reiterating the point he made in verses 35-49 during the discussion of the type of resurrection body. It is not the mortal body that is resurrected: "I tell you this, brothers: flesh and blood cannot inherit the kingdom of God, nor does the perishable inherit the imperishable". He identifies clearly that the mortal body that dies is not the body resurrected in two ways, first by describing the body as flesh and blood which cannot inherit the spiritual kingdom of God, and secondly as a perishable body that does not inherit the imperishable kingdom. As with the new creation inner man, the body is not a perfecting of the old but a new creation body. Then Paul declares, "Behold! I tell you a mystery". What is this mystery? If the mystery Paul was informing the church was, that one would enter heaven as a soul without a body, until the final trumpet on Judgment Day, then he could have easily explained it in clear terms here. But he did not. He again misses this opportunity to declare, if true, this huge time delay in the receipt of the resurrection body. Why didn't he explain this delay? Because it does not exist. A delay in our transformation from mortal to immortal is not the mystery he is speaking to them about, rather he is again emphasizing the immediacy of the transformation. Just as when death meant immediate resurrection life for those who previously died, in this case these living saints are immediately transformed and taken to heaven on the Last Day. The earlier verses explained the transition of the body from a mortal to imperishable form prior to entry into the heavenly kingdom and this section shoes that the same is true for those alive at the end time. This is what Paul shows when speaking of the immediate transformation in verses 51-53.

Paul is not declaring a common resurrection of all at the Last Trumpet here as is commonly taught. The dead item being raised to new life in this passage is the mortal body of the person alive at Christ's coming for judgment, not the dead from all eternity. This entire section only describes the process of those alive, who did not die (sleep) at the Last Trumpet because all other resurrections had already been addressed in verses 12-34. Those alive will be changed immediately into their imperishable state at the Last Trumpet. He continues speaking about this group of believers. When Paul says, "and the dead shall be raised, and we shall be changed", what is the dead item that will be changed? The mortal body of these people. What is raised imperishable? The mortal body of those alive at the Last Trumpet. The certainty of this analysis being their mortal body spoken of is confirmed as Paul restates the point that the mortal/perishable body must put on its immortal/imperishable qualities in verse 53.

Paul completes this section dealing with the final generation of elect alive at the Last Trumpet by stating that death has finally been defeated for the entire number of all the elect. At the same time, the final defeat of death for the kingdom is commencing and will be completed by the death of all unbelievers left on earth who will then be brought to judgment along with all the unbelievers previously held in the abyss to meet their eternal fate along with Satan and his evil spiritual companions. Thus, death itself will be completely destroyed.

Paul closes his entire doctrinal teaching on resurrection here in 1 Corinthians, (which he will further clarify in 2 Corinthians), with encouragement to the Corinthian believers to be steadfast in their faith, knowing that their time or labor while here on earth in Satan's domain is not in vain, but will be rewarded with resurrection life at death in the heavenly and spiritual Kingdom of our Lord He will destroy death and turn the completed new creation including his people and the new heaven and earth back to the Father thus ending his reign after perfecting the people and the kingdom. The work of the Messiah during his "week" prophesied by Daniel will have been accomplished.

Finally, in keeping with the entire exposition including the order of the 3 resurrection groups, (first Christ, then the elect who have died, and finally the elect alive at his final coming at the Last Trumpet), all his people thus match Christ's resurrection pattern which is resurrection life and outer glory upon entrance into the heavenly kingdom, as they receive their glorious body and reign with him in heaven, awaiting his destruction of the earthly kingdom so that they may then reign with him on earth fulfilling both Adam's original mandate and the revelation in Johns Apocalypse of the heavenly city coming down and uniting with the new earth.

CHAPTER 7

RESURRECTION OF THE
BODY IN 2 CORINTHIANS

G. K. Beale shows the tie between new life thru regeneration and resurrection in his section on resurrection and new creation from 2 Cor. 2:14-16 and 4:10-11. He states:

> The "triumph" in which God "leads" Paul and that exudes "the sweet aroma of the knowledge" of God includes "a fragrance of Christ to God among those who are being saved," which Paul further says is "an aroma from life to life, "a probable reference to resurrection life. Here we see a likely link, if not virtual equation, between "being saved" and "life" (it may even be [inaugurated resurrection] life to [consummative resurrection] life.[23]

> The reason why such trials do not annihilate Christians is that they are "always carrying about in the body the dying of Jesus, so that the life of Jesus also may be manifested in or body" (4:10). The comparison here to Christ's "dying" and the "life of Jesus" is not mere analogy. Rather, they are truly and really identified with Jesus' death and

---

[23] Beale, G. K.. A New Testament Biblical Theology: The Unfolding of the Old Testament in the New. (Grand Rapids: Baker Academic, 2011), 264.

resurrection, as I have argued in Rom. 6 and 1 Cor. 15 and will argue again in 2 Cor. 5:14-17. This means that they really have begun to die to the old cosmos through their union with Christ's death, and they have begun to live in the new order through their union with his resurrection. Although they have not yet physically died and been raised, they have begun to do so in a literal yet nonmaterial sense. [24]

Beale appears to be making the same point I am in this book, namely, that death is a transfer to the heavenly realm in our new body. Paul began his teaching on the resurrection of the body in 1 Corinthians, therefore it provides the basis for the interpretation of the 2 Corinthian texts. The two can only be understood as one continuous doctrine or thought.

> For we do not want you to be unaware, brothers, of the affliction we experienced in Asia. For we were so utterly burdened beyond our strength that we despaired of life itself. Indeed, we felt that we had received the sentence of death. But that was to make us rely not on ourselves but on God who raises the dead. He delivered us from such a deadly peril, and he will deliver us. On him we have set our hope that he will deliver us again. (2 Cor. 1:8-10)

Paul ties the persecution he experienced with death, describing the situation as "burdened beyond our strength that we despaired of life" and "we felt that we had received the sentence of death". Paul's hope resides not in himself but in "God who raises the dead", who had delivered him, and would deliver him again. The point Paul keeps emphasizing is the tie between physical death and the end of our work on earth, and the hope provided at that time—in God who raises the dead. The tie is not to a Judgment Day raising of him from death to life, but upon his death, that is where his hope is focused. Paul was fearless because he understood the gospel of good news meant bodily resurrection life at death, or put another

---

[24] Beale, G. K.. A New Testament Biblical Theology: The Unfolding of the Old Testament in the New. (Grand Rapids: Baker Academic, 2011), 267-8

way, that the new life he experienced at regeneration would rescue him from death when his mortal body perished, and experience continued life through resurrection to heaven. He understood that death's hold on him had already been broken by Christ's first resurrection. There is no mention of a separation from his body, instead there is a transformation. The sentence of death Paul felt he might be experiencing was only a death to his outer body. Paul clearly sets our hope not on the Last Day but solely on Christ. When do we unite with this hope in Christ? No other time than our entrance into heaven at death, through the gospel of death to resurrection life.

> And it is God who establishes us with you in Christ, and has anointed us, and who has also put his seal on us and given us his Spirit in our hearts as a guarantee. (2 Cor. 1:21-22)

The Spirit's indwelling in our inner man which has been recreated anew and become a part of the heavenly spiritual realm at regeneration is also the seal which guarantees our future transformation into the fullness of our glorious body upon death. This spiritual identity, called the new creation man, is already united with the heavenly kingdom. Thus, Paul can describe the saint as seated with Christ in the heavenly realm. The most explicit statement of the uniting of the heavenly realm or spiritual nature of the regenerate saint with God who is Spirit is in Colossians 1:13:

> For he has rescued us from the dominion of darkness and brought us into the kingdom of the Son he loves.

Here Paul makes it clear we have already become part of the new creation even while still residing here on earth. Interestingly, Paul says "the kingdom of the Son", not the kingdom of God. I believe Paul is describing the entire work of the Messiah as the completion of his redemption of the cosmos, a redemption which began at his first advent and will end at the final destruction of the kingdom of Satan on the Last Day of Judgment. Paul, you will recall, made reference to this reign of the Son ending upon his messianic work being completed and returning the finished glorious product back over to the Father in 1 Cor. 15:24-28:

> Then comes the end, when he delivers the kingdom to God the Father after destroying every rule and every authority and power. For he must reign until he has put all his enemies under his feet. The last enemy to be destroyed is death. For "God has put all things in subjection under his feet." But when it says, "all things are put in subjection," it is plain that he is excepted who put all things in subjection under him. When all things are subjected to him, then the Son himself will also be subjected to him who put all things in subjection under him, that God may be all in all.

It seems the kingdom of the Son, which includes all the elect and the new heavens and earth, is given back to the Father and God becomes all in all. The heavenly and earthly kingdoms have become one, whereas our recreation in the kingdom of the Son while on earth was separated from the heavenly kingdom until our resurrection at death.

> But thanks be to God, who in Christ always leads us in triumphal procession, and through us spreads the fragrance of the knowledge of him everywhere. For we are the aroma of Christ to God among those who are being saved and among those who are perishing, to one a fragrance from death to death, to the other a fragrance from life to life. 2 Cor. 2:14-16

Here Paul uses the image of Christ's triumphal procession into heaven, which Christ led upon his resurrection and ascension, which initially consisted of the OT saints.

> Therefore it says, "When he ascended on high he led a host of captives, and he gave gifts to men." (Eph. 4:8)

But Paul is speaking to saints still on the earth and his leading of them to heaven, not his original procession to heaven with the OT saints.

The procession began at his ascension or resurrection into heaven and is a continuing procession of leading saints to heaven during the gospel era ending upon the Last Day when Judgment Day arrives and the opportunity for salvation has expired— "Christ always leads us in triumphal procession, and through us spreads the fragrance of the knowledge of him everywhere" (v. 14). This procession begins for the saint first in terms of our new life (regeneration) while remaining here on earth. We continue to spread the fragrance of the knowledge of him through our witness for him during our earthly life of suffering for Christ as we experience persecution from the world and the Satanic powers of darkness who govern this present world. This passage is referring to our wilderness journey now—there is no longer a need to spread the knowledge of Christ once we arrive in heaven. But this passage also refers to resurrection life in heaven, the ending of the procession to heaven.

The resurrection to life in heaven is seen beginning in verse 15. Paul describes this fragrance as the aroma of Christ to both the elect ("being saved") and to the lost ("those who are perishing"). The Gospel, which is the fragrance of Christ being proclaimed by those who are in Christ and who are being saved or whose ultimate salvation still awaits in heaven, results in one of two different ends at death for each class of person on earth: either being saved or perishing. Those two ends are a continuing state of either death or life, as verse 16 explains: "to one a fragrance from death to death, to the other a fragrance from life to life." The believer goes from "life to life"—from indwelling life of the Spirit to the addition of outward resurrection life via the new glorious body. Conversely, the lost go from "death to death" for they resided in a state of death while on earth in their mortal body and continue in this state of death when their body perishes, but no resurrection life for their body awaits them. Both outcomes at death result in an escalation of their state: the believer receives his reward and completion of his redemption but the lost await their final judgment and their second death on Judgment Day.

"Life to life" cannot be understood to represent only the continuation of new life via the soul alone as the intermediate state doctrine teaches. Paul eliminates this possibility later in chapter 5. This phrase reaffirms the doctrine of Paul in 1 Corinthians 15 covered in the last chapter. Death to the physical body results in a judgment whereby the final determination of man's standing before God is sealed but whereas the believer transitions immediately to his final or escalated state, the lost are held until Judgment Day where their escalated final state is rendered to them. At this point resurrection life for the new body begins for those in Christ as they transition from their earthly body to their heavenly body. Secondarily, the lost lose their mortal body at death but are not given a new glorious body at death. They will remain "naked" which is synonymous with the outer body, awaiting not a resurrection of their former bod, but a resurrection or raising from the abyss for final judgment. The image of the lost then becoming "naked" or without their outer covering hearkens back to the original fall in Eden. More importantly, Paul uses the same terminology to describe what happens to the believer in 2 Cor. 5:2-5:

> For in this tent we groan, longing to put on our heavenly dwelling, if indeed by putting it on we may not be found naked. For while we are still in this tent, we groan, being burdened—not that we would be unclothed, but that we would be further clothed, so that what is mortal may be swallowed up by life. He who has prepared us for this very thing is God, who has given us the Spirit as a guarantee.

These texts depict a transition at death from life to life or from mortal body to immortal body at death—refuting the intermediate state again. The life one has via the Spirit is escalated at this point via the adornment of outer glory, thus life to more life. Christ stated this idea in Matt. 13:12:

> For to the one who has, more will be given, and he will have an abundance, but from the one who has not, even what he has will be taken away"

In John 10:10 he states: "I came that they may have life and have it abundantly". In this passage he is the great shepherd leading his sheep to heaven where abundant life (bodily glorification) exists after having received new life at regeneration. The intermediate state is one of nakedness. Paul denies this will occur for the elect as seen above. The lost do experience the "nakedness" or lack of outer adornment in a glorified body.

Paul teaches that the coming of the new creation is a permanent, glorious coming:

> Now if the ministry of death, carved in letters on stone, came with such glory that the Israelites could not gaze at Moses' face because of its glory, which was being brought to an end, will not the ministry of the Spirit have even more glory? For if there was glory in the ministry of condemnation, the ministry of righteousness must far exceed it in glory. Indeed, in this case, what once had glory has come to have no glory at all, because of the glory that surpasses it. For if what was being brought to an end came with glory, much more will what is permanent have glory.
>
> Since we have such a hope, we are very bold, not like Moses, who would put a veil over his face so that the Israelites might not gaze at the outcome of what was being brought to an end. But their minds were hardened. For to this day, when they read the old covenant, that same veil remains unlifted, because only through Christ is it taken away. Yes, to this day whenever Moses is read a veil lies over their hearts. But when one turns to the Lord, the veil is removed. Now the Lord is the Spirit, and where the Spirit of the Lord is, there is freedom. And we all, with unveiled face, beholding the glory of the Lord, are being transformed into the same image from one degree of glory to another. For this comes from the Lord who is the Spirit. (2 Cor. 3:7-18)

Again, it is helpful to point out what is not brought out here—a glory for the soul but not the body. Instead, there is a singular coming of permanent glory. The question for us is does the saint receive this permanent glory upon entry into heaven or is it awaiting the eschaton and resurrection on Judgment Day? This coming of glory is obtained in two stages: first via an inner glory at regeneration, and then upon death when the outer glory is revealed as we are transformed into our glorious body and our mortal body is laid to rest.

Paul continues to describe this glory as a hope we possess with boldness, presenting our present state of glory as a partial manifestation of glory now, when he says, "And we all, with unveiled face, beholding the glory of the Lord, are being transformed into the same image from one degree of glory to another." The unveiled face of New Testament believers is contrasted with that of the temporary nature of Moses face of glory in the Old Testament. The ultimate permanence of our glory represented by our glorious face, with the totality of glory to the entire person which is obtained at death is much greater than the glory of Moses which was receding and could never result in outer glory. The face is used to represent that our inner glory is present via the Spirit's indwelling, but our outer glory is still veiled by our mortal body until this veil is removed at death. Paul describes this process as "one of one degree of glory to another [degree of glory]". This is the same process described as "life to life" in 2 Cor. 2 and I identified as an escalation of life (glory), now Paul expresses it even more clearly here via "one degree to another".

We are "being transformed" from one glory to another. We see a picture of this transformation process for mankind in nature, one example being a caterpillar transforming into a butterfly. Paul used the metaphor of a seed planted in the ground in 1 Cor. 15, transitioning into the new glorious spiritual body. There is no break indicated in this transformation such as taught in the intermediate state. The thought conveyed is that of our union with Christ represented by our inner glory of the Spirit transitions to a more glorious or escalated condition through the removal of the veil of the body. He says that this transformation "comes from the Lord who is the Spirit", clearly indicating the power of this transformation resides in the saint through the indwelling Spirit, not through a delayed command executed by Christ at his visible personal coming on the Last Day. Granted Christ and his Spirit are the same, but Paul specifically highlights the presence of the Spirit who is the Lord not the Lord reigning in heaven who comes to destroy Satan's kingdom. This cannot be ignored. The kingdom has already come for the believer, awaiting the crushing of the entire kingdom of death at the Last Day. Christ told his disciples to wait in Jerusalem for the Spirit who would empower them, thus indicating his enthronement and return to his glorious state.

The transition from one state of glory to an escalated glorious state can be seen elsewhere in the New Testament. In Acts 7:2-4 Stephen introduced the connection of future glory in the Promised Land at the beginning of his speech:

> Brothers and fathers, hear me. The God of glory appeared to our father Abraham when he was in Mesopotamia, before he lived in Haran, and said to him, 'Go out from your land and from your kindred and go into the land that I will show you.

The manifestation of the glorious face of Stephen at his death before the Jewish council, in which his face shone like an angel, can easily be understood to teach that his glorious face resulted from his union with Christ. Also, it testified to all that his death would result in transforming glory of the entire person in heaven upon his death and entrance to the true Promised Land.

Another example is seen at the transfiguration when Christ exhibited full outer glory. Stephen only displayed a partial glory to the face while awaiting his complete glory in heaven, but during the transfiguration before his passion, Christ's inner glory which had been shrouded by his earthly body was transformed into outer glory of his entire body. Christ was giving a glimpse into his future return to glory after his resurrection and exaltation, which resulted in his outer glory forever. The resulting return of Christ's outer glory initiated the giving of the Spirit of Glory to the church at Pentecost in order to build his Temple. The glorious face of Steven was indicated a pre-ultimate state of glory (inner glory awaiting outer), whereas Christ retained all of his glory (although veiled by his human form prior to his ascension) and therefore a full body glorification image was shown. He was showing them his future, and the saints future as well.

At the close of chapter 3 Paul highlights the new, glorious ministry of the Spirit. He states that the Lord and Spirit are one and follows by teaching that the Spirit among other things brings the light and thus the glorious radiance of Christ and gives it to his image bearers.

> And even if our gospel is veiled, it is veiled to those who are perishing. In their case the god of this world has blinded the minds of the unbelievers, to keep them from seeing the light of the gospel of the glory of Christ, who is the image of God. For what we proclaim is not ourselves, but Jesus Christ as Lord, with ourselves as your servants for Jesus' sake. For God, who said, "Let light shine out of darkness," has shone in our hearts to give the light of the knowledge of the glory of God in the face of Jesus Christ. (2 Cor. 4:3-6)

The fullness of this glorious radiance is expressed only upon the removal of our mortal body and receipt of our glorious body upon entrance to heaven. The point to be made here is the mechanism for this complete work of glorious restoration is the gospel which begins at regenerating new earthly inner life/light/glory and finishes at heavenly resurrection life with a glorious outer body. The gospel relates only to the elect and is good news as they escape Final Judgment via resurrection to heaven prior to the Judgment Day reserved for those who rejected the gospel. The gospel as in Christ's example ended with his resurrection to heaven and restoration to his fully glorious state. Thus, the salvation thru the gospel is completed for the elect image bearers of Christ's glory upon resurrection to heaven and restoration to their full glorious state. The gospel does not extend to a Judgment Day restoration of the glorious body for the elect. The offer of the "good news" ended upon the arrival of Judgment Day, there are no further resurrections to life as the elect have already been transported into heaven. Thus, Judgment Day is described as a day without light, darkness, gloom, and destruction and is the polar opposite of the gospel light. As Christ's work of securing the salvation of his people upon his death and resurrection is complete, so is our work on earth finished and glory manifested outwardly upon our resurrection to heaven. This means there is not a heavenly state for the saint without the glorious body. I believe that this means the intermediate state doctrine corrupts the gospel because it teaches that Christ's resurrection was not enough to accomplish our glorious state, but that we must wait past our resurrection to heaven until a Day of Judgment and darkness. This confuses the gospel era of the church with the judgment of the unbelievers. Nowhere is the gospel of salvation spoken of in terms of a Last Day deliverance. The path to glory of Christ exactly matches the path of his image bearers.

But how is this brought out in this section of chapter 4? Paul begins by describing the veiling of the gospel by Satan to those who are perishing, "to keep them from seeing the light of the gospel of the glory of Christ, who is the image of God". The gospel is the glory and results in glorification. This unbelief or non-glorious state is contrasted with the light of the gospel, which is the glory of Christ, who is the exact glorious image of God. During the gospel dispensation one either remains in a state of death whereby future glorification is not attained due to unbelief in the gospel, or one believes the gospel and is on a path from partial glorification at regeneration to full glorification upon resurrection. Glorification has begun in the believer and is not all reserved for the resurrection into heaven. It is the gospel that results in glorification. Here Paul uses three distinct descriptions to illustrate the common end time for the redemption of the individual saint, which is upon resurrection to heaven. These descriptions are 1) the gospel, 2) the glory of Christ, and 3) the image of God. All three point to glorification, which is the end point because once we are remade into his image there is no further escalation in status. The last two need no explanation as glorification is apparent. The gospel needs clarification in that it is the pathway or process to deliver the believer at the glorified state in heaven, which is upon resurrection. The theme of this book put in the shortest 3-word synopsis is resurrection means glorification. Resurrection life which was restored to Christ's earthly body and in which he remained on the earth for 40 additional days was not the completion of his work. Resurrection must be understood to be fulfilled in its entirety only when the person has been raised to heaven resulting outer glorification. Christ after his resurrection and witness on earth for 40 days, had not yet attained outer glory as it was still veiled in his earthly human body. Outer glory waited for Christ until he was taken to heaven via the glory cloud, as the Son of Man passage of Daniel 7:13-14 prophesied:

> I saw in the night visions, and behold,
>> with the clouds of heaven
> there came one like a son of man, and he
>> came to the Ancient of Days

and was presented before him. And to
   him was given dominion
and glory and a kingdom, that all peoples,
   nations, and languages
should serve him; his dominion is an
   everlasting dominion,
which shall not pass away, and his kingdom
   one that shall not be destroyed.

This prophecy depicts Christ's return to glory upon his resurrection to heaven. This is proven due to his coming to the Father in heaven from his prior earthly position and his being given "glory". It does not depict the time of the final state of the kingdom to be accomplished on his descent to Judgment. Although the saints benefit from the destruction of the kingdom of this world, as it initiates the new earth/heavens, by this point the full number of the elect had already been translated into the heavenly kingdom and received their completed glorification as a result of the gospel which is the life, death, and resurrection of Christ. It is a misrepresentation of the gospel to separate resurrection to heaven from complete glorification. Heavenly status, when we are in the presence of the King of Glory, results necessarily in our own body reflecting his glory and thus becoming his image bearers. The veil covering the mirror has been removed at death and entrance to glory.

Paul, in verse 6, speaks only of the present inner glory described as seeing the face of Christ as opposed to the entire body in heaven because they still reside on earth with the veil of their mortal body. Paul presents again, as in 3:18, the picture of our displaying inner glory via regeneration while on earth while waiting a future glorious body here, "For God, who said, 'Let light shine out of darkness,' has shone in our hearts to give the light of the knowledge of the glory of God in the face of Jesus Christ". The idea again is that we are only able to display Christ's glory through our "face" as we have only a partial manifestation of it while in our mortal body as opposed to our future full glorification. The similar idea is we only see Christ partially now, thru faith, awaiting our arrival in heaven where we will see him via sight. Both examples end in glorification in heaven.

Next Paul explains that this treasure or glory is held in vessels of clay.

> But we have this treasure in jars of clay, to show that the surpassing power belongs to God and not to us. We are afflicted in every way, but not crushed; perplexed, but not driven to despair; persecuted, but not forsaken; struck down, but not destroyed; always carrying in the body the death of Jesus, so that the life of Jesus may also be manifested in our bodies. For we who live are always being given over to death for Jesus' sake, so that the life of Jesus also may be manifested in our mortal flesh. So death is at work in us, but life in you.
>
> Since we have the same spirit of faith according to what has been written, "I believed, and so I spoke," we also believe, and so we also speak, knowing that he who raised the Lord Jesus will raise us also with Jesus and bring us with you into his presence. For it is all for your sake, so that as grace extends to more and more people it may increase thanksgiving, to the glory of God. So we do not lose heart. Though our outer self is wasting away, our inner self is being renewed day by day. For this light momentary affliction is preparing for us an eternal weight of glory beyond all comparison, as we look not to the things that are seen but to the things that are unseen. For the things that are seen are transient, but the things that are unseen are eternal. (2 Cor. 4:7-18)

Paul continues the image of inner glory vs. the outer body (described as a clay vessel), highlighting that this surpassing power of glory from God is inside the saint presently. It is not a power to be received on the Last Day. The image is one of hidden or unseen glory moving to revealed glory when the outer vessel of clay or mortal body is removed. He teaches that we carry the death of Jesus in our bodies now. Thru his death on the cross which killed our old man, even now in this state we manifest the life of Christ in these mortal bodies while on earth. But his point is not only the manifestation of his life in our dead bodies now, it carries the meaning of this body's transformation from death to life upon the physical death of the mortal body, and the body's transformation into a glorious spiritual body, enabling us to dwell in heaven.

Paul had already made clear that there are only two choices when speaking of bodies in 1 Cor. 15 and no identification of a bodyless time period was taught. Either a mortal or immortal, an earthly or heavenly state were presented. Paul now states, "we also believe, and so we also speak, knowing that he who raised the Lord Jesus will raise us also with Jesus and bring us with you into his presence." Paul is not teaching a singular moment on the Last Day where all will be resurrected. He says Jesus will raise us and bring us into his presence. Here resurrection is stated in clear terms as occurring when we enter his presence in heaven as opposed to at the eschaton. He equates the resurrection of Christ (raised him) with our resurrection (will raise us also), with the time period for our resurrection (bring us into his presence). He does not state the raising up and bringing into his presence is a singular event, but promises that he, the apostles, and these Christian believers will be raised by Christ and brought into his presence. This cannot be a resurrection or raising at one time, such as a singular resurrection on the Last Day, for it speaks of being brought into his presence, and all teach we are brought into his presence upon death, and they did not die on the same day. This is not a resurrection of the soul only, for the soul is not the context here or in the previous chapters of 2 Corinthians. Nor going back to the basis of the doctrine begun in 1 Corinthians 15— the topic consistently has been the resurrection of the body. So, when Paul says, "raise us with Jesus and bring you into his presence", he is undeniably speaking of the bodily resurrection happening when we are "brought into his presence", and not after we have been in heaven during an Intermediate state, and then resurrected on the Last Day. The context is of earthen vessels here on earth in which we reside.

Why are we not to lose heart (v.16)? Paul then describes our hope of heaven. When do we arrive there? We arrive only at death. At death faith and hope no longer "remain" as Paul explained in 1 Cor. 13:12-13:

> For now we see only a reflection as in a mirror; then we shall
> see face to face. Now I know in part; then I shall know fully,

even as I am fully known. And now these three remain: faith, hope and love. But the greatest of these is love.

When we obtain entrance into heaven at death, faith and hope in things not seen, have become things realized by sight, when we are face to face with Christ. Therefore, a hope or faith possessed by the heavenly saint awaiting the Last Day is contrary to these texts when related to the individual saint's redemption. Our hope does not reside in the future events of the Last Day which deal with the kingdom of Satan, our hope is in Christ and being in his presence. To deny the attainment of our hope when we are with Christ in heaven and teach the promise of more to gain later is contrary to the gospel, for Christ is the gospel, and the gospel is his death and resurrection. Paul further describes this transformation as currently taking place now, "our outer man is wasting away", or heading towards death, but our "inner man is being renewed day by day", or being conformed to the image of Christ, and proceeding to "an external weight of glory", which is the outer body fully mimicking the glorious body of Christ such as appeared to Paul on the Damascus Road.

Returning to 2 Corinthians 4, heaven is the unmistakable place of this crowning with the external weight of glory, described as "a place beyond comparison" (v. 17) and further described by comparing the present state—"things that are seen" with their future state in heaven as "things that are unseen" (v.18). The former are transient, the latter eternal. The outer "man" is thrown away and the inner man is renewed or given a new glorious body. Paul is not speaking in terms of two different men, but of an alive new man whose body in seed form is present in the new inner creation but is residing in the dead (spiritually) outer body. This topic of the body as a seed was detailed in the exposition of 1 Corinthians 15. Kenneth Wuest, teacher Emeritus of New Testament Greek at The Moody Bible Institute, in his NT translation of 1 Cor. 15:7-8 puts it this way:

> After that he appeared to James, then to all the apostles, and in the last of all his appearances, he appeared also to me, an unperfected, stillborn embryo.[25]

---

[25] Kenneth Wuest, The *New Testament: An Expanded Translation*, (Grand Rapids, Eerdmans, 1984), 411.

Here Wuest describes Paul's status, prior to his regeneration on the road to Damascus, as "an unperfected stillborn embryo". This image of a dead embryo in an unregenerated man, representing the fallen image of God residing in an unbeliever can be used to then understand the idea of the regenerated believer containing, in embryonic or seed form, the spiritual body which Paul describes here and in the 1 Cor. 15 sections, when the embryo is described as a seed to be planted in the ground. The thought may be expressed as this progression: 1) a dead embryo in a lost person, 2) given new life and transformed into a live embryo encased in a dead mortal body, which is 3) transformed at death into the fullness of the original Adam. The redeemed man (Adam's progeny) has then returned to heaven (Eden) and been restored to Adam's original place (described in Ezekiel 28 where Adam is identified as "an anointed guardian cherub"). Adam's expulsion from heaven because and therefore all his progeny, (for whom he was the federal head), because of his sin, has come full circle. The second Adam has entered heaven and paved the way for those he represented to return to their previously intended glory. The concept of a return to heaven without a glorious body or covering via the immediate state is inconsistent with this model and example. Heaven is a return to glory, not an unfulfilled redemptive placeholder for man who is awaiting Judgment Day with the rebels.

Paul details our transformation into heaven in 2 Cor. 5:1-9:

> Now we know that if the earthly tent we live in is dismantled, we have a building from God, an eternal house in heaven, not built by human hands. For in this tent we groan, longing to be clothed with our heavenly dwelling, because when we are clothed, we will not be found naked. So while we are in this tent, we groan under our burdens, because we do not wish to be unclothed but clothed, so that our mortality may be swallowed up by life. And God has prepared us for this very purpose and has given us the Spirit as a pledge of what is to come. Therefore, we are always confident, although we know that while we are at home in the body, we are away from the Lord. For we walk by faith, not by sight. We are

confident, then, and would prefer to be away from the body and at home with the Lord. So we aspire to please Him, whether we are here in this body or away from it.

These verses clearly present an immediate transformation from our earthly body into our glorious body, not a bodyless existence of the soul in heaven until the Last Day. Christ made the promise that he was going to heaven to prepare a place for us in Jn. 14:1-3:

Do not let your hearts be troubled. You believe in God; believe in Me as well. In My Father's house are many rooms. If it were not so, would I have told you that I am going there to prepare a place for you? And if I go and prepare a place for you, I will come back and welcome you into My presence, so that you also may be where I am.

This indicates that our heavenly home (body) awaits only our coming to heaven to obtain it. Christ promises to come back and welcome us into his presence. The coming described is not a final coming but refers initially to the coming of Christ thru his sending (coming) of the Spirit at Pentecost, and continuing comings of the Spirit throughout this age. These comings unite us with Christ through his Spirit making us a temple of his presence. This indwelling presence is the guarantee of the transformation at the death of our mortal body so that whether we are here on earth (unglorified state) or in heaven (glorified state) the entire "man" is present with Christ. 2 Cor. 5:1-9 makes the connection between these two states of man in the repeated references to the unity of the body and soul. We see this first through his identification that while in this tent or temporary body, we long to be clothed with our permanent heavenly home. Again, this text does not indicate a separation from the outer body, Remarkably, Paul makes it clear that he is not speaking of a time where we would be in an unclothed state (without our heavenly covering) or time of separation between body and soul. He says, "For in this tent we groan, longing to be clothed with our heavenly dwelling, because when we are clothed, we will not be found naked" (v.4). This groaning to be further clothed is synonymous with our desire to be in heaven with Christ and our receipt of a glorified (body) state. Paul refutes the teaching of unclothed saints without their outer glorious body in heaven, by stating, "we will not be found naked".

This understanding is confirmed in the parable of the wedding feast where those without the proper garment for the occasion were cast into utter darkness (Matt. 22). It is utterly indefensible to equate the lost who are without the proper clothing in the parable, with the current teaching of saints in heaven as naked or unclothed, as they represent different classes of people. The point of being able to differentiate the unclothed lost, from the properly clothed saints endowed with their glorious body, is then nullified, contradicting the clear teaching of the parable. Verse 12 indicates that the lack of proper adornment is the critical point: "And he said to him, 'Friend, how did you get in here without a wedding garment?" Thus, the requirement for the first day or entry into the heaven of his glorious presence, is adornment of the glorious garments, it is not a condition obtained on the Last **Day**. The feast does represent Judgment Day in that on the Last Day the lost will appear before Christ, but only to be judged and then removed from his presence forever, as the parable describes. Until that day only glorified saints are before his throne. The parable makes no mention of the adorning of the saints as it presupposes the process defended in this book, resurrection is glorification at death. The error lies in not recognizing the continuing resurrection of the saints throughout the messianic age, as Christ progressively builds the Temple in heaven until it is complete, resulting in Judgment Day, with the singular resurrection to judgment of the lost on the Last Day of the kingdom of Satan.

The doctrine of a one-time resurrection day for all mankind, is not scripturally based. The depiction of this feast being only a Last Day feast is untenable as even in this present age we confess and celebrate our communion with Christ through the Lord's supper, waiting here on earth until we can continue to partake of it with him in heaven. It is therefore a present feast we participate in, a real presence with Christ through his Spirit indwelling us, which continues until we eat it again with him in heaven, as Christ taught in Matt. 26: 27-29:

> Then He took the cup, gave thanks, and gave it to them,
> saying, "Drink from it, all of you. This is My blood of the

covenant, which is poured out for many for the forgiveness of sins. I tell you, I will not drink of this fruit of the vine from now on until that day when I drink it anew with you in My Father's kingdom."

It was Christ who would not drink the cup again until he was resurrected to his heavenly kingdom. He drinks it with us as he is in the kingdom in heaven, while we have the kingdom of God (Spirit) within us, awaiting the day we join him in heaven. Drinking the cup is clearly described as beginning when we drink it anew with Christ in the kingdom. If we are to experience a real presence with Christ here when we celebrate the Lord's Supper, it must have begun when Christ returned or ascended into heaven. Denying this presence by relegating this feast until the Last Day alone removes the power and grace of this supper to the church in this age. This is a serious but warranted warning. As the feast teaches our attainment of our outer glorious body when in heaven, the supper teaches our attainment of inner glory now by the indwelling presence of the Holy Spirit, which blossoms into an outer glory of our resurrection bodies at death. As we have seen, Paul described this in 2 Cor. 4:16-18:

> Though our outer self is wasting away, yet our inner self is being renewed day by day. For our light and momentary affliction is producing for us an eternal glory that is far beyond comparison. So we fix our eyes not on what is seen, but on what is unseen. For what is seen is temporary, but what is unseen is eternal.

The Old Testament example of the manna from heaven eaten during Israel's wilderness journey mirrors this New Testament type of the supper—both point to the ultimate bread of life which we receive by faith when partaking of the emblem of the real bread of life. the Lord's Supper is the sign and seal of the present reality of our union with him, not of a future blessing we obtain. Likewise, the wilderness journey was celebrated in the Feast of Tabernacles in which the Israelites would remember the wilderness journey by building temporary huts to remain in for 7 days. This feast contains the picture of the huts, representing our temporary outer mortal bodies, unable to reflect outer glory while we are overshadowed by the glorious presence of God during the earthly journey, represented by the fire and the cloud. The temporary hut was abandoned along with the Tabernacle when the Israelites pass the Jordan River and enter the Promised Land where the permanent Temple (Christ) resides. So too, we also abandon our mortal body at death.

Returning to the text above in 2 Corinthians, Paul further eliminates any chance of mistaking the immediacy of the change from one body into another and the negation of a transition to a state of nakedness or one without a body by stating we do not wish to be unclothed, but clothed, so that our mortality may be swallowed up by life. This refutes the idea of a Christian desiring or the teaching of a state of nakedness without a body. This text clearly teaches a transformation directly from one state to another by using the phrase "swallowed up by life". This is not described as a death of the old body followed by a long period of nakedness only to be reunited at the Last Day, rather as a transformation from death to life in an immediate process of transition described as one destroying or swallowing up the other. The victory over death was won at the cross, but its elimination is progressive. One must differentiate the swallowing or elimination of death for the individual with that of the entire cosmos. This "destroying" described by swallowing up by life refers not to the ultimate destruction of the evil kingdom, but only to the saint upon his entry into the eternal kingdom of heaven. The end of death and transition for the saint or individual is at the death of the mortal body, after all curse of Adam has been removed. But death, as represented in the earthly kingdom and Satan the king, is not destroyed at an individual's death as death continues to operate in this fallen world. However, death's final grip over the saint was removed by the removal of the outer body of death, resulting in resurrection life for the body. The ultimate victory over the kingdom of Satan is accomplished on Judgment Day, when death itself and therefore Satan's kingdom, is destroyed entirely and forever.

Although we are given new life at our regeneration when we are created anew, given the Spirit, and placed by the Spirit into his body, and although the Spirit is the guarantee of the future transformation at death, while on earth we await the final victory, the final swallowing up of death when we put aside our body of death and are gloriously transformed. Through

Christ's death on the cross we are baptized into Christ's death and our mortal body is killed with respect to its ability to control us, and we await the final freedom from what Paul calls "our body of death" in Rom. 7:24. The individual obtains victory over death when the dead body is removed and we are clothed with the new body. So, the picture or timeline Paul teaches is:

1. regeneration and indwelling by the Spirit and placement into the body of Christ in his heavenly Temple.
2. our wilderness journey here on earth in which we are endowed with the protection and overshadowing of the Spirit to be his ambassadors or witnesses to the world until our work is done at physical death.
3. Transformation into his glorious image when we remove the earthly outer garment of our mortal body and it returns to the ground. We are transformed and clothed with our new glorious body fit for heaven and taken there: the place filled and illuminated continuously by his glory, for there is no darkness or night in heaven because our Lord cleansed it once for all by his blood on the cross, destroying death's hold on his people and casting the devil who previously had access to the heavenly realms to the earth to await the Last Day—for he knows his time is short.

Resurrection is more than just a movement up to the higher dimension or simply an escalation in earthly benefits where we no longer suffer the travails of pain and suffering in this wilderness life, or even being freed from our body of death which tempted us. Resurrection at its core is the transformation of the fallen sons of Adam back to Adam's original glorious pattern. Resurrection is a return to the image of God with which we were created but lost, requiring God to cloth us with earthly garments at the fall, as seen in Gen. 3:21. "And the LORD God made garments of skin for Adam and his wife, and He clothed them." Only when we are returned to our glorious state upon entry to heaven is redemption for the individual completed.

Returning again to 2 Cor. 5, Paul describes the giving of the Spirit to the saint in verse 5 as the promise of this transformation at death, saying,

"He who has prepared us for this very thing is God, who has given us the Spirit as a guarantee." He continues, reiterating that there only two states: either in the body on earth, or in our heavenly body in heaven.

> we know that while we are at home in the body, we are away from the Lord. (v.6)
> . . . and would prefer to be away from the body and at home with the Lord (v.8)
> So we aspire to please Him, whether we are here in this body or away from it. (v.9)

The contrasts presented in these verses are between our presence with the Lord on earth in our mortal body, or our presence in heaven with our spiritual, glorious, resurrected body. If we are in this body we are away from heaven and we desire to put aside this body and be with Christ in heaven, but we desire to please him in either this body or in the next. Here in the most detailed description of resurrection, nothing other than two options—an earthly body or a heavenly body—is found. No instruction is given of an intermediate state. The description of "home" with the Lord, is another way of describing us in heaven where he went to prepare a place for us. There is not a middle phase of nakedness for those united with Christ, who have a resurrection like his.

Paul continues the use of only two choices by identifying our current mode as being by faith—awaiting our heavenly body, and the future mode in heaven as being by sight—our glorious body. There is not a depiction of a middle mode in heaven where we are in sight of our risen Lord but still living by faith awaiting the Last Day for our body. It is either living by faith waiting for the future glorious body, or by the sight having obtained it. Faith or sight. A body is present in both locations. He closes the section by referring our confidence in this future work, to the fact that we have the promise of the indwelling Spirit not the promise of a future command or final coming of Christ. As the Spirit came and recreated us in Christ's image through regeneration, so the Spirit indwells us during our wilderness journey on earth, then upon death of the mortal body this same indwelling Spirit fulfills the guaranteed promise by transforming us into his glorious image as he takes us to his presence in heaven. He takes the entire man, not only a part of us to heaven. A resurrection like our Lord.

2 Cor. 5:10 has been a major cause of the propagation of the common resurrection of all mankind on Judgment Day. This text is an important pivot point and understanding its meaning and the conclusion one then draws about resurrections, then leads to a correct or a faulty interpretation. Does this teach only one resurrection to Christ's Judgment seat for all on Judgment Day? The text states:

> For we must all appear before the judgment seat of Christ, that each one may receive his due for the things done in the body, whether good or bad.

The text implies that Christians desire to please Christ because we know that all mankind will be judged by Christ for the actions performed on the earth in the body. It also serves as a warning for the lost, that they also will be judged according to what they did in the body, as they refused Christ's salvation per the gospel and are subject to his future wrath. This is a statement of an almost universal belief by all mankind: a judgment after death where all actions will ultimately meet a just sentence. If I was to summarize the text, I would say "every person will someday face God for judgment". This is one example of a text that is used to defend doctrines not supported by the text. The text does *not* state:

- That all are resurrected at the same time
- That all are judged at the same time
- This happens entirely on the Last Day
- Degrees of rewards for saints will be obtained in heaven

Rather, it only states that all mankind will appear at Christ's judgment seat to receive a judgment. Further it clarifies that two different judgments will be rendered, good or bad.

Perhaps we should consider the suggestion that if two different verdicts are rendered, then a singular judgment day is not reasonable. All believe the lost receive a judgment at death but await their final judgment until the Last Day when they are resurrected and appear before the throne of Christ.

Does it not follow that the same would be true for the elect, which is they receive their final judgment upon the loss of their mortal body, and receipt of their glorious outer body upon entrance to heaven at death? All believe the saints go to heaven where Christ's throne is upon death. So, it seems reasonable to ascribe the final judgments to be given to either the elect or the lost directly upon their resurrection to heaven. The general theme of scripture is God extending his offer of grace and building his holy nation progressively, all the while delaying his final judgment and ultimate fury of his wrath until Judgment Day. The 2 Cor. 5:10 text only identifies two classes of people and two rewards. "All must appear" refers to only two categories of people—elect and lost—and matches the only two awards to be received from the time in the body—either good or bad rewards. No mention of degrees of rewards are in the text. So, there is a direct correlation between 2 people groups and 2 reward categories. Second, verse 10- only states that all will appear at the throne or judgment seat of Christ, it does not state they arrive there at the same time. Traditional eschatology understands the saint arriving in heaven at their death but without their glorious body, however it certainly is logical to understand this arrival in heaven as meaning their arrival before Christ's judgment seat. Christ is currently sitting at the right hand of the Father. Why cannot this be acknowledged as the same time the elect receive their positive judgment for their good works done in the body on earth?

The previous discussions dealt extensively with the topic of earthly suffering resulting in heavenly glory as our earthly race (period of works) ends upon entrance to heaven with Christ. It seems silly not to understand a judgment occurring at death for both classes. The elect receive their final judgment and reward at death when they arrive in heaven, but the lost receive their preliminary judgment at death but wait in Sheol until the Last Day judgment or final judgment for them and resurrection to their second death. There is not a necessity to separate Christ's current position in heaven on his throne from also being his judgment seat, or more clearly to not properly understand heaven's attainment as the end of sin and further judgments. Christians arrive in heaven upon death and the lost arrive on judgment Day on the Last Day. I understand Paul is addressing the church, but as the congregation is a mixture of true and false believers, Paul warns them all of their future appearance before the throne where either a good or bad judgment will be rendered. The next verse, "Therefore, knowing the fear of the Lord, we persuade others", carries forward the thought that Paul has both lost and believers in mind and emphasizes our commission to declare the gospel to the lost world. But there is not a sliding scale portrayed for either group where degrees of rewards can be defended. How can one get more or less of Christ who is our great reward? One is either in or out of Christ.

The ESV Reformation Study Bible states:

> Degrees of reward in heaven are taught in this verse. Though Christians have their sins forgiven and will never suffer the punishment of hell, (Rom. 6:23; 8:1). They will all nonetheless stand before Christ at the Day of Judgment, to receive various degrees of reward for what they have done in this life (Matt. 6:20; Lk.19:11-27; 1 Cor. 3:12-15). This judgment will include a disclosure and evaluation of the motives of our hearts (1 Cor. 4:5)[26]

However, the Romans references used to support the first sentence do not support degrees of rewards for Christians:

> For the wages of sin is death, but the free gift of God is eternal life in Christ Jesus our Lord (Rom.6:23)

> There is therefore now no condemnation for those who are in Christ Jesus. (Rom. 8:1)

The first supports my identification of only two rewards or outcomes of either death or eternal life. The second clearly states there is no more of what is here translated as condemnation. Strong's concordance defines word used here for condemnation as:

> Usage: punishment following condemnation, penal servitude, penalty.

---

[26] Study note for 2 Cor. 5:10 in R.C. Sproul, Ed., *ESV Reformation Study Bible*, (Orlando: Ligonier Ministries, 2005)

Cognate: 2631 *katákrima* (from 2596 /katá, "*down*, according to," intensifying 2917 /kríma, "the results of *judgment*") – properly, the exact *sentence* of condemnation handed *down* after due *process* (establishing guilt)[27]

So, the reference given in the Reformation Study Bible as a basis to defend a judgment but not a final judgment, rather of rewards for Christian service, uses an incorrect definition of condemnation. The condemnation word used is for a judgment or casting down, that is, a final judgment and sentence after a finding of guilt that can only refer to the judgment of the lost.

Furthermore, Paul completes his definition or thought of what "no Condemnation" means in Rom. 8:1 further in verses 10-11:

> But if Christ is in you, although the body is dead because of sin, the Spirit is life because of righteousness. If the Spirit of him who raised Jesus from the dead dwells in you, he who raised Christ Jesus from the dead will also give life to your mortal bodies through his Spirit who dwells in you.

No condemnation means future resurrection life for the body at death via the guarantee or seal of the indwelling Spirit. So going back to 2 Cor. 5:10 reference to "all" which includes the elect, it means the Spirit brings the believer, who has the Spirit of Christ's righteousness inside, to Christ's heavenly judgment seat sinless through the indwelling Spirit at death. We do not experience death but receive more life through resurrection life to our outer body.

Two further texts defend my position that judgment of the elect ends at death when we are finally released from our mortal body which is still corrupted by Adam's fall. The first is 2 Thess. 1:5 which says,

> All this is evidence that God's judgment is right, and as a result you will be counted worthy of the kingdom of God.

---

[27] Strong's Concordance: 2631. κατάκριμα (katakrima) -- penalty (biblehub.com)

The kingdom is already inside us; thus judgment has been rendered, and we will proceed to the heavenly kingdom which we already have been granted access. Kingdom entrance means the end of judgment. The second text is Jn. 5:24:

> Truly, truly, I say to you, whoever hears my word and believes him who sent me has eternal life. He does not come into judgment, but has passed from death to life.

This passing from judgment commenced at regeneration and ends at death and heavenly entry. Christ clearly teaches here that we do not come under judgment. This refutes the doctrine of the elect participating in the judgment or penalty assigned to the lost on their Final judgment on the Last Day. The elect in heaven are witnesses of the judgment of the lost, not recipients of end time judgment. Christ clearly taught we will judge the world, and our participation as witnesses at their judgment fulfills this proclamation of Christ. The idea of God recalling in heaven our previous sins or failures, which Christ removed from us, and assigning degrees of rewards is a Pre-Reformation carryover and error of a soteriology of works in our doctrine. The only reward in heaven is being before the throne or judgment seat of Christ with our adornment of his righteous robes obtained at death. Therefore, 2 Cor. 5:10 teaches two classes of people before the judgment seat: one in their righteous robes and one without. It does not teach degrees of rewards for the elect. The additional references in the Reformation Study Bible don't support varying rewards either. This is especially the case regarding the reference to 1 Cor. 4:5 r which states the opposite of judgment for the believer as in his faults will be brought to light at that time, for is states "Then each one will receive his commendation from God". This matches the earlier statement of two rewards, as here the elect are described as only being commended, the equivalent of Christ stating well done good and faithful servant. The context of the 1 Cor. 4:5 text is not to render judgments on each other now but to await Christ's commendation. It has nothing to do with a Last Day judgment for the elect.

A final comment regarding the Reformation Study Bible note stating, "Degrees of reward in heaven are taught in this verse". The New Testament speaks of those entering heaven being purged via a fire by Paul in 1 Cor. 3:11-15:

> For no one can lay a foundation other than that which is laid, which is Jesus Christ. Now if anyone builds on the foundation with gold, silver, precious stones, wood, hay, straw—each one's work will become manifest, for the Day will disclose it, because it will be revealed by fire, and the fire will test what sort of work each one has done. If the work that anyone has built on the foundation survives, he will receive a reward. If anyone's work is burned up, he will suffer loss, though he himself will be saved, but only as through fire.

The Day is our entrance into heaven, not the final judgment day, when we pass through the "fire" symbolized in the flaming torches guarding Eden in Genesis. As we enter back through the fire on our entrance into heaven the refining work of the Holy Spirits ongoing work in the life of the believer is completed. This is contemporaneous with the adornment of outer glory. The final purification is then accomplished by the Holy Spirit not on the Last Day but upon our "first" day in heaven, as he removes any dross and refines us upon entry. Death is described as a passage through fire, but the fire does not destroy us. This is when we are purged and "judged". The idea of a last day judgment for works for the saint after having been in heaven is derived from the wrong assumptions of a common resurrection and judgment day for the elect and the lost.

There are differing abilities and calls which God has given to different saints, such as an apostle, but as all graces or gifts come from God they need to be viewed as deriving from the heavenly Father, as the potter forming his vessels of clay, and constructing the vessels differently to accomplish his purposes, and not as a result of our own works.

The final section in 2 Corinthians we will explore, 2 Cor. 5:12-18, is a very interesting commentary by Paul relating to resurrection, the type of resurrection body, and the nature of the union of body and soul before and after our resurrection to heaven.

We are not commending ourselves to you again but giving you cause to boast about us, so that you may be able to answer those who boast about outward appearance and not about what is in the heart. For if we are beside ourselves, it is for God; if we are in our right mind, it is for you._For the love of Christ controls us, because we have concluded this: that one has died for all, therefore all have died; and he died for all, that those who live might no longer live for themselves but for him who for their sake died and was raised. From now on, therefore, we regard no one according to the flesh. Even though we once regarded Christ according to the flesh, we regard him thus no longer. Therefore, if anyone is in Christ, he is a new creation. The old has passed away; behold, the new has come. All this is from God, who through Christ reconciled us to himself and gave us the ministry of reconciliation.

Paul begins in verse 12 speaking of those who boast about outward appearance instead of what is in the heart, thus creating this inner glory vs. outer fleshly veil comparison.

We must return to Genesis to compare the original creation of Adam to the final form to which the second Adam returns mankind. They must be identical mirror images, but more importantly, the timing of these transitions must match as well, with either an immediate transition or that of a period of time between the bodily transitions from fleshly to glorious.

The model of our transformation to our resurrection body Paul describes in his Corinthian letters, is one of the new inner person transforming into the full-grown man clothed with glory, which is revealed upon the removal of the outer body of flesh at death. It is not the transformation of the old body, but the revelation of the new creation body implanted via the Holy Spirit at regeneration. If true, this destroys the idea of a resurrection of the glorious body on the Last Day and confirms the thesis of this book, as it means that death is just the revealing of the present inner glorious reality. The body of "flesh" is to be understood as part of the judgment rendered to Adam after his sin, not a part of the original nature of Adam, who was created soul and body, in a spiritual body before God clothed him with garments of "flesh" or skin. Adam's original creation of body and soul was altered into a different body and he was given the spiritual nature of the tempter. We see the serpents' skin, which has the ability to shed itself, and God's covering of Adam with skins, portraying from the beginning the inner person cloaked with the body type of the new master. I think there was a transition in Adam's body at the point of his sin to one of an earthly or flesh and blood body which is then typologically represented in circumcision via the partial cutting away of the foreskin. The judgment rendered to Adam upon his sin was death, and that death resulted in his being adorned by a mortal body of flesh which would then perish upon the loss of the breath of God. A judgment is a casting down, from the heavenly realm to the earthly which is what Adam experienced.

Adam transitioned from a glorious body into a body of flesh upon the judgment. Therefore, the redemptive cure must be that of transitioning from the body of death and into the glorious body as I described, a resurrection or a raising back up to the heavenly realm. A fleshly and visible body vs. a spiritual and invisible body, as Paul describes the body's characteristics in 1 Cor. 15. As Adam went immediately from a glorious spiritual body into a fleshly earthly body, so does Christ return us immediately from an earthly fleshly body into a spiritual glorious body at death to the mortal body. Both Adam's transition from heavenly to earthly and our transition from earthly to heavenly occur instantaneously, without an intermediate state breaking of the unity of the body and soul. This is the same language and immediate change description Paul uses in 1 Cor. 15:50-51 where he says, "but we shall all be changed, in a moment, in the twinkling of an eye" where he describes those on earth at his final coming and their bodily transitions as they enter into heaven, further supporting an immediate transition when entering the glory cloud of heaven. Christ's ascension into heaven was the time of his change from earthly body into glorious one and was the final confirmation. The belief that Christ's body upon his rising from the grave and remaining on earth is his glorified body, rather than the body Christ was adorned with upon his ascension, has caused enormous damage to the gospel in relation to the resurrection body for the saint. Viewing Christ's earthly body as the glorified body in heaven leads to errors. Adam's original model is confirmed by Christ as one of immediate transformation, therefore as Paul explains we follow the same immediate transformation at death.

Paul proceeds, in verses 14 -15, to describe how Christ's death for all resulted in the death of the sin nature for all his elect, resulting in new life via the Spirit. Paul is talking to believers still on earth in their mortal bodies, so when he refers to "therefore all have died" (v.14), he is speaking of the spiritual death to the old nature (man) now recreated in Christ's image, but also to the mortal body of flesh which the death of Christ's body of flesh killed when he died. Although this mortal body is still breathing, its future death is secured. He is referring to the baptism into death the Christian experiences at regeneration when the old nature has been killed, but also to the ultimate physical death of that body which then results in bodily (spiritual) resurrection life in heaven. The resurrection body is spiritual, as 1 Cor. 15:44 states, "it is sown a natural body; it is raised a spiritual body. If there is a natural body, there is also a spiritual body". Second, "those who live . . . for him" (v.15) are these same believers, who begin to live for Christ at regeneration but in the future at their death will then live with Christ in heaven at the death of their mortal body. This was accomplished by Christ, "who for their sake died and was raised" (v. 15). As believers died with Christ at regeneration, being raised with Christ refers not to the indwelling of the Spirit as the primary meaning but rather to the resurrection to heaven and the receipt of the glorious image. The inner glory of the Spirit is the stage of promise, awaiting future completion in heaven with Christ. The gospel of death and resurrection means resurrection into heaven, for inner glory on earth in a mortal body is not our Blessed Hope. Paul is making the astonishing point that the inner glory of the Spirit bestowed upon regeneration resulted in the death of the old person and recreation of the new glorious man now housed in a mortal body of flesh. The outer body of flesh awaits its death when the breath of life which God gives ceases, and it returns to the ground.

But the most interesting part is verse 16, where he states we are not to view any person renewed by the Spirit as "according to the flesh" because they are a new man in Christ. Second, Paul states that we are not even to consider Christ according to the flesh any more now that he is resurrected to his glorious body even though Christ did reside on earth in a fleshly body so as to be able to pay our debt: "Even though we once regarded Christ according to the flesh, we regard him thus no longer". Paul is stating that there was a period of time where Christ was in the flesh, but we are no longer to regard or think about Christ in this manner any longer. Why? Because Christ took on human form in order to suffer the penalty of death fallen mankind deserved, but upon the completion of his work he returned to his glorious and spiritual nature in heaven. Many fail to recognize that the body Christ rose and resided on earth was the same flesh and blood body that was killed, but at his ascension into the invisible realm via the glory cloud is when the transition from earthly to spiritual body occurred. A spiritual body is still a body. Paul here is tying both Christ's and the believer's transition from the earthly body into the heavenly body. A picture of the fleshly body preventing the entrance back into the presence of God is provided in the Old Testament types seen in both the Tabernacle and the Temple.

> And you shall hang the veil from the clasps, and bring the ark of the testimony in there within the veil. And the veil shall separate for you the Holy Place from the Most Holy. (Ex. 26:33)

> But he shall not go through the veil or approach the altar, because he has a blemish, that he may not profane my sanctuaries, for I am the Lord who sanctifies them. (Lev. 21:23)

> And behold, the curtain of the temple was torn in two, from top to bottom. And the earth shook, and the rocks were split. (Matt. 27:51)

> By the new and living way that he opened for us through the curtain, that is, through his flesh. (Heb. 10:20)

The veil or curtain was our fallen mortal body of flesh given to us via Adam's judgment, the barrier bocking our return to the Holy of Holies. Christ by his death in his "time in the flesh", removed the barrier for his people. The curtain was not placed on Christ to enter the Holy of Holies but was thrown down to open the way.

This mortal body has already perished when seen thru the lens of it being the outer body housing the newly created inner man. Additionally, the man that is now alive is the inner new creation man Paul described in 1 Cor. 15 and Kenneth Wuest translated as "embryo", because Christ's life is the animating principle in the believer. This also follows Paul's declaration that "*it is not the body that is to be raised*" when he described the mortal body. Therefore, this adds up to the transformation process for the believer as transitioning from inner to outer glory as that of an unveiling of the inner "embryo" into the fully mature man displaying his outer glory, when unveiled at the death of the old body. Resurrection may entail the flowering of the seed of the Spirit into manifestation of the outer body, but in no manner is it the old body. Paul states in verse 17, "Therefore, if anyone is in Christ, he is a new creation. The old has passed away; behold, the new has come." The old perishes and another creative act like that of genesis creates the new man.

CHAPTER 8

CHRIST'S COMING AND
JUDGMENT DAY
IN 1 THESSALONIANS

The closing chapters will focus on two primary points. First, that the completed redemption of the elect in heaven occurs before the Judgment Day events. The return of Christ on Judgment Day is his final elimination of all things standing in opposition to his rule. The removal of the elect from the earth is a necessary precursor to his Final Judgment. This is covered in my 1 Thessalonians 4:14-5:11 exposition. The statement in 4:16, "and the dead in Christ will rise first", is presented as a rising to stand up rather than the common description of a bodily resurrection. This verse is a critical hinge on which the doctrine of bodily resurrection is grounded.

Following upon the above premise, this last section will deal with the broad topic of the "Revelation of Jesus Christ," defined as: when God's creatures, human or angelic, come to the realization that The Lord is ruler of heaven and earth. The timing of this revelation of Christ follows the separation in time of the judgments of the elect and the lost: first to the elect as savior and then finally to the fallen creatures remaining on Judgment Day. This is critical for several reasons. First, the revelation of Christ for the elect begins at regeneration and is completed when Christ is revealed to us as our faith becomes sight when we enter heaven at death because the Lord is fully revealed in all his glory to his people at this time.

Second, the revelation of Christ to the lost occurs on Judgment Day as this day is solely the revelation of Christ to all who have rejected him. Third, this revelation of Christ had already resulted in the salvation of the elect prior to Judgment Day. So, my charge for the reader is to contemplate what revelation of Christ is being presented in each text, whether that of faith or that of horror on Judgment Day when his fury is kindled against them. Put another way, will the following chapters point the saint towards the goal of their faith being union with Christ at death or Judgment Day?

1 Thessalonians 4:13-18: Christ's Coming for the Elect Prior to Judgment

> But we do not want you to be uninformed, brothers, about those who are asleep, that you may not grieve as others do who have no hope. For since we believe that Jesus died and rose again, even so, through Jesus, God will bring with him those who have fallen asleep. For this we declare to you by a word from the Lord, that we who are alive, who are left until the coming of the Lord, will not precede those who have fallen asleep. For the Lord himself will descend from heaven with a cry of command, with the voice of an archangel, and with the sound of the trumpet of God. And the dead in Christ will rise first. Then we who are alive, who are left, will be caught up together with them in the clouds to meet the Lord in the air, and so we will always be with the Lord. Therefore encourage one another with these words.

Before discussing this section in detail, I will finish the discussion began in chapter 6 regarding the Last Trumpet which signals the beginning of the Final Judgment for the lost by comparing it with 1 Cor. 15:50-55:

> I tell you this, brothers: flesh and blood cannot inherit the kingdom of God, nor does the perishable inherit the imperishable. Behold! I tell you a mystery. We shall not

all sleep, but we shall all be changed, in a moment, in the twinkling of an eye, at the last trumpet. For the trumpet will sound, and the dead will be raised imperishable, and we shall be changed. For this perishable body must put on the imperishable, and this mortal body must put on immortality. When the perishable puts on the imperishable, and the mortal puts on immortality, then shall come to pass the saying that is written:

"Death is swallowed up in victory."
"O death, where is your victory?
O death, where is your sting?"

These two texts by Paul discuss the same topic, namely the bodily resurrection of believers alive on earth at the Last Trumpet. We must keep in mind that Paul has specifically identified this group of saints as a separate discussion from when the resurrection of all of the saints from eternity occurs. They are a special case. This is critical to identify, as this refutes the common doctrine of a resurrection of all mankind at the Last Trumpet on the Last Day. As we saw in chapter 6, the saints who already died prior to the Last Trumper were resurrected at their death throughout the church age. If the Last Trumpet signaled the resurrection of the body for every saint, then Paul would have clearly and simply stated such in the following manner: "All saints go to heaven as only a soul upon death and await the resurrection and reuniting with their heavenly body, until the Last Trumpet sounds the end of the Day of Salvation (church age) and the Day of Judgment has arrived." Paul never states this either here or anywhere else in a similar clear exposition because he never intended to. It was not his intention to make a simple doctrine more complicated, but to explain that the order and sequence of resurrection is upon death for the saint and on the Last Day for the lost who are held until that time. Therefore, Paul is forced to give these two clear passages on the resurrection of those saints still alive at the Last Trumpet. He separates their resurrections from all previous believers because they are unique in that they did not die on earth. Zechariah 14:6-7 describes the Last Day as a unique day:

On that day there will be no light, no cold or frost. It will be a day known only to the LORD, without day or night; but when evening comes, there will be light.

John's Revelation gives the trumpet pattern of six continuing trumpet warnings throughout the church age until the Last (seventh) Trumpet signals the end. The pattern is thus a continuing resurrection at death until this final resurrection at the Last Trumpet. The Last Trumpet in Paul's writing is synonymous with the seventh Trumpet in John's revelation. C. F Keil gives the correct understanding of the number seven as used in scripture and is helpful here:

> Seven is the measure and signature of the history of the development of the kingdom of God, and all the factors and phenomena significant for it…the signature for all the actions of God, in judgment and in mercy, punishments, expiations, consecrations, blessings, connected with the economy of redemption, perfecting themselves in time.[28]

The number seven identifies the restoration of the cosmos, the perfecting, or finishing of the recreating work of Christ who makes all things new again. In these two texts along with Revelation, the Last Trumpet signals this completion. Therefore, the resurrection of all on the Last Day doctrine falls. Why? The Last Trumpet signals the end of the gospel dispensation and Christ raptures to heaven the final elect members from earth in order to commence Judgment Day. The Last Trumpet sounds first and the Final Judgment events follow including the resurrection of the lost. Christ returns to judgment after the resurrection of these saints to heaven. This final prior resurrection to heaven is before the singular resurrection of all the lost. The mystery Paul will explain in 1 Cor. 15:50-58 and I Thess. 4:13-18, signaled by the seventh Trumpet, is this unique day of a resurrection of only this group of believers alive on Judgment Day on earth. The misinterpretation of these two texts by applying this resurrection to a singular bodily resurrection of all humanity at one time

---

[28] C.F Keil and F. Delitzsch, *Commentary on the Old Testament*, (Grand Rapids: Eerdmans, 1973), 9: 153

has created a critical error in teaching the gospel, whereby earthly death does not result in resurrection life for the entire Christian man (mankind) or in perfection in heaven, but only a need for a continued faith for Christ to finish his work. In this model, faith in a future resurrection of the glorious body is still required even when residing in heaven which is the epitome of glory and conflicts with 1 Jn. 3:2:

> Beloved, we are God's children now, and what we will be has not yet appeared; but we know that when he appears we shall be like him, because we shall see him as he is.

This verse teaches that we will be like his glorious body when we see him in his glorious body in heaven, as the glorious body has not appeared while we reside on earth in our mortal body. This New Testament example of God rescuing his people out of this world, which Paul is describing as mysterious due to their not experiencing physical death, is foretold by the example of Enoch in the OT. Here these saints are the antitype to the Old Testament type of Enoch, the 7th from Adam, who also never experienced death:

> Enoch walked with God, and he was not, for God took him. (Gen. 5:24)

> By faith Enoch was taken up so that he should not see death, and he was not found, because God had taken him. Now before he was taken, he was commended as having pleased God. (Heb. 11:5)

> Enoch, the seventh from Adam, also prophesied about them: "Behold, the Lord is coming with myriads of His holy ones to execute judgment on everyone, and to convict all the ungodly of every ungodly act of wickedness and every harsh word spoken against Him by ungodly sinners." (Jude 14-15)

The Genesis text alludes to the same kind of transition from earth to heaven without death as the Corinthian and Thessalonian texts describe.

Hebrews clearly states Enoch did not see death which further confirms the same tie. Interestingly, Jude includes the indicator of the number seven to Enoch's ascension into heaven, which is the time marker of the completion of the restoration of the kingdom. This also ties it to the Last or Seventh Trumpet signaling Judgment Day in Revelation. Jude further indicates the separation of resurrections between the lost and the elect, as he uses the same "Behold" introduction Paul used to introduce the Last Day resurrection in 1 Cor. 50, "Behold! I tell you a mystery". Here in Jude 14 "Behold" is used to highlight not those to be resurrected, but to emphasize that those who previously died and were resurrected into heaven will be returning with Christ. Behold in scripture is used to ensure the reader or audience pays specific attention what follows. Thus, this final coming with the holy ones includes the church already in heaven in totality, body and soul, before the Last Day. In Genesis, Enoch's life prophesies that the beginning of resurrection life is upon the completion of the saint's time on the earth. The Hebrews text highlights his walking with God in faith and then being taken to God (resurrected) after pleasing God. Jude identifies Enoch as prophesying that Gods holy ones (saints) will be a part of the Glory Cloud of angels who return with the Lord to execute judgment on all the ungodly. The saints must have been resurrected prior to the sounding of the Seventh Trumpet in order to be able to return with Christ on Judgment Day. The resurrection of the saints is to life: body and soul. The resurrection of the godless is not a bodily resurrection but a resurrection to judgment, preceded by the gospel age of resurrection of the saints to heaven. 1 Thess. 4:13-18 describes this same return of Christ with the resurrected saints in heaven from Jude 14 to meet those on earth.

The coming of Christ for his remaining people on earth is the first action on the commencement of Judgment Day which Paul will discuss in chapter 5. Christ must remove all those who are his in order to destroy the evil kingdom and its remaining rebellious inhabitants on earth. The class of people Paul is speaking about is solely those alive at the final coming of Christ, and how they enter the glory cloud or heaven. These verses do not teach that every saint receives glorification at the Last Trumpet. Paul begins by giving assurance to those alive at the time of the writing of this letter and the hope of their own resurrection at death in contrast to those without Christ who have no hope of resurrection life at death or on the

Last Day. Paul again ties Christ's present resurrection reality with that of those who have already died stating, "For since we believe that Jesus died and rose again, even so, through Jesus, God will bring with him those who have fallen asleep" (v.14). This is the same point Paul made in section two of 1 Cor. 15 discussed earlier. Since Christ's bodily resurrection after death is true, it is also true for those who have died in him, and their resurrection will take place in the same manner—directly upon death. It is a present reality for them as surely as Christ is raised. "Even so" in verse 14 means "in the same manner" and cannot be reduced to a spiritual resurrection of the soul only, for that happened at regeneration. A resurrection like Christ's is the only pattern. For Christ will bring with him those who have died, for they ascended into heaven in the same manner as that of Christ's resurrection to heaven, which is upon ascension to heaven via the Glory Cloud.

The Glory Cloud on which Christ ascended to heaven is seen in his return via the cloud with the saints in verse 17,

> Then we who are alive, who are left, will be caught up together with them in the clouds to meet the Lord in the air, and so we will always be with the Lord. Therefore encourage one another with these words.

Those left on earth will join the congregation already in the Glory Cloud. To be in the Glory Cloud is to see the glorified Christ, to have a glorified body, to reside in his glorious Temple, and is the final stage to our incorporation into his body. In this section Paul presents *again* the order of resurrections which was previously discussed: first Christ's, second the dead saints upon entry into heaven, third those on the Last Day. If he was intending to teach a common resurrection day, he would not separate these two people groups in time or inform the Thessalonians that those who had already died have already been resurrected and will return with Christ in the Glory Cloud, at which time they will be united with those resurrected from the earth at his Final Coming. If a singular resurrection for the elect is true, Paul would tell them what is the current doctrine of the church: those on earth are not glorified when they enter heaven's Glory Cloud, rather they enter heaven unglorified and await their future resurrection with those already unglorified in the Glory Cloud and with the lost, who by the way do not receive a new resurrection body, which adds another nonsensical component to this doctrine.

The whole point of this text in 1 Thessalonians is that Christ and the saints in heaven are descending within the glory Cloud to the atmosphere where these saints on earth will arise and meet them and be incorporated to the heavenly realm and be transformed into their glorious heavenly bodies. It is the final harvesting of the earth of its good fruit. If there was a single resurrection at Judgment Day, there would be no need for Paul to indicate whose resurrection occurred first (Christ's), second (the elect who has died in faith), or last (those alive at Judgment Day). But he does differentiate the timing of the respective resurrections in the exact same manner he did in 1 Cor.15. He does this by stating, "For this we declare to you by a word from the Lord, that we who are alive, who are left until the coming of the Lord, will not precede those who have fallen asleep" in verse 15. Who will not proceed whom? Those on the earth will not proceed those who have already died. Proceed in what? A resurrection. Why will they not proceed in resurrection those who have already died? Because the dead in Christ are already resurrected and with Christ in heaven. It teaches a resurrection order in time rather than a common resurrection is indicated here by Paul. Paul clearly tells his readers in Thessalonica that those who are left on earth at his final coming will not precede those who had died, but that those who have died have already experienced resurrection life in the body and will be brought back with the Lord, "For since we believe that Jesus died and rose again, even so, through Jesus, God will bring with him those who have fallen asleep" (v.15). Why does he state this truth here? He states it to give hope of resurrection to heaven to those still on the earth: "But we do not want you to be uninformed, brothers, about those who are asleep, that you may not grieve as others do who have no hope" (v.13). There is hope for those on earth in the knowledge of the completion of the resurrection of their loved ones who have died, which is contrasted with the dead without Christ who have no hope of a resurrection to new resurrection life but only a resurrection for judgment. What supplies this hope? They have hope because their loved ones who died in faith in Christ's resurrection are, in the same manner as Christ, already resurrected and with him. Those in heaven and a part of the Glory Cloud (God's heavenly residence) have already experienced resurrection life and are with Christ and are counted among the "holy ones" returning with Christ. If you believe Christ rose again, "even so", you must believe they are resurrected and coming with him as promised.

Jude 14, as we saw above, states the same thing: that Christ returns "with myriads of his holy ones". All beings in heaven, whether angelic or human, are "holy ones" and "glorious". It is patently absurd to consider inglorious saints in heaven, which is the epitome of glory, who are unable to reflect Christ's glory. This first act by Christ's return to judgment where he removes or saves the saints on earth is necessary so Christ can commence the execution of his judgment on all the lost from eternity who have not been incorporated into this Glory Cloud, due to their hardness of heart manifested by unbelief. Paul states the same thing in 1 Thessalonians 3:11-13:

> Now may our God and Father himself, and our Lord Jesus, direct our way to you, and may the Lord make you increase and abound in love for one another and for all, as we do for you, so that he may establish your hearts blameless in holiness before our God and Father, at the coming of our Lord Jesus with all his saints.

Here Paul describes the group descending within the Glory Cloud as saints (v. 13), rather than just "holy ones" as in Jude 14, confirming they are indeed the triumphant church in heaven and not only angelic beings. This is the final coming for salvation which results in the Final coming to Judgment on the earth and its dwellers.

We now arrive at part of this passage, which has confused most commentators and has led to the erroneous teaching of a Last Day Resurrection of all mankind—verses 16b to 18. The misunderstanding centers on the meaning of the word "rise":

> . . . and the dead in Christ will rise first. After that, we who are still alive and are left will be caught up together with them in the clouds to meet the Lord in the air. And so we will be with the Lord forever. Therefore encourage one another with these words. (NIV)

"Rise first" (v.16b) refers to those who had already died and reside in heaven; however, it does not denote a resurrection of the body, but simply a rising to stand up. The word translated "rise" in this verse is used only four times, each to stand upright:

ἀναστήσονται (anastēsontai)— 4 Occurrences:

Matthew 12:41: "of Nineveh will stand up with this" (NASB)

Luke 11:32: "of Nineveh will stand up with this" (NASB)

Acts 20:30: "men will arise, speaking" (NASB)

1 Thessalonians 4:16: "in Christ will rise first." (NASB)[29]

Additionally, Strong's Exhaustive Concordance has this definition:

arise, jump up, stand up. From ana and histemi; to stand up (literal or figurative, transitive or intransitive) – arise, lift up, raise up (again), rise (again), stand up(-right).[30]

But what was Paul's meaning and purpose for the inclusion in the text in 1 Thessalonians of the resurrected saints in heaven rising to stand at the Last Trumpet? What scriptures can be used to further support the meaning of those already in heaven "rising first" meaning to stand up and not depict a resurrection of the body to heaven? The procedure of rising to stand in a court of law prior to the proclamation of a verdict or judgment is still followed today in our justice system. It is out of respect for the one rendering the judgment and the justice of the sentence rendered. A general explanation of this imagery of rising to stand is to be understood as a contrast of transitioning from a position of resting to a position of standing upright. Christ describes this standing up or rising to shut the door of salvation and initiate the Last Judgment in Lk. 13:24-25:

---

[29] Englishman's Concordance #450 – biblehub.com
[30] Strong's Exhaustive Concordance #450, anistemi - biblehub

Make every effort to enter through the narrow door, because many, I tell you, will try to enter and will not be able to. Once the owner of the house gets up and closes the door, you will stand outside knocking and pleading, 'Sir, open the door for us." But he will answer, "I don't know you or where you come from." (NIV)

The thought here is that the saints already in heaven have entered into their eternal rest and security. They have been taken out of the world and its tribulation and are seated with Christ around his heavenly throne. Christ is seated on his throne as his work to secure salvation for his people has been accomplished via his death and resurrection. This resting with his people also depicts the fact that indeed his resurrection brought resurrection life already for those in heaven and will continue until the Last Day when he will gather the remaining elect on earth to heaven signally the completion of his Temple building which is the elect. His work of redemption is complete for the people when his rest or sitting ends and he stands up to come as King of Kings and judge and execute the covenant curses.

The final rest and ultimate security for all the elect has not been achieved upon their entry to heaven as the kingdom of darkness on earth ruled by Satan has not been destroyed and judged. Therefore, the rising to stand by the elect who are already resurrected and in heaven indicates the Day of Judgment signaled by the Last Trumpet has arrived as Christ stands as well to begin the end time holy war and finish his work of destroying death and sin in totality thru the destruction of the kingdom of evil or the present heavens and earth, the false prophet, and Satan. For on Judgment Day at the white throne judgment all will appear before his throne, as the lost and the elect will be gathered to receive their final rewards; the elect having already experienced resurrection life with Christ and who have already been at the throne, will be joined by the resurrection of the lost. Thus, the elect will witness the completion of the Kingdom as heaven and earth will once again be united and forever purified.

One additional comment concerning the standing of the elect versus the body position for the lost: the entirety of scripture has a central theme of separating humanity into two classes of people. It chronicles the eternal destiny for both the righteous and the profane, culminating here at the heavenly throne at the conclusion of time. The righteous will be able to stand on the Day of Judgment and witness and rejoice in the day, whereas the lost will not be able to stand due to their fear and horror as they realize they shall suffer the wrath of him whom they have rejected and mocked. Revelation 6:17:

> For the great day of their wrath has come, and who can withstand it? (NIV)

The rhetorical answer is not the lost. This text gives us the answer that only those wearing the righteous robes washed in the blood of Christ will be able to stand on the great Day of Wrath. One must not be dogmatic in this area as some scriptures speak of the lost also standing before the throne, perhaps after rising to hear their fate. An Old Testament text which supports rising to judgment or to conquer is found in Numbers 10:35-36 where the Israelites are set to leave Mount Sinai on their way to the promised land:

> And whenever the ark set out, Moses said, "Rise up, Lord! May your enemies be scattered; may your foes flee before you." Whenever it came to rest, he said, "Return, Lord, to the countless thousands of Israel." (NIV)

This Old Testament example in which the Israelites rose to conquer more territory and nations, but rested in a time of peace as the glory cloud and pillar of fire protected the nation is another basis for the "rise first" referring to the saints in heaven rising to judgment and to conquer with Christ as he rises on Judgment Day. This example is typological of both the ultimate end time war to defeat of Satan's kingdom and the entry into the eternal rest of heaven. See other texts relating to this question of rising/ standing below.

> Who are you to judge someone else's servant? To their own master, servants stand or fall. And they will stand, for the Lord is able to make them stand. (Romans 14:4 NIV)

he exerted when he raised Christ from the dead and seated him at his right hand in the heavenly realms, (Ephesians 1:20 NIV)

You, then, why do you judge your brother or sister? Or why do you treat them with contempt? For we will all stand before God's judgment seat. (Romans 14:10 NIV)

After this I looked, and behold, a great multitude that no one could number, from every nation, from all tribes and peoples and languages, standing before the throne and before the Lamb, clothed in white robes, with palm branches in their hands. (Revelation 7:9 NIV)

And I saw the dead, great and small, standing before the throne, and books were opened. Another book was opened, which is the book of life. The dead were judged according to what they had done as recorded in the books. (Revelation 20:12 NIV)

The men of Nineveh will stand up at the judgment with this generation and condemn it, for they repented at the preaching of Jonah; and now something greater than Jonah is here. (Luke 11:32 NIV)

Paul began this section in 1 Thessalonians by explaining the tie between Christ's resurrection and the resurrection of the saints who have died, that is, they occur in the same order and manner as Christ's by stating "For we believe that Jesus died and rose again, and so we believe that God will bring with Jesus those who have fallen asleep in him" (v. 14). Paul had made this same point in the beginning of 1 Cor. 15, explaining that if it is true that Christ has been resurrected, then those who died had been resurrected as well: Christ first, then the elect who died in faith in Christ, and now these who would be left on earth at the final Trumpet. Here, Paul states their hope in resurrection is based upon Christ's resurrection and the completed resurrection of those who are asleep (dead). He makes it beyond dispute by stating as Jesus rose directly after death upon his ascension, "even so", are those who died also resurrected and he will bring them back with him at the Last Trumpet. The dead saints were resurrected to heaven first, at their death, before those left on earth who will be resurrected at the Last Trumpet signaling the Final Judgment. Therefore, it is impossible for Paul to now contradict what he has already made clear, (which is that those who have died have already been resurrected even as Christ is), by stating here that "the dead in Christ will rise first" and mean that this refers to a resurrection of the body at a future time at the Last Trumpet. This mistake perpetuates the belief in the intermediate state in which those saints who have died and entered heaven do so as only a soul and will receive their resurrection body at the Last Trumpet. The meaning of "rise" being to "stand up" and the entire context of Paul's 1 and 2 Corinthian exposition denies this conclusion. Paul concludes this section by telling them to encourage one another with these words, as he had based their confidence in the status of their loved one's current resurrection on nothing other than their confidence in the resurrection of Christ which gives them a sure hope as they anticipate their future reunion with them either in heaven before the Last Trumpet or on that day when he brings all the saints with him to join those left on earth and bring them to heaven.

The writer of Hebrews, whom I believe is Paul, offers the same encouragement to the readers of Hebrews, in Hebrews 12:1-2:

> Therefore, since we are surrounded by such a great cloud of witnesses, let us throw off everything that hinders and the sin that so easily entangles. And let us run with perseverance the race marked out for us, fixing our eyes on Jesus, the pioneer and perfecter of faith. For the joy set before him he endured the cross, scorning its shame, and sat down at the right hand of the throne of God. (NIV)

Again, the saints are described as a "cloud of witnesses" indicating their union with the resurrected Christ in heaven. Paul, in 1 Corinthians and 1 Thessalonians, and here in Hebrews, offers the fact of the dead saints' resurrection and union with Christ in the Glory Cloud in heaven as the hope for the earthly saints undergoing persecution. If the saints of old are not resurrected now, then their example is not one of completed resurrection, and therefore could not offer them any resurrection hope for the only resurrection having been accomplished already would be Christ's. The tragedy of denying their resurrection reality while with Christ in heaven is that it breaks our unity with Christ's resurrection at death and does not give Christians complete hope at death, but extends the hope past our death to a future work of Christ to be accomplished at the Last Trumpet when he is alleged to summon the resurrection body to rise at that time, which is based on this mistaken interpretation of "rise first". Thus, the gospel of Christ's death and resurrection and his work of salvation was not completed upon his ascension for the elect but awaits Judgment Days last Trumpet.

1 Thessalonians 5:1-11: Initiation of Judgment Day

Following the removal of the elect from the earth in the coming of Christ in chapter 4, Paul proceeds to instruct them on the "Day of the Lord" which is Judgment Day.

> Now, brothers and sisters, about times and dates we do not need to write to you, for you know very well that the day of the Lord will come like a thief in the night. While people are saying, "Peace and safety," destruction will come on them suddenly, as labor pains on a pregnant woman, and they will not escape. But you, brothers and sisters, are not in darkness so that this day should surprise you like a thief. You are all children of the light and children of the day. We do not belong to the night or to the darkness. So then, let us not be like others, who are asleep, but let us be awake and sober. For those who sleep, sleep at night, and those who get drunk, get drunk at night. But since we belong to the day, let us be sober, putting on faith and love as a breastplate, and the hope of salvation as a helmet. For God did not appoint us to suffer wrath but to receive salvation through our Lord Jesus Christ. He died for us so that, whether we are awake or asleep, we may

live together with him. Therefore encourage one another and build each other up, just as in fact you are doing. (I Thess. 5:1-11 NIV)

There will be no visible signs to warn the lost that Judgment Day has come. They will have a false sense of peace and security until the sudden realization of the promised judgment and wrath of the visible Messiah in the sky has arrived. There will be no hiding or escaping his gaze. The important point for our topic, is that we see clearly the resurrections to heaven for the elect is separated from the Day of Wrath resurrections. The exposition in Corinthians revealed a transformation from earth to heaven and earthly body to heavenly body upon death and entrance into heaven for the elect. For the elect, Paul states here, "God did not appoint us to suffer wrath" (v. 9), disassociating them from the Day of Wrath. He also contrasts it with their future association with Christ in heaven, "to receive salvation through our Lord Jesus Christ. He died for us so that, whether we are awake or asleep, we may live together with him" (vv.9b, 10). If there is a common reunion on Judgment Day as per the intermediate state, Paul would certainly not state we are not destined for the Day of Wrath. This is the clearest statement of the error of the intermediate state identifying the Day of Wrath as the time of our resurrection to our new immortal body. He states that the Judgment Day or Day of Wrath (which is the same "day"), is not our destiny. Paul described the final removal of the last elect from earth to heaven in chapter 4, and now the lost will be resurrected to judgment on this Last Day. Two separate chapters for two different outcomes for two different classes of people: the Last Day of Salvation in chapter 4 where the final elect are resurrected, and the Last Day of Judgment in chapter 5 where the lost are judged and condemned. When the elect are removed from the earth in totality the heavenly temple, which is made up of his people, has been completed. Dealing with the lost follows in the timeline. Paul instructs and encourages the saints by reminding them that Christ died in order that whether we were still awake (living on earth at his final coming for them) or asleep (died and already raised to life with Christ in heaven), all would live with him and escape this Day of Wrath.

CHAPTER 9

THE REVELATION OF JESUS CHRIST IN PAUL

This chapter compares Paul's points so far with the balance of other New Testament texts to determine if the focus of the end of the believer's life of suffering on earth is new resurrection life in a glorious body upon entry to heaven, or if the weight of those texts point our hope towards Judgment Day. Secondarily, one must come to terms, after completing this section, with why there is not an exposition of the intermediate state in Scripture. It is not credible that the central point of the gospel, the resurrection to life in body and soul for Christ's people is left without multiple texts stating it in clear terms.

The Revelation of Jesus Christ

How is the phrase "the revelation of Jesus Christ" to be understood? This section will attempt to summarize the broad meanings inherent in the various usages of this phrase. The broadest meaning of revelation of Christ for the elect occurs progressively: beginning at incarnation and culminating in the final revelation of Christ's glory as King of Kings, as he pours out his wrath on his enemies at the consummation. This same revelation reveals either his final glory or wrath to the intended recipients. The revelation of Christ to the unbeliever is only obtained at the final judgment. Everyone experiences either a return to the glorious image of Christ in which we were created, or the fury of his wrath. My argument is these judgments of glory or wrath reach finality at different times, as opposed to concurrently at the Final Judgment, as taught in the intermediate state and reformers.

The elect are glorified at death on entrance to the kingdom. The revelation of Christ's wrath to all mankind, which can be quenched via the gospel, was the mystery hidden to previous generations but disclosed by the manifestation of Christ visibly via his first coming in the flesh as the Messiah, the sin bearer and giver of new spiritual life. This first visible manifestation ended upon Christ's ascension back into the heavenly or spiritual realm which we are unable to perceive with our natural sight. The gospel era or "Day of Salvation" which is the offering of the good news of forgiveness of sins will terminate upon the second visible appearance of Christ as the Lord of Lords on the "Day of Darkness" or "Day of Wrath" when he returns in glory (light) to execute his righteous wrath upon the dark world and all of those who rejected the message of the gospel. The first step of his appearing to judgment will be the removal of the elect left on earth as they rise to meet him in the clouds (heaven). The world will then be totally in darkness as all his people (the light of the world) have been removed and no light remains on the earth. The gospel era is the revelation of Christ to the elect. The first and last appearances are two visible manifestations of Jesus Christ: one to proclaim an offer of salvation, and the other to execute his final judgment and pour out his wrath upon all unbelievers. Between these visible revelations or manifestations are invisible manifestations or revelations of Christ to those on earth which become visible upon translation to heaven and Christ's personal presence. We must access the revelation of Christ by faith until we are united with and see him in heaven.

Within the timeframe of the first and last visible revelations, the elect and the unbelievers experience the revelation of Christ at different times. The revelation of Christ's glory (salvation) to the elect begins at regeneration, continues throughout life on earth via sanctification, and culminates via sight of the Messiah in heaven. The believer ultimately receives the revelation of Christ's wrath on the Last Day judgment as the elect in heaven witness the execution of that wrath upon those who rejected him as Messiah. For the unbeliever, the entire revelation of Christ occurs on the Last Day as they are resurrected to judgment and experience his wrath, but also come to the realization that they rejected the Lord of Glory. Both elect and the lost witness the revelation of both Christ's glory and wrath at the judgment, but experience only one or the other on that day.

A subset inside of this bookended visible manifestation of the revelation of Christ, is the invisible revelation of Christ to those who are given the Spirit by grace through their faith in Christ as the Messiah. Although this group has not seen Christ visibly, they are, by virtue of the indwelling of the Spirit, adoption of sons, etc., partakers of the revelation of Christ which will eventually culminate in their sight of the Messiah when they are united with him in the heavenly kingdom. So, for the elect, the revelation of Christ has three phases: 1) the initial invisible revelation at regeneration and ongoing increasing sanctification and understanding; 2) the visible revelation which occurs at death when we transition to heaven and see Christ in glory; and 3) Judgment Day where the visible revelation of Christ in both his glory and wrath is realized. Therefore, when one comes across the phrase "Christ's revelation" or words such as coming, appearing, manifestation, etc., we must determine via the context which time frame is being referenced. A problem is evident in expositions where the "revelation of Christ" is mistakenly identified with his final visible manifestation or revelation on the Day of Judgment or Wrath (which consists of both his glory and wrath), but the context does not support this understanding. The argument of this book means that the revelation of Christ's glory on Judgment Day must be understood not as the first receipt of glory for the elect but as the extension of his glory beyond heaven (where they already reside in glorious bodies), to encompass the entire cosmos as Christ eliminates darkness and death forever. The lost will acknowledge his glory at that time but will wail and cry out in realization that the Day of Salvation had ended, and only his wrath awaits them.

Revelation of Christ in Romans (Chapters 1-8)

As the writer of 13 or 14 New Testament books, the apostle Paul was given extraordinary revelations concerning the gospel. Paul gives expression to the nature of our soul and body in terms of an inner and outer man as well as in our transformation to glory from the inner spiritual seed of the Holy Spirit into our glorious heavenly body. In the first 7 chapters of Romans, Paul chronicles the bondage of mankind in sin and proceeds to the gospel that delivers us from that bondage and God's judgment of wrath. Chapter 8 culminates in the future realization of our inheritance of glory in Christ in heaven. Chapter 7 ends with this question:

> So I find this law at work: Although I want to do good, evil is right there with me. For in my inner being I delight in God's law; but I see another law at work in me, waging war against the law of my mind and making me a prisoner of the law of sin at work within me. What a wretched man I am! Who will rescue me from this body that is subject to death? Thanks be to God, who delivers me through Jesus Christ our Lord! So then, I myself in my mind am a slave to God's law, but in my sinful nature a slave to the law of sin. (Rom 7:21-25 NIV)

Paul is instructing his readers that the final deliverance from our struggle against sin will be at death, when we are freed from the residual effects of the sin nature residing in our mortal bodies. Commentators acknowledge this in part but do not tie this deliverance from sin in our body at death, to our immediate transition to glory in Christ, which Paul summarizes in Chapter 8. Instead, an intermediate state is taught when we are united with Christ in heaven, but still without a glorified body. Chapter 8 would be another perfect chance for Paul to defend and clearly explain that the deliverance from "this body that is subject to death" results not in glory but only an inglorious state for us while we reside with our glorious Lord, waiting glorification on the Last Day resurrection to our glorious body. But he does not and again the reason is that it is not true. Paul does not somehow neglect this critical step and therefore hide it from his audience, nor does he expound it other places.

Is it possible that I have overemphasized glorification at death as being the main theme of chapters 1-8? The following brief summary specifically highlights "glory". Any good writer begins with the main point in the introduction. Paul open Romans with the death and resurrection of Christ, in 1:1-4

> Paul, a servant of Christ Jesus, called to be an apostle and set apart for the gospel of God—the gospel he promised beforehand through his prophets in the Holy Scriptures regarding his Son, who as to his earthly life was a descendant of David, and who through the Spirit of holiness was appointed the Son of God in power by his resurrection from the dead: Jesus Christ our Lord.(NIV)

Paul ties Christ's incarnation, becoming a son of David, to his declaration to be a "Son of God" by his resurrection from the dead. The gospel is Christ's taking on human flesh, dying in our stead in order to obtain resurrection life for us at the death of our mortal body. It is our time of death when he delivers resurrection life. That is the gospel—his death so we do not experience the death we deserved. This central truth of life at death cannot be changed to death to our body resulting in a continuing in a state of death for our body. He continues his focus on our future hope in heaven in 5:1-2:

> Therefore, since we have been justified through faith, we have peace with God through our Lord Jesus Christ, through whom we have gained access by faith into this grace in which we now stand. And we boast in the hope of the glory of God. (NIV)

Our "hope" in the glory of God ends when we receive it and come face to face with our glorified Christ in heaven where faith has become sight. Heaven is not a place for hope or faith in a future glorification for the temple pieces, but only a hope for the glorification of the cosmos.

Paul contrasts our current state on earth as a baptism into death, (the death to the bondage to sin residing in our mortal body or flesh), to our uniting with Christ in heaven in a resurrection like Christ's in Romans 6:4-7.

> We were therefore buried with him through baptism into
> death in order that, just as Christ was raised from the dead
> through the glory of the Father, we too may live a new life.
> For if we have been united with him in a death like his,
> we will certainly also be united with him in a resurrection
> like his. For we know that our old self was crucified with
> him so that the body ruled by sin might be done away
> with, that we should no longer be slaves to sin—because
> anyone who has died has been set free from sin. (NIV)

Christ's glory was returned upon his return to heaven, therefore so is ours for our resurrection is like his—exactly like his. Resurrection in Paul's thought is primarily to the new glorious life in heaven, not simply new life on earth. All of this leads to our need to be released from this body of death to obtain our future glorious body. This mortal body is the only impediment to future glory.

As we begin the exposition of chapter 8, recall the conclusion to Paul's first 7 chapters ended with this question, "Who shall deliver me from this body of death?" (v.24). The question was followed by the answer, "Jesus Christ my Lord" (v.25). The final goal of Christ's redemption plan was glorification and the return to our original image of God made in the likeness of the Son of God. This likeness was lost in Eden resulting in both our future death and immediate expulsion from Eden. Here Paul contrasts the two curses, death and expulsion from heaven, to the two cures, which are restoration to life and a return to the heavenly realm upon our death. The initial promise to the elect of creation to new life, which began upon regeneration with the accompanying seal of the Holy Spirit, ensures our future release from death. This release will reach completion in our adoption and receipt of our inheritance, which is Christ, in heaven and is summarized by the word glorification. The inner glory becomes outer. New life on earth in our mortal body was not the end goal; Christ, after his resurrection to life and his 40-day time on earth, told his disciples he must return to heavenly glory in order to be able to then send his Spirit, effectively stating that new life on earth must reach resurrection life to glory, for him and therefore for us.

I will divide chapter 8 into 4 sections: verses 1-11, verses 12-17, and verses 18-39. Let's begin Romans chapter 8.

Section 1: 8:1-11

Therefore, there is now no condemnation for those who are in Christ Jesus, because through Christ Jesus the law of the Spirit who gives life has set you free from the law of sin and death. For what the law was powerless to do because it was weakened by the flesh, God did by sending his own Son in the likeness of sinful flesh to be a sin offering. And so he condemned sin in the flesh, in order that the righteous requirement of the law might be fully met in us, who do not live according to the flesh but according to the Spirit. Those who live according to the flesh have their minds set on what the flesh desires; but those who live in accordance with the Spirit have their minds set on what the Spirit desires. The mind governed by the flesh is death, but the mind governed by the Spirit is life and peace. The mind governed by the flesh is hostile to God; it does not submit to God's law, nor can it do so. Those who are in the realm of the flesh cannot please God. You, however, are not in the realm of the flesh but are in the realm of the Spirit, if indeed the Spirit of God lives in you. And if anyone does not have the Spirit of Christ, they do not belong to Christ. But if Christ is in you, then even though your body is subject to death because of sin, the Spirit gives life because of righteousness. And if the Spirit of him who raised Jesus from the dead is living in you, he who raised Christ from the dead will also give life to your mortal bodies because of his Spirit who lives in you. (NIV)

Paul begins by declaring that we are free from condemnation or judgment due to Christ's death in the flesh on the cross. We are no longer animated by the former nature and have been declared righteous and justified. This statement should awaken those who await glorification on the Day of Judgment, as "free from condemnation" makes clear the Day of Judgment or a casting down, cannot define the saint's role on Judgment

Day. Condemnation is defined as "an adverse sentence (the verdict)", in Strong's Concordance[31]. The saints, per justification, have already received their acquittal. Paul goes so far as to describe our new life as "not in the realm of flesh" but "in the realm of the Spirit" in verse 9. Paul is referring here to our regeneration while we are on earth in our mortal bodies. We are now animated by the indwelling Spirit as we are a "new Creation" in Christ and have the new nature of Christ inside us. The power over the fallen nature, described as our fleshly mortal body, has been crucified (killed) as we await its removal. We have begun our transformation from fleshly to spiritual beings.

At the end of verse 9 Paul changes from "the Spirit of God in you" to "the Spirit of Christ" to describe the same indwelling. Why? I believe the point is to link our union in Christ now via the Spirit while still on earth and residing in our mortal body with the Spirit of God the Father who raised Christ from the dead, thereby giving us assurance of the same promise of resurrection life at death in heaven that Christ received. As God the Father raised Christ, his only son, so will the Father raise us at death to heaven. As Christ was endowed with the Spirit internally prior to his death and resurrection but endowed with glory upon his resurrection to heaven, so are we as we await our resurrection to heaven. He is saying that if we are united with or "in Christ" now, how much more will we be united with and "in Christ" when we are in heaven. In verse 11, Paul clearly describes this transformation from our mortal (dead fleshly) body to our resurrection to life in our glorious life, "he who raised Christ from the dead will also give life to your mortal bodies because of his Spirit who lives in you". God the Father, being the Spirit that raised Christ, will therefore give resurrection life to our mortal bodies by the Holy Spirit who dwells in us. It is impossible to understand this in any other manner that resurrection life at death through the Holy Spirit residing within us. It is a transformation from a dead body to a body of life, summarized as glorious resurrection life. This is the death to life experience typified in the Jordan River crossing to the Promised Land. And critical to the proof of the mischaracterization of the intermediate state glorification on the Last Day, here Paul gives the power for this transformation to the Spirit, residing in the saint, not a future Last Day one-time command of Christ.

---

[31] Strong's Exhaustive Concordance: 2631. κατάκριμα (katakrima) -- penalty (biblehub.com)

Each saint rejoices in their possession of the guarantee of the promise of resurrection life which is the Spirit, or what I would call the Blessed Hope.

To remove any doubt that this is referring to our glorious body, Paul calls this "the redemption of our bodies" in verse 23. Here "redemption" is from the word apolutrósis, which Strong's defines as, a release effected by payment of ransom[32]. What definition or word could more clearly articulate our release from our mortal body to our glorious new body paid for by Christ's death on the cross. Paul uses the same word, apolutrósis, to describe our release from our body of death causing us to sin, by the sealing Spirit within us in Eph. 4:30

> And do not grieve the Holy Spirit of God, with whom you
> were sealed for the day of redemption. (NIV)

This day of redemption is at death, and not as attributed by almost all to the resurrection of the lost, on Judgment Day. This release at death is our hope of future blessedness with Christ in our glorious body.

Section 2: 8:12-17

> Therefore, brothers and sisters, we have an obligation—
> but it is not to the flesh, to live according to it. For if you
> live according to the flesh, you will die; but if by the Spirit
> you put to death the misdeeds of the body, you will live.
> For those who are led by the Spirit of God are the children
> of God. The Spirit you received does not make you slaves,
> so that you live in fear again; rather, the Spirit you received
> brought about your adoption to sonship. And by him we
> cry, "Abba, Father." The Spirit himself testifies with our
> spirit that we are God's children. Now if we are children,
> then we are heirs—heirs of God and co-heirs with Christ,
> if indeed we share in his sufferings in order that we may
> also share in his glory. (NIV)

---

[32] Strong's Exhaustive Concordance: 629. ἀπολύτρωσις (apolutrósis) -- a release effected by payment of ransom (biblehub.com)

Paul again contrasts life on earth in the fleshly body with "you will live" (v.13), referring to resurrection life in the new glorious spiritual body of "life" in heaven. He provides the basis of this future confidence in our resurrection at death to our being "led by the Spirit" (v.14) and our receipt of the Spirit which brought about our "adoption to sonship" (v.15) by which we can call the Spirit of God, "father". The future to which these evidences and promises guarantee is then stated in verse 17, where this relationship leads to our future inheritance in heaven with the glorified Christ after our wilderness journey on earth consisting of suffering, trial, and persecution from the worldly spiritual powers— "if indeed we share in his sufferings in order that we may also share in his glory". We share his suffering to await sharing his glory. Paul's question at the end of chapter 7 "who will deliver me from this body of death?" Is answered: Christ via his Spirit has already given us as the down payment at our new creation in him.

Section 3: 8:18-25

I consider that our present sufferings are not worth comparing with the glory that will be revealed in us. For the creation waits in eager expectation for the children of God to be revealed. For the creation was subjected to frustration, not by its own choice, but by the will of the one who subjected it, in hope that the creation itself will be liberated from its bondage to decay and brought into the freedom and glory of the children of God. We know that the whole creation has been groaning as in the pains of childbirth right up to the present time. Not only so, but we ourselves, who have the firstfruits of the Spirit, groan inwardly as we wait eagerly for our adoption to sonship, the redemption of our bodies. For in this hope we were saved. But hope that is seen is no hope at all. Who hopes for what they already have? But if we hope for what we do not yet have, we wait for it patiently. (NIV)

The natural reading of verse 18 is that of a time of suffering on earth for the saints, immediately followed by a time of glory. Again, there is no hint or discussion of any break between these two periods. The absence of an allusion to, insertion of, or clear description of an intermediate state is evidence in favor of its rejection. Paul begins this section with "the glory that will be revealed in us" after our suffering, and next describes this transformation as "the children of God to be revealed". As we saw in the opening of this chapter, revelation has the meaning of unveiling or making visible, therefore it is clear that this revealing of glory is of the sons (and daughters) of God. In the previous section Paul had already told us who these sons of God are, stating, "For those who are led by the Spirit of God are the children of God" (v.14). So, the sum of this is that all believers, by virtue of the inner glory of the Spirit, though veiled by our mortal body, will be revealed in outer glory when we reach our promised inheritance (the redemption of our body) in heaven. Paul had stated that the Spirit was the Spirit of adoption which witnesses with our spirit that we are children of God (vv. 15-16). The very simple thought being conveyed is that the glory now being revealed or unveiled will extend to the entire man, an escalation of the glory previously veiled (invisible to us) by our mortal body (flesh), is now revealed to us, "in order that we may share in his glory" (v.17), now stated as, "the glory that will be revealed in us" (v. 18). The simple point being made is that when we are united in heaven with him, we are glorified with him, and this glory is revealed to us at that time, for when we can see Christ's glory revealed to us in heaven, we will also see our outer glory with our eyes. Revelation is always one direction, from God to us.

In verses 19-22, Paul expands on the glory to be revealed to us and speaks of creation awaiting the freedom of the sons of God, but also creation's revealing of its own former glory. "Will be set free" and "obtain" (v.21) are both future events for creation. The redemption or release from bondage of our mortal bodies will occur first, and this revealing sets the stage for creation to obtain its freedom as well. The whole creation consisting of both the cosmos and the sons of God has been waiting and groaning for the revealing of the sons of God "right up to the present time" (vv.22,23). The revelation of the long-awaited glory of the sons of God has come, their wait was ended with Christ's first coming. This is a startling and monumental statement proving that with the first advent of Christ and his return to glory, the new age of creation and redemption of the sons of God has begun. It is not just the age of inner glory on earth but glory in heaven. Current theology admits an "already/not yet eschatology", but still has glorification not occurring during this age, but on the Last Day. This is irreconcilable with Paul's teaching both here in Romans and as we saw in 1 Corinthians 15. Our glorification is not awaiting the Last Day, it began with Christ's resurrection from death to glory and has been realized now in his saints. Death for them now means resurrection glory in heaven. While it is true that glory and renewal still await the cosmos until the Last Day events, the combining of these two events in time on the Last Day is in error.

Although glorification has come for those who died in faith in the prior age of promise, the Old Testament saints, and for those present age saints who have already died, Paul returns to the present state of his audience who are still awaiting their revealing of glory as a son of God by possession of the "firstfruits of the Spirit" in verse 23. He makes this same point in 1 Cor. 15:20, "But Christ has indeed been raised from the dead, the firstfruits of those who have fallen asleep." There Christ is described as the "firstfruits" or guarantee, which we have via his indwelling Spirit, guaranteeing the harvest of our new body at death. These readers are waiting in hope for this adoption to be finalized with the redemption of their "dead" body, through their faith in the gospel. We need faith to see or hope for those things that are not revealed or visible to us now. Although creation is still awaiting it's release from bondage from Adam's sin on the Last Day, the freedom and glory of the sons of God has come in Christ, this is the waiting "up to the present time" (v.22). The "Light of the World" has come shining his light in our souls till we reach the "Father of Lights" in heaven.

The kingdom came in fullness for his people upon his ascension to glory, leading the Old Testament former captives with him, and the giving of his Spirit at Pentecost. Glory for those who have gone before is now complete, but Christ's final coming or appearing to Judgment will bring the release from bondage to the cosmos.

Section 4: 8:26-39

In the same way, the Spirit helps us in our weakness. We do not know what we ought to pray for, but the Spirit himself intercedes for us through wordless groans. And he who searches our hearts knows the mind of the Spirit, because the Spirit intercedes for God's people in accordance with the will of God. And we know that in all things God works for the good of those who love him, who have been called according to his purpose. For those God foreknew he also predestined to be conformed to the image of his Son, that he might be the firstborn among many brothers and sisters. And those he predestined, he also called; those he called, he also justified; those he justified, he also glorified. What, then, shall we say in response to these things? If God is for us, who can be against us? He who did not spare his own Son, but gave him up for us all—how will he not also, along with him, graciously give us all things? Who will bring any charge against those whom God has chosen? It is God who justifies. Who then is the one who condemns? No one. Christ Jesus who died—more than that, who was raised to life—is at the right hand of God and is also interceding for us. Who shall separate us from the love of Christ? Shall trouble or hardship or persecution or famine or nakedness or danger or sword? As it is written: "For your sake we face death all day long; we are considered as sheep to be slaughtered." No, in all these things we are more than conquerors through him who loved us. For I am convinced that neither death nor life, neither angels nor demons, neither the present nor the future, nor any powers, neither height nor depth, nor anything else in all creation, will be able to separate us from the love of God that is in Christ Jesus our Lord. (NIV)

Paul continues to focus on the goal of Chapters 1-8, our glorification, in verse 30 with, "he also glorified," which is the final stage of the salvation process which began with foreknowledge. He begins by describing our current state on earth as "weakness" in verse 26. This contrasts with our future glory to be revealed, but the Spirit is the common thread in our state of weakness or glory. He continues the focus of glory in verse 29, "predestined to be conformed to the image of his Son," which is a glorious image. Verse 30 is another example of the clear teaching of no break in time from the transition from justified to glorified: "And those he predestined, he also called; those he called, he also justified; those he justified, he also glorified". There is no stage between justification and glorification after death as claimed in the intermediate state—if true it should have been included here. Verses 31-34 reminds the readers that they are free from a future judgment from God, as it was God who justifies us. A death without a glorious body is a judgment which was just described as impossible for the believer, for the lost suffer this judgment at death —they do not have a future glorious body awaiting after their mortal body returns to the earth per Adam's curse. They await their resurrection to judgment not the resurrection to life which awaits the elect at death. More than just forgiveness, we have the love of God, in that Christ is praying for us in heaven and his prayers are always answered. Recall his priestly prayer before the cross was for the father to glorify his people with the glory he had previously (Jn. 17:24).

The closing verses, 35-39, identify nothing shall separate us from the love of Christ, neither "persecution or famine or nakedness or danger or sword" (v.35), "nor anything else in all creation" (v.39). We are more than conquerors at death, as our savior defeated death and has gone before us to bring us safely home in glory to him. Notice more than conquerors over death, not a death while still requiring a faith of a future resurrection of our body on the Last Day. If we await a future redemption of our body at death, then death has not been conquered at our death when we enter heaven, for death still has its depraved hold on us as we are still under the curse of Adam as the new body has not been united with us. Then the Spirit inside us, as the guarantee of the redemption of our bodies, did not produce at death the result stated earlier, "but we ourselves, who have the firstfruits of the Spirit, groan inwardly as we wait eagerly for our adoption to sonship, the redemption of our bodies. For in this hope, we were saved" (vv.23,24). The redemption of our mortal body is the hope the gospel was to produce, so if the redemption of our body is not accomplished when in heaven, we await still in hope. Hope and faith ended upon entry to heaven and Christ's kingdom. All our faith pointed towards the goal of glorification and our life in the Spirit in our spiritual bodies in heaven. Assigning hope to the next age conflicts with the text and the entire message of the gospel. No mention is made of an inglorious intermediate state in the entire 8 chapters, but only future glory with Christ.

The following sections on Philippians, 1 and 2 Timothy present the

"Revelation of Jesus Christ" as occurring upon the saints' entrance to heaven at death rather than on Judgment Day. Paul's use of "Day of Christ" in Philippians should be understood as the time when Christ is "revealed" to the saint entering heaven by sight for the first time. This "Day of Christ" is the eternal day where no darkness exists and is to be contrasted with the realm of Satan described as darkness or night and is coming to an end. It is a contrast between the Kingdom of light and the kingdom of darkness. During this age Christ established and is building his kingdom. Paul tells his readers we are a part of the "day", where day identifies us with the eternal day in heaven, in contrast with Christ's day of darkness when final judgment is executed on the kingdom of darkness.

Second, Paul continually focuses our attention toward the goal of being present with Christ in heaven, not to the end time judgment. Christ is our primary focal point, and although the events on Judgment Day do have significance for the saints, it is secondary to our entrance into his presence. Paul will make this clear in 2 Timothy where he speaks of "that day" which is his death and entrance into heaven. The "Day" he is looking for is when his work on earth is done and his Lord will present is rewards to him "on that day".

Last, these points fall within the broad topic of resurrection: resurrection from this evil world into the world already purged from sin's defilement. Upon our resurrection into heaven all the promises are fulfilled and the rewards or "crowns" representing all his blessings are complete for the saint—our restoration is complete. The remaining event is the conquering of death by his coming to Judgment and restoration of the cosmos.

Revelation of Christ at Death in Philippians

Section 1: 1:6-11

> being confident of this, that he who began a good work in you will carry it on to completion until the day of Christ Jesus. It is right for me to feel this way about all of you, since I have you in my heart and, whether I am in chains or defending and confirming the gospel, all of you share

in God's grace with me. God can testify how I long for all of you with the affection of Christ Jesus. And this is my prayer: that your love may abound more and more in knowledge and depth of insight, so that you may be able to discern what is best and may be pure and blameless for the day of Christ, filled with the fruit of righteousness that comes through Jesus Christ—to the glory and praise of God. (NIV)

"The Day of Christ Jesus" that Paul refers to in verse 6 is his own day of death, a day which ends in heaven. He is encouraging the reader to be pure and blameless on their Day as well (vv.9-11). He refers to his death again in the next section, confirming the Day of Christ refers to the end of his work on earth at death.

Section 2: 1:18-26

Yes, and I will continue to rejoice, for I know that through your prayers and God's provision of the Spirit of Jesus Christ what has happened to me will turn out for my deliverance. I eagerly expect and hope that I will in no way be ashamed, but will have sufficient courage so that now as always Christ will be exalted in my body, whether by life or by death. For to me, to live is Christ and to die is gain. If I am to go on living in the body, this will mean fruitful labor for me. Yet what shall I choose? I do not know! I am torn between the two: I desire to depart and be with Christ, which is better by far; but it is more necessary for you that I remain in the body. Convinced of this, I know that I will remain, and I will continue with all of you for your progress and joy in the faith, so that through my being with you again your boasting in Christ Jesus will abound on account of me. (NIV)

Paul credits the indwelling Spirit, who is the guarantee of resurrection life in the new body, for his deliverance (v.19). Then he only expresses a life with a body, not one without a body: "Christ will be exalted in my body, whether by life or by death" (v.20). Clearly either his life in a body now or his life after death in a body will give honor to Christ, but he does not say he will somehow honor Christ for a period of time without a body until a Last Day resurrection. He then makes it clearer, "to live is Christ, to die is gain" (v. 21). It is impossible and contrary to every inclination of scripture to understand Paul as meaning his death, which would result in his loss of a body until the Last Day, is a "gain". The heart of the gospel and the Old Testament typology teach death means resurrection life. He further states, "I desire to depart and be with Christ" (v. 23) in which his death and pending glorification mimic Christ's departure from earth and glorification in heaven. Christ instructed his disciples concerning his death but further explained the need for him to depart after his resurrection and return to heavenly glory in order to send his Spirit.

Section 3: 2:5-11

> In your relationships with one another, have the same mindset as Christ Jesus: Who, being in very nature God, did not consider equality with God something to be used to his own advantage; rather, he made himself nothing by taking the very nature of a servant, being made in human likeness. And being found in appearance as a man, he humbled himself by becoming obedient to death—even death on a cross! Therefore God exalted him to the highest place and gave him the name that is above every name, that at the name of Jesus every knee should bow, in heaven and on earth and under the earth, and every tongue acknowledge that Jesus Christ is Lord, to the glory of God the Father. (NIV)

Here Paul uses Christ's example of obedience until death and resulting exaltation to glory, to instruct the readers to have this same mindset. Again, no break is mentioned.

Section 4: 2:14-17

> Do everything without grumbling or arguing, so that
> you may become blameless and pure, "children of God
> without fault in a warped and crooked generation." Then
> you will shine among them like stars in the sky as you hold
> firmly to the word of life. And then I will be able to boast
> on the day of Christ that I did not run or labor in vain.
> But even if I am being poured out like a drink offering
> on the sacrifice and service coming from your faith, I am
> glad and rejoice with all of you. (NIV)

Paul again ties his death or sacrificial offering with faith, "hold firmly to the word of life" (v.16). In verse 16 he again links "the day of Christ" with his death and entry into heaven and the eternal day where no darkness exists because Christ reigns. This contrasts with the current day/night cycle representing the reprobate /elect mix of peoples in the two kingdoms on earth. Paul describes the elect on earth as "children of God without fault" and says, "you will shine among them like stars in the sky". If Paul can describe the saints as shining as lights, displaying the glory of Christ while on earth in an inglorious body, does it not seem inescapable that when we proceed to heaven we will then further shine as more glorious lights via our glorious resurrection body? There is nothing clearer. Nothing in heaven is inglorious, except the doctrine of the intermediate state postulates this exact impossibility. We glorify Christ in our body on earth, only to glorify Christ in the new body in heaven, there is not a third option.

Section 5: 3:1-21

> Further, my brothers and sisters, rejoice in the Lord! It is
> no trouble for me to write the same things to you again,
> and it is a safeguard for you. Watch out for those dogs,
> those evildoers, those mutilators of the flesh. For it is we
> who are the circumcision, we who serve God by his Spirit,
> who boast in Christ Jesus, and who put no confidence
> in the flesh— though I myself have reasons for such

confidence. If someone else thinks they have reasons to put confidence in the flesh, I have more: circumcised on the eighth day, of the people of Israel, of the tribe of Benjamin, a Hebrew of Hebrews; in regard to the law, a Pharisee; as for zeal, persecuting the church; as for righteousness based on the law, faultless. But whatever were gains to me I now consider loss for the sake of Christ. What is more, I consider everything a loss because of the surpassing worth of knowing Christ Jesus my Lord, for whose sake I have lost all things. I consider them garbage, that I may gain Christ and be found in him, not having a righteousness of my own that comes from the law, but that which is through faith in Christ—the righteousness that comes from God on the basis of faith. I want to know Christ—yes, to know the power of his resurrection and participation in his sufferings, becoming like him in his death, and so, somehow, attaining to the resurrection from the dead. Not that I have already obtained all this, or have already arrived at my goal, but I press on to take hold of that for which Christ Jesus took hold of me. Brothers and sisters, I do not consider myself yet to have taken hold of it. But one thing I do: Forgetting what is behind and straining toward what is ahead, I press on toward the goal to win the prize for which God has called me heavenward in Christ Jesus. All of us, then, who are mature should take such a view of things. And if on some point you think differently, that too God will make clear to you. Only let us live up to what we have already attained. Join together in following my example, brothers and sisters, and just as you have us as a model, keep your eyes on those who live as we do. For, as I have often told you before and now tell you again even with tears, many live as enemies of the cross of Christ. Their destiny is destruction, their god is their stomach, and their glory is in their shame. Their mind is set on earthly things. But our citizenship is in heaven. And we eagerly await a Savior from there, the

> Lord Jesus Christ, who, by the power that enables him
> to bring everything under his control, will transform our
> lowly bodies so that they will be like his glorious body.
> (NIV)

Paul has no confidence in his "flesh" or human lineage (vv.1-8), but only in his faith in Christ towards "the righteousness that comes from God on the basis of faith. I want to know Christ—yes, to know the power of his resurrection" (vv.9b-10). The simple gospel message is that at the death of our mortal bodies we rise to life in our resurrected glorious bodies. Paul points to the end point of our salvation, "I press on toward the goal to win the prize for which God has called me heavenward in Christ Jesus" (v.12). I pray this book and Paul's statement will bear the fruit of our acknowledgment that the goal, prize, and end point of the Christian life on earth, is the upward call, our resurrection to heaven at death, and not a longing for Judgment Day. Paul cements the point by telling them the timing of this resurrection to life, "But our citizenship is in heaven. And we eagerly await a Savior from there, the Lord Jesus Christ, who, by the power that enables him to bring everything under his control, will transform our lowly bodies so that they will be like his glorious body" (vv.20-21). This transformation is not described as waiting for Christ to return from heaven to judgment, but as already in heaven. We are moving towards heaven, awaiting the day faith becomes sight at the revelation of Christ when we see him. Paul is not stating Christ leaves heaven to bring our citizenship to us. Paul again lays out this transformation from mortal to immortal body, (which I have been tirelessly repeating), occurs at death; it awaits us in heaven where Christ will award it and give us our crown of glory at death. No interim bodyless state is included in this clear and simple presentation of the gospel which brings the dead to life.

Section 6: 4:19-20

> And my God will meet all your needs according to the
> riches of his glory in Christ Jesus. To our God and Father
> be glory for ever and ever. Amen. (NIV)

Our greatest need post regeneration is to be delivered from our wretched body of death. This greatest of riches, as it is the final release from Adams curse of death, awaits us in glory in Christ Jesus, which is heaven. It awaits us in heaven: this is the substance of things hoped for in faith. It awaits in heaven as our Lord went before us to prepare it and incorporate us into his body. Paul does not say we go to heaven as a soul and await our riches and fullness until the Last Day.

Revelation of Christ at Death in 1 Timothy

Section 1: 3:16

> Beyond all question, the mystery from which true godliness springs is great: He appeared in the flesh, was vindicated by the Spirit, was seen by angels, was preached among the nations, was believed on in the world, was taken up in glory. (NIV)

This is Paul's clear declaration of what the early church confessed. Christ was made manifest (visible) through his descension and by taking on the form of humanity, thus becoming a Son of Man. He was declared to be innocent (justified) as the sinless Son of God by his resurrection by the Spirit to life. Angels witnessed his resurrection to life at the tomb and his resurrection was proclaimed to the known world by the disciples and, after his 40-day earthly witness, he was taken to heaven in glory. Christ's redemptive work for the elect ended upon entry into heaven with the restoration of his glorious adornment. Paul is using Christ's example for our encouragement because we follow the same pattern.

Section 2: 4:8-10

> For physical training is of some value, but godliness has value for all things, holding promise for both the present life and the life to come. This is a trustworthy saying that deserves full acceptance. That is why we labor and strive,

because we have put our hope in the living God, who
is the Savior of all people, and especially of those who
believe. (NIV)

Paul encourages Timothy to train himself in godliness, the conforming
of our life into the image of Christ. Paul then describes only two lives:
the life Timothy has on earth in his mortal body, and the future life in
his glorious immortal body. Paul again uses the life-to-life phrase he uses
in 2 Cor. 2:16. The Christian moves from new life in Christ residing
in a body of death to new resurrection life in the new body in heaven.
There is not a period of nakedness without a body as described in the
intermediate state. Paul declares that "the life to come" (v. 8), which can
only be understood as life in heaven upon death, is the goal or reward
of the believer and why we "labor and strive" (v.10) or persevere in faith
during our period on earth. The end is entrance into heaven, the life to
come, therefore not a Last Day judgment. He removes all doubt the goal is
heaven by continuing to make the point of all the scriptures: the goal is to
unite us with Christ in heaven. This completes the return of the fallen sons
of Adam, made in his fallen nature, to their place as Sons of God made
in Christ's image, as then the fallen image of Adam born by all humanity
will have been transformed back into the glorious image of the eternal Son
of God in whose image we were created with in Eden. This "hope" is not
to be deferred until a Judgment Day resurrection for the believer, for the
hope is clearly completed upon our reuniting with Christ. The theology
of awaiting as bodyless souls while with Christ until Judgment Day, is
insulting to Christ and his work, and contrary to every intent of scripture.
Christ is our only hope and goal, the Son of Man of Daniel returned to
heaven and was given dominion and glory and a kingdom, Dan. 7:13,14.
Christ as the firstfruits, was foretold in the Son of Man in Daniel by his
return to heaven, which foretold Christ opening the door for the elect to
follow in his train into heaven as seen in Psalm 68:18:

When you ascended on high, you took many captives; you
received gifts from people, even from the rebellious—that
you, Lord God, might dwell there. (NIV)

Section 3: 6:12-16

> Fight the good fight of the faith. Take hold of the eternal
> life to which you were called when you made your good
> confession in the presence of many witnesses. In the
> sight of God, who gives life to everything, and of Christ
> Jesus, who while testifying before Pontius Pilate made
> the good confession, I charge you to keep this command
> without spot or blame until the appearing of our Lord
> Jesus Christ, which God will bring about in his own
> time—God, the blessed and only Ruler, the King of kings
> and Lord of lords, who alone is immortal and who lives in
> unapproachable light, whom no one has seen or can see.
> To him be honor and might forever. Amen. (NIV)

Paul continues to describe the salvation of Christ's people in terms of a
singular event bringing them into the kingdom, uniting them with him
via his Spirit, as well as the corresponding progression of this new life in
the Spirit from that on earth as witnesses in our time of suffering which
ends when we are in heaven in our final glorified state with Christ. We
have Christ's glory now on earth, but still await the fullness of the complete
manifestation of our glory until when we arrive in heaven. This is the same
veiling of his inner glory that Christ exhibited during his first advent and
displayed at the transfiguration, so this thought should not appear strange
to our sensibilities.

Paul begins by telling Timothy to fight in the holy war being waged
here on earth (v.12). He does this by taking hold of the eternal life already
possessed via his calling and placement in his kingdom by the Spirit and
fighting with the spiritual armaments Paul outlines in Ephesians 6. We
have already entered into eternal life, have already been resurrected, already
possess the inner glory though veiled by our flesh. He encourages Timothy
to be blameless until the appearing of our Lord Jesus Christ (v.14). As I
have stated elsewhere the "appearing" of our Lord Jesus Christ is not to be
understood only as his final return to earth for judgment, where he is then
manifested to the only class of humanity not already united with him—
those lost from all eternity. The "appearing" of our Lord Jesus Christ is also

to be understood as when the elect reach heaven and Christ who was only visible by faith then becomes sight, so Christ appears to us upon our death and immediate translation into the heavenly kingdom. We see examples of this understanding of appearing throughout the New Testament but specifically in Christ's post-resurrection appearances to the disciples prior to his ascension. These were not supernatural events where Christ passed through physical doors, but simply the common understanding of the arrival of a person at a gathering, where they appeared to the crowd at the event, as we could describe when a guest singer appeared at a concert to join with the original band. This is the manner Christ appeared at various times. But both appearing to us in heaven and at the final advent are in view. Our focus on meeting him in heaven encourages the saints to persevere under trial here on earth, and the final advent to judgment gives us confidence that the ultimate end of all suffering and death is in the future. Paul states Christ will display his appearance at the proper time, he does not t say he will only appear to all at the same time. This is misunderstood as meaning he will only appear to all at the Final Judgment, but it does not preclude his prior appearing to the saint when they enter heaven. Thus, he appears first to the saints, and then to all on Judgment Day.

Revelation of Christ at Death in 2 Timothy

Section 1: 1:8-14

> So do not be ashamed of the testimony about our Lord or of me his prisoner. Rather, join with me in suffering for the gospel, by the power of God. He has saved us and called us to a holy life—not because of anything we have done but because of his own purpose and grace. This grace was given us in Christ Jesus before the beginning of time, but it has now been revealed through the appearing of our Savior, Christ Jesus, who has destroyed death and has brought life and immortality to light through the gospel. And of this gospel I was appointed a herald and an apostle

and a teacher. That is why I am suffering as I am. Yet this is no cause for shame, because I know whom I have believed, and am convinced that he is able to guard what I have entrusted to him until that day. What you heard from me, keep as the pattern of sound teaching, with faith and love in Christ Jesus. Guard the good deposit that was entrusted to you—guard it with the help of the Holy Spirit who lives in us. (NIV)

Paul speaks of his (our) holy calling ("life" here in the NIV, v. 9), and Christ's ability to guard the gospel in Paul's care until "that day" (v.12). The day is not the Last Day but Paul's last day on earth. This epistle carries only this thought because Paul understands the day of his death is eminent. He only looks forward to his death and his upward calling to heaven. No mention of his awaiting the Last Day for his own salvation to be completed. He instructs Timothy to follow his "pattern of sound teaching" (v.13), or the gospel, Christ and the gospel are the pattern. The gospel is the good news of the opportunity to come to Christ, not the bad news of Judgment Day. Christ death and resurrection to heaven is the pattern we follow to glorification. In verse 14 Paul again gives the reason for the promise of both our ability to persevere till death "Guard the good deposit that was entrusted to you", and then the power for the transformation into our new body at death "guard it with the help of the Holy Spirit who lives in us": the Holy Spirit will bring us faithfully to our day of death, to then translate us in glory to heaven.

Section 2: 2:3-10

Join with me in suffering, like a good soldier of Christ Jesus. No one serving as a soldier gets entangled in civilian affairs, but rather tries to please his commanding officer. Similarly, anyone who competes as an athlete does not receive the victor's crown except by competing according to the rules. The hardworking farmer should be the first to receive a share of the crops. Reflect on what I am saying,

for the Lord will give you insight into all this. Remember
Jesus Christ, raised from the dead, descended from David.
This is my gospel, for which I am suffering even to the
point of being chained like a criminal. But God's word is
not chained. Therefore I endure everything for the sake
of the elect, that they too may obtain the salvation that is
in Christ Jesus, with eternal glory. (NIV)

The earthly race ends with heavenly crowning with glory. Paul tells
Timothy to remember Christ's example of rising from the dead (v.8) to
glory in heaven, which is also our example: "for the sake of the elect"
(v.10). When Paul states "that they too may obtain the salvation that is in
Christ Jesus with eternal glory" (v.10), he is telling them when they leave
this temporal world for the eternal world in heaven they will manifest the
salvation of Christ with their "eternal glory", and therefore this is not a
Last Day resurrection to a glorified body.

Section 3: 2:16-18

Avoid godless chatter, because those who indulge in it
will become more and more ungodly. Their teaching will
spread like gangrene. Among them are Hymenaeus and
Philetus, who have departed from the truth. They say that
the resurrection has already taken place, and they destroy
the faith of some. (NIV)

Paul is not stating that those who have died are not currently resurrected
with their glorified bodies, but that some are falsely spreading lies that the
resurrection period has ended.

Section 4: 4:6-8

For I am already being poured out like a drink offering,
and the time for my departure is near. I have fought the
good fight, I have finished the race, I have kept the faith.

> Now there is in store for me the crown of righteousness,
> which the Lord, the righteous Judge, will award to me on
> that day—and not only to me, but also to all who have
> longed for his appearing. (NIV)

Paul, as stated earlier, is looking forward to the day of his death and departure into heaven. The race ends at that point and no further future escalation in status is mentioned after arriving in heaven. He then ties this time of death with the immediate receipt of his and all other saints' crowns (glory) as well upon "that day" (v.8). This irrefutably ties the crowning of glory with the day of departure or his and every saint's death. The words "Now there is in store for me" (v.8) can mean nothing other than immediately following the death we are crowned with our glory. But the critical point is "that day" excludes any other day, eliminating the Day of Judgment. A judgment is rendered at death, it is final for the elect, but only preliminary for the lost for although their fate is assured, their final judgment does await the Last Day. Kenneth Wuest provides a clear exposition marking this as the end,

> I like a wrestler have fought to the finish…My race, I like
> a runner have finished, and at present sitting at the goal…
> Henceforth there is reserved for me the victor's laurel
> of righteousness, which the Lord will award me on that
> day…and not only to me but to those…. who have their
> love fixed on it.[33]

Wuest adds the thought that this is the target to which we are to keep our gaze focused: the risen glorified Christ as Lord in heaven, we are not to cast our gaze to the Last Day, as so many do, and confuse the church with erroneous teachings with altered the goal posts. Those who advocate for the Intermediate state place the saint on a treadmill while in the place of eternal rest, seeking rest on the Last Day. This is a sad perversion of the gospel.

---

[33] Kenneth Wuest, The *New Testament: An Expanded Translation*, (Grand Rapids, Eerdmans, 1984), 506.

CHAPTER 10

THE REVELATION OF JESUS CHRIST IN PETER

This last chapter, looks at how Peter understands the Revelation of Christ in 1 and 2 Peter, concentrating on entrance into heaven as the goal of glorification and resurrection of the body, as the Old Testament typology section argued. I have broken this chapter into 3 sections: 1 Peter 1, 1 Peter 2-5, and 2 Peter.

The Revelation of Christ in 1 Peter 1

Peter, an apostle of Jesus Christ, To God's elect, exiles scattered throughout the provinces of Pontus, Galatia, Cappadocia, Asia and Bithynia, who have been chosen according to the foreknowledge of God the Father, through the sanctifying work of the Spirit, to be obedient to Jesus Christ and sprinkled with his blood: Grace and peace be yours in abundance. Praise be to the God and Father of our Lord Jesus Christ! In his great mercy he has given us new birth into a living hope through the resurrection of Jesus Christ from the dead, and into an inheritance that can never perish, spoil or fade. This inheritance is kept in heaven for you, who through faith are shielded by God's power until the coming of the salvation that is ready to be revealed in the last time. In all this you greatly rejoice, though now for a little while you may have had to suffer grief in all kinds of trials. These have come so that the proven genuineness of your faith—of greater worth than gold, which perishes even though refined by fire—may result in praise, glory and honor when Jesus Christ is revealed. Though you have not seen him, you love him; and even though you do not see him now, you believe in him and are filled with an inexpressible and glorious joy, for you are receiving the end result of your faith, the salvation of your souls. Concerning this salvation, the prophets, who spoke of the grace that was to come to you, searched intently and with the greatest care, trying to find out the time and circumstances to which the Spirit of Christ in them was pointing when he predicted the sufferings of the Messiah and the glories that would follow. It was revealed to them that they were not serving themselves but you, when they spoke of the things that have now been told you by those who have preached the gospel to you by the Holy Spirit sent from heaven. Even angels long to look into these things. Therefore, with minds that are alert and fully sober, set your hope on the grace to be brought to you when Jesus Christ is revealed at his coming. As obedient children, do not conform to the evil desires you had when you lived in ignorance. But just as he who called you is holy, so be holy in all you do; for it is written: "Be holy, because I am holy." Since you call on a Father who judges each person's work impartially, live out your time as foreigners here in reverent fear. For you know that it was not with perishable things such as silver or gold that you were redeemed from the empty way of life handed down to you from your ancestors, but with the precious blood of Christ, a lamb without blemish or defect. He was chosen before the creation of the world, but was revealed in these last times for your sake. Through him you believe in God, who raised him from the dead and glorified him, and so your faith and hope are in God. Now that you have purified yourselves by obeying the truth so that you have sincere love for each other, love one another deeply, from the heart. For you have been born again, not of perishable seed, but of imperishable, through the living and enduring word of God. For, "All people are like grass, and all their glory is like the flowers of the field; the grass withers and the flowers fall, but the word of the Lord endures forever." And this is the word that was preached to you. (1 Pt. 1:1-25 NIV)

Peter addresses his letter to the "elect exiles," referring to Christians who are on earth and exiled from the ultimate result of their faith, which is the heavenly city of Jerusalem. He also is describing the current state of exile of the readers from the earthly city of Jerusalem due to persecution. So, he is making a comparison between both their dispersion from the heavenly Jerusalem and their exile from the earthly Jerusalem at the same time. If he wanted to include all exiles from the Dispersion from Jerusalem, both elect and unbelieving Jews, he would not have needed to qualify the audience as only "elect exiles". Peter is therefore able to bring to their mind the Old Testament wilderness journey in which they were away from the Promised Land but by faith would enter later. Peter then ties the Old Testament exile typology to the current reality of their exile from heaven ending with their time on earth (death). He describes their exile again in verse 17 as "your time as foreigners". The critical point of this "exile is how Peter will describe the result of their exile's end when they are in heaven.

It is clear our time of exile here on earth is being contrasted with our union with the glorified Christ in heaven, "the grace to be brought to you when Jesus Christ is revealed at his coming" (v. 13). The comparison of exile resulting in the revealing of Jesus Christ twice: first in verse 7, and again in verse 13. This revealing (visible manifestation) of Jesus Christ at the end of our exile, cannot be describing his revelation at the Last Day of Judgment because that event does not occur when we end our exile on earth and enter heaven Instead, it occurs only after all of the elect have been resurrected to heaven during the church age. The Coming to

Judgment is Christ's revelation or manifestation to the evil Kingdom. Therefore, this passage is not his revealing himself to the fallen world and his coming to the earth to judge on the Last Day. The "revelation of Jesus Christ" which Peter is describing is when Christ is revealed to the saints as they enter heaven and see the risen Lord. Prior to entrance into heaven all of the benefits of Christ could not be seen but were only received by faith as what cannot be seen. This type of misinterpreting a "revelation of Christ" which is speaking of our coming to Christ, to his final coming to earth is one of the root causes that has theologians attempt to rectify by constructing the intermediate state. They fail to understand the collateral damage they do to the gospel message. That tis his revelation speaking of our coming to Christ was confirmed earlier when our exile resulted in entrance to heaven and is confirmed in verse 7 as it results in "praise, glory, and honor". This verse is describing the saints receiving these things as the result of their faith. The glory received is the important one for the purpose of identifying this glory with our new resurrection body.

The indwelling glory is described by Paul as "inner glory" and the adornment of our glorious immortal body as "outer glory", also described as "white robes" or "wedding garments". The outer glory we receive at the end of our exile from earth is our glorious body. We had already received the inner glory of the Spirit upon regeneration. The clear implication of this is that the gospel provides life to our mortal body at death via the adornment of our glorious body. Why is it difficult to understand we need a new body upon the death of the previous body? It is tragic to make the simplicity of the gospel complex. Christ rose body and soul from the grave and resided on earth for 40 additional days to demonstrate to everyone the gospel pattern, but somehow, we have created another pattern to follow. Peter instructs the believers in verse 13 to set their hope "fully sober" on this day of the revelation of Christ. He does not say this is an important first stage, but you will be fully glorified and united with your body at some future time, but "fully" on this reward at the end of their earthly race. That is why I describe our resurrection at death to heavenly glory as the "Blessed Hope", for Peter tells us to place our hope (faith) fully or completely in that day when Christ is first revealed to us visibly in heaven, thus eliminating the doctrine of our requiring a future hope of a glorious body on Judgment Day. Peter makes no mention of an intermediate stage between exile on earth and glory in heaven.

Peter makes it clear in multiple places in this text that this glorious hope of our body is obtained at the end of the exile when we arrive in heaven:

- Verse 4: "This inheritance is kept in heaven for you"
- Verse 5: faith for the "salvation that is ready to be revealed in the last time".
- Verse 6: In this you "rejoice, though now for a little while"
- Verse 9: "receiving the end result of your faith, the salvation of your souls"
- Verse 11: "the sufferings of the Messiah and the glories that would follow".
- Verse 12: "by those who preached the gospel to you by the Holy Spirit"
- Verse 20: "chosen before the creation of the world but was revealed in these last times for your sake."
- Verse 21: "Through him you believe in God, who raised him from the dead and glorified him, and so your faith and hope are in God."
- Verse 23: "you have been born again, not of perishable seed, but of imperishable, through the living and enduring word of God."
- Verses 24,25: "All people ('flesh'—ESV) are like grass, and all their glory like the flowers of the field; the grass withers and the flowers fall, but the word of the Lord endures forever. And this is the word that was preached to you"

Peter describes our exile as beginning with being born again, then progressing to our possession of our inheritance that is kept in heaven. These two different reference points of earthly exile and heavenly completion are the keys to understanding Peter's instruction. Peter, in verses 3-5, describes our being born again by the Spirit into a living hope of our future inheritance in heaven as faith and hope are needed until we see Christ face to face in heaven. He describes our "inheritance" not in terms of an end time fulfillment, but rather in terms of an "imperishable" inheritance (v.3). Paul uses "imperishable" in 1 Cor. 15:42 to describe the resurrection body. There is an unmistakable link here between entrance to heaven after our exile on earth and receipt of our new body, as Peter links imperishable with our inheritance and Paul uses it to define our resurrection body. Peter describes this inheritance as "kept in heaven for you" (v. 4), insinuating receipt upon arrival in heaven, after our exile. This matches Christ's statements of going to heaven before us to prepare for us a home (body) in heaven, which home is Christ's body as we become a part of his heavenly Temple. The inheritance is only waiting for our arrival.

"Kept in heaven for you" is further explained when Peter offers encouragement to the elect with the promise that they "through faith are shielded by God's power until the coming of the salvation that is ready to be revealed in the last time" (v. 5). The "last time" is not the Last Day of wrath as explained by many, but rather the gospel era which ends at the second visible coming of Christ as judge. This gospel era is the last and only time of opportunity to acknowledge Christ as Lord. It is the "first resurrection" when each time a saint finishes their exile at death, the salvation awaiting in heaven is revealed to them upon ascension into the heavenly kingdom where our inheritance awaits us. The "first resurrection" of the elect is contrasted with the "second resurrection" of the lost. For the elect then, death to our body means resurrection life via our resurrection body of life, as Paul makes clear when he describes our mortal body as "body of death". Put another way, the "last time" is the final time the saint is on earth, until death translates them to heaven. Last time is this current age, contrasted with the eternal age without "time", which is ushered in fullness at the second coming.

Peter continues to contrast the exiled condition with the completed inheritance upon entering heaven in verses 6-9. He says to "rejoice" for only "a little while" or a short period of time of suffering or trials is necessary for them to be tested, both are indicative of our earthly sojourn. "A little while" is indicative of the relative short duration of our life on earth compared to eternity and cannot be taken to mean a time extending until the Last Day as this inheritance was previously described as "kept in heaven for you" (v.4) or awaiting our receipt when we arrive, and not as a future award on the Day of Wrath. The "revelation of Christ" to the elect had to have already been completely accomplished prior to the beginning of Judgment Day, for no potential for forgiveness is possible via a revelation of Christ as savior once Christ's visible coming and appearing to the entire cosmos for Judgment has commenced. Grace and forbearance have ended for the Satanic Kingdom. This inheritance in heaven is said to result in glory, this glory is the glorious resurrection body.

Verses 8-9 continue to validate this conclusion of the glorious body, When Peter contrasts their current state of living by faith in Christ and not by sight (his visible presence in heaven), which is their future glorious outcome in heaven throughout this section. He first identifies their "glorious joy" (v.8), which is the glory of the inner Holy Spirit which through faith will grant them the salvation of their souls which will be consummated in glory in heaven. This inner glory began at their initial revelation of Christ by faith at regeneration and continues to grow in them until outer glory is manifested in heaven. He follows this train of thought as he mentions the Spirit of Christ that was in the prophets, predicted this grace of glory which the New Testament elect possesses in verse 11. Here Peter is making the point that Christ first experienced his suffering on earth and glory immediately following when he ascended into heaven. No one questions Christ return to glory when he left the earth, but the intermediate state denies this same pattern to the elect. Peter is encouraging the recipients of his letter by reminding them of Christ's pattern of suffering followed by glory, reminding them that though they are now exiled and walking the path of suffering and trial, they will soon obtain glory in the same manner and timing as Christ did. He is our pattern and our resurrection to glory mimics his. Peter, in verse 12, continues this thought that the prophets were serving the recipients of the gospel, or these believers, who responded to the good news, described here as suffering and subsequent glory. A period of suffering, persecution, and trials can only be "good news" when accompanied by future glory. Paul stated the same thought when he spoke of his close encounters with death in 1 Cor. 15:32:

> If I fought wild beasts in Ephesus with no more than human hopes, what have I gained? If the dead are not raised, "Let us eat and drink, for tomorrow we die. (NIV)

Paul knew as well as Peter that earthly death results in a glorious resurrection life. Peter then repeats the theme, tying "raised from the dead" with "glorified him" in verse 21. His point is here clear, as Christ was raised from the dead and then received glory, so too will these saints (and all saints) upon death and the end of their exile on earth experience glorification in heaven. The path for Christ, and therefore his people, is earthly exile to heavenly revelation (visibility) of Christ in his glory, and the receipt of our glorious body. This is the movement from faith to sight Paul explained.

At the end of chapter 1, Peter brings a clinching conclusion. He moves from metaphors of exile/heaven, unseen/sight, and promise/inheritance, all of which contrast the earthly body with the outer glorious body, to the metaphor of perishable and imperishable seed (v.23). The mortal bodies of all people return to the ground just like dead grass or the petals of earthly flowers (v.24). This is perishable seed. The word of the Lord, which is the indwelling Spirit and the guarantee of the redemption of our mortal bodies into glorious bodies on entry to heaven, is the imperishable seed. This is the same metaphor that we saw Paul use in 1 Cor. 15: 42-44 (see Ch. 6).

> So will it be with the resurrection of the dead. The body that is sown is perishable, it is raised imperishable; it is sown in dishonor, it is raised in glory; it is sown in weakness, it is raised in power; it is sown a natural body, it is raised a spiritual body. (NIV)

The Temple must be completed prior to Judgment Day, with our glorious white robes adorning us, to enable Christ to separate us from the improperly adorned lost without their wedding garments at their resurrection on Judgment Day.

Revelation of Christ in 1 Peter 2-5

1 Peter 2:4-5 offers a synopsis of the "Revelation of Christ" beginning in our exile and culminating in glorious new life in our body in heaven, throughout the rest of the book. As in the previous chapter, I break the

text down into shorter sections to show how Peter addressed the revelation of Christ in relation to resurrection.

Section 1: 2:4-5 (synopsis)

> As you come to him, the living Stone—rejected by humans but chosen by God and precious to him— you also, like living stones, are being built into a spiritual house to be a holy priesthood, offering spiritual sacrifices acceptable to God through Jesus Christ. (NIV)

Peter affirms the topic of 1 Peter is our coming to Christ in heaven and not his coming to earth as he states, we come to him (v.2). This verse is a clear delineation of my doctrine of the resurrection of the saints, who are the living stones of the heavenly Temple, coming to Christ at death, and being incorporated into the Temple. The "living stone" is referring to resurrected life in heaven. This affirms my premise of the Temple building occurring during the church age and ending upon the last saint being resurrected to new life in heaven as the Temple is then complete and initiating the end time judgment and second resurrection of the lost. How can the Temple stones in heaven at the completion of the Temple be considered inglorious, meaning without the outer covering of the new body? Paul in 1 Cor. 15:40 (NIV) describes only two bodies, and they are both glorious:

> There are also heavenly bodies and there are earthly bodies; but the splendor of the heavenly bodies is one kind, and the splendor of the earthly bodies is another.

For even the body of the fallen man retains remnants of the original glory of Adam, but Paul never discusses a period without a body for the saint, and directly refutes it. But we insert an intermediate state Temple with inglorious stones in heaven, with no scriptural warrant, and a direct refutation by Paul, covered in the 1 Cor.15 section previously n detail. There is only a glorious Temple in heaven, it is absurd to consider another type.

Section 2: 2:9

> But you are a chosen people, a royal priesthood, a holy
> nation, God's special possession, that you may declare
> the praises of him who called you out of darkness into his
> wonderful light. (NIV)

Another clear two-part transition from one stage directly into another,
from darkness to light, one kingdom into another, there is no intermediate
kingdom without glory. Light is synonymous with glory. The transition
to the heavenly kingdom allows for the inner glory of the earthly saint to
become manifested in outer glory by the removal of the outer skin of flesh.

Section 3: 2:11-12

> Dear friends, I urge you, as foreigners and exiles, to
> abstain from sinful desires, which wage war against your
> soul. Live such good lives among the pagans that, though
> they accuse you of doing wrong, they may see your good
> deeds and glorify God on the day he visits us. (NIV)

Here our earthly exile will result in our good deeds being visible to the
apostate world as we come back with Christ in his glory at the second
coming, already adorned with robes of glory prior to Judgment Day.
This is the final coming to judgment, notice though, it is God visiting
us on earth as opposed to the other revelations or comings which are the
saints entering the heavenly domain. One is a downward and the other an
upward movement, we are coming up to the light, Christ is coming down
as light to the darkness.

Section 4: 2:21-25

> To this you were called, because Christ suffered for you,
> leaving you an example, that you should follow in his
> steps. "He committed no sin, and no deceit was found

in his mouth." Then they hurled their insults at him, he did not retaliate; when he suffered, he made no threats. Instead, he entrusted himself to him who judges justly. "He himself bore our sins" in his body on the cross, so that we might die to sins and live for righteousness; "by his wounds you have been healed." For "you were like sheep going astray," but now you have returned to the Shepherd and Overseer of your souls. (NIV)

The issue in the current "already" and "not yet" eschatology is the failure to understand the sending of the Spirit to indwell believers resulted in the heavenly kingdom of God coming to earth in the believer who are united with Christ via the inner glory of the Spirit and are already incorporated into the Temple (Christ) because we are a part of his body now while on earth. That is why Peter describes us as "living stones" now. Their failure is to not bring the totality of the new creation work of Christ in the lives of the elect forward to when we ascend into heaven. The error is not understanding that the guarantee the Spirit gives, what the inner glory while on earth proves, and why Peter can describe us as "living stones", is our "resurrection to new life" has already been initiated. The only part not initiated is that these "living stones" remain on earth in inglorious mortal bodies which will be transported (resurrected) to heaven at death when the inner glory breaks forth in outer glory. In fact, the new body can (should?) be understood not as another body, but simply a visible revelation of the new creation man created at regeneration, when the outer veil is removed. God creates man body and soul. Paul hints at this in 1 Cor. 15 where he speaks of the imperishable seed of the Spirit, or "word of God," implanted (sown) in believers. This seed flowers into the glorious form in heaven. Peter sates we follow his steps, and thus have a "resurrection like Christ's". He bore or sins so we might die to sin and live to righteousness, because of our baptism into Christ's death and receipt of life at regeneration we have the "life" now, we have been healed. We have now already returned to our Shepherd, via union with his Spirit, while still on earth. We await only our escape out of the earthly exile.

Section 5: 3:18-22

> For Christ also suffered once for sins, the righteous for
> the unrighteous, to bring you to God. He was put to
> death in the body but made alive in the Spirit. After
> being made alive, he went and made proclamation to the
> imprisoned spirits—to those who were disobedient long
> ago when God waited patiently in the days of Noah while
> the ark was being built. In it only a few people, eight in
> all, were saved through water, and this water symbolizes
> baptism that now saves you also—not the removal of
> dirt from the body but the pledge of a clear conscience
> toward God. It saves you by the resurrection of Jesus
> Christ, who has gone into heaven and is at God's right
> hand—with angels, authorities and powers in submission
> to him. (NIV)

Christ's death to his fleshly or earthly body resulted in resurrection life
via the Spirit in heaven. This is the gospel. In the same way as Christ, our
death to our body of flesh results in resurrection life at regeneration, where
the old body or man was killed. The old man that was killed (spiritually
rendered unable to dominate us in sin) at regeneration, and called our
body of death, is removed at its death and loss of breath, resulting in new
life in heaven. The water crossing of the Jordan to heaven and the exodus
water crossing are in view, but throughout is the transition to heaven and
not new life in the wilderness. Baptism is the corresponding sign of this
transition from physical death to resurrection life. This is the picture
water baptism portrays: death to the fleshly body, up out of the watery
grave via the Spirit to resurrection life in heaven via our new spiritual
and glorious body. Water baptism is often truncated to refer only to new
life at regeneration typified in the exodus crossing in the Old Testament.
The context of the correlation of Christ's death in the flesh to life in the
Spirit in verse 18 must be connected to our death to our fleshly body at
death and heavenly resurrection life, for that is the example provided by
Christ when his fleshly body died and quit breathing, as he did not need
a regeneration. This is not primarily speaking of new life at regeneration

for here it is speaking of our returning to heaven via the Spirit after the death of the mortal and fleshly body, as mentioned in Christ's fleshly body in verse 19 and his going into heaven in verse 22. The work of Christ's Spirit in the elect must be seen as heaven coming to earth in regeneration, followed by heaven as in the Spirit within the saint returning to the heavenly kingdom upon completion of their earthly witness. Why? The final and permanent uniting of heaven and earth awaits the second advent and elimination of the Satanic kingdom, which is revealed in Revelation 21:1-2:

> Then I saw "a new heaven and a new earth," for the first heaven and the first earth had passed away, and there was no longer any sea. I saw the Holy City, the new Jerusalem, coming down out of heaven from God, prepared as a bride beautifully dressed for her husband. (NIV)

Residence in heaven is the ultimate manifestation of a place without any darkness It cannot ever be associated with the elect without their glory per the intermediate state, which is founded upon a misapplication of the difference between final glory in heaven for the elect and the final glory of the cosmos which is accomplished on the Last Day Judgment. To perceive the elect in heaven unable to reflect the glory of Christ while in heaven should cause a sincere reflection on the theology which defends this conclusion, but unfortunately it is dominating the church.

Section 6: 4:4-6

> They are surprised that you do not join them in their reckless, wild living, and they heap abuse on you. But they will have to give account to him who is ready to judge the living and the dead. For this is the reason the gospel was preached even to those who are now dead, so that they might be judged according to human standards in regard to the body, but live according to God in regard to the spirit. (NIV)

The section presents a contrast between judgment awaiting the lost and resurrection life awaiting the elect on earth. Believers have passed from judgment to life, as Christ states in John 5:24:

> For this is why the gospel was preached even to those who are dead, that though judged in the flesh the way people are, they might live in the spirit the way God does.

The lost are "judged in the flesh" at death per Adam's curse, but die without resurrection life for the body, as opposed to the elect whose bodily death results in resurrection life in the new body in heaven.

Section 7: 4:13-14

> But rejoice inasmuch as you participate in the sufferings of Christ, so that you may be overjoyed when his glory is revealed. If you are insulted because of the name of Christ, you are blessed, for the Spirit of glory and of God rests on you. (NIV)

In keeping with the period of suffering on earth resulting in glory when we reach heaven, Peter encourages these believers because they will rejoice and be glad when his glory is revealed to them. Again, this is not referring to the Last Day judgment where Christ's glory is revealed to the lost and they are forced to acknowledge it but are still judged. Here he is speaking to believers. This revelation of Christ's glory is when they appear in heaven after death and are in his presence. Additionally, Peter tells them they are already "blessed" since the "Spirit of glory and of God rests upon you". They do not have outer glory resting on them at this time, so this must refer to the inner Spirit's dwelling in them, understood as the inner man awaiting the unveiling of this glory upon arrival in heaven as the outer body of death (flesh) is laid aside. This matches Paul's teaching in which the Spirit is the guarantee of the redemption of the body, which is an exchange of a dead mortal body with a glorious body at death. God, through the Holy Spirit, will bring us safely and completely, soul with glorious body, into our glorious eternal home.

Section 8: 5:1, 4

> To the elders among you, I appeal as a fellow elder and
> a witness of Christ's sufferings who also will share in the
> glory to be revealed: . . . And when the Chief Shepherd
> appears, you will receive the crown of glory that will never
> fade away. (NIV)

Peter combines his witness to the suffering of Christ with being a partaker
(sharer) in the "glory to be revealed". Peter states we possess or are partakers
of Christ's glory now, although it is veiled by our mortal body. So, the
question becomes when will this glory be revealed? In other words when
is the revelation, manifestation, or outer adornment of the current inner
glory of the Spirit? Before answering the question with the text, let's
consider closely the strange position the intermediate state postulates, as
it postpones this adornment of outer glory and resurrection body until
the Final Judgment or Day of Wrath. This view removes the outer veil of
the inner glory, which is our mortal body, which should expose the inner
glory. Consider the transfiguration, why would this event make more sense
to them after Christ's resurrection to heaven? Part of the reason is because
that is when Christ transitioned from mortal body to glorious body. The
removal of the mortal body should reveal the inner glory, and perhaps this
is why it is sometimes called the crowning with glory or receiving a crown
of glory to indicate the finish of the race ran on earth and receipt of our
inheritance in heaven. Saints transition from glory to glory per 2 Cor. 3:18:

> And we all, who with unveiled faces contemplate the
> Lord's glory, are being transformed into his image with
> ever-increasing glory, which comes from the Lord, who is
> the Spirit. (NIV)

Verse 4 tells us that Christ appears to the saint when they enter heaven.
The appearing of the chief Shepherd is equivalent to the "revelation of
Christ" and simply means when we are in Christ's presence and can see
him in his glory. This is mistakenly understood as the appearing of Christ
to the apostate world at his appearing to judgment at the end of the age. As

I have said before, the revelation or appearing to the elect which is a visible manifestation of Christ had already been accomplished prior to his second advent as all of the elect had been resurrected to heaven before that time. In fact, the New Testament marker of the initiation of the Last Day is the trumpet call of the archangel. The first action upon this call is described as the removal of those on earth who are Christ's, to be changed and meet the heavenly church in the clouds. This then results in the Day of Darkness, as all light has been removed by this last remnant of his witness on earth. This is not referencing the final appearance to judgment where he becomes visible to the lost but our entrance into heaven and his appearance to us at that time. If I make a trip to the President's home, he appears to me when I enter the room where he is present. That is the thought here when we enter into the heavenly realm which is where Peter described our inheritance as waiting for us. The crown of glory is received after we have finished our "race" on earth, that is the termination point-when we reach heaven and not on the Last Day. Paul uses the same metaphor when he states in 2 Tim. 4:6-8:

> For I am already being poured out like a drink offering, and the time for my departure is near. I have fought the good fight, I have finished the race, I have kept the faith. Now there is in store for me the crown of righteousness, which the Lord, the righteous Judge, will award to me on that day—and not only to me, but also to all who have longed for his appearing. (NIV)

The crown here is "righteousness," but we will share many crowns at the end of our race on earth. The other crowns are described elsewhere as crowns of life, gold, saints, imperishable, and victors, but they all derive from our resurrection life in the Spirit. There is not another race to run during an intermediate state in order to receive our crowns.

Section 9: 5:6-10

> Humble yourselves, therefore, under God's mighty hand, that he may lift you up in due time. Cast all your anxiety on him because he cares for you. Be alert and of sober

mind. Your enemy the devil prowls around like a roaring lion looking for someone to devour. Resist him, standing firm in the faith, because you know that the family of believers throughout the world is undergoing the same kind of sufferings. And the God of all grace, who called you to his eternal glory in Christ, after you have suffered a little while, will himself restore you and make you strong, firm and steadfast. (NIV)

Here at the close of his letter, Peter, as is common in writing letters, returns to the theme he began in 1:3-4, namely, that our short time of suffering will result in our calling to our eternal glory in heaven:

Praise be to the God and Father of our Lord Jesus Christ! In his great mercy he has given us new birth into a living hope through the resurrection of Jesus Christ from the dead, and into an inheritance that can never perish, spoil or fade. This inheritance is kept in heaven for you. (NIV)

The earlier text describes it as this inheritance is kept in heaven for you, not as a blessed hope on the Last Day judgment. In 5:6-10 he closes with the encouragement that at the proper time God would exalt them, echoing Joshua and Christ's entrances to the typological and real Promised Land in heaven. He indicates the time as a little while until the God who called them to his eternal glory in Christ, will restore the glory Adam lost and establish them in the heavenly kingdom. Christ is in heaven having already been returned to his glory prior to his descending to earth. This glorious inheritance is obtained by us in heaven upon the revelation of Christ before our eyes.

Revelation of Christ in 2 Peter

Section 1: 1:3

His divine power has given us everything we need for a godly life through our knowledge of him who called us by his own glory and goodness. (NIV)

Peter continues the focus on our calling to Christ's glory, and in effect our glory in heaven as well, that we saw in 1 Pet. 5:10 where he says, "who called you to his eternal glory in Christ". Now Peter states all things that pertain to life and godliness have been granted unto us. They are our possession now. The life already granted to us is resurrection life, which is the Spirit, and therefore we have also already been granted the means of transformation into our glorious spiritual nature at death. Christ is not awaiting the Last Day to award this to us, and this must be emphasized because Peter does not allude to a glory for them to be obtained on the Last Day but makes the point that our calling is to be conformed to the glorious image of Christ who has already gone before us into heaven where his glory was restored to him. The absence of this opportunity and many others like it to explain that our return to heaven and Christ's glory does not result in our outer bodily glory, but is delayed until final judgment, is evidence by exclusion of its fallacy. Peter is clearly equating our calling with our return to heaven, which results in our glorification. The rest of the 2 Peter text reinforces this conclusion.

Section 2: 1:10-11

> Therefore, my brothers and sisters, make every effort to confirm your calling and election. For if you do these things, you will never stumble, and you will receive a rich welcome into the eternal kingdom of our Lord and Savior Jesus Christ. (NIV)

We have an upward or heavenly calling. Our life on earth is not our ultimate calling, that is in heaven when we are completely transformed. Peter ties his previous reference to this call as one to glory in the previous section, to our entrance into heaven here. This refutes a resurrection to bodily glory on Judgment Day. "Rich welcome" is the escalated glorious state to be obtained, as taught here and elsewhere, upon entrance to the heavenly kingdom. It contrasts with Christ's lowly estate upon his humiliation on earth and ours as well. Our "riches" are in heaven and those awaiting gold and silver rather than glorious adornment will be disappointed. If Peter was attempting to distinguish a difference between entrance to heaven and our glorious calling this would have been the time to clearly inform us our arrival into the kingdom in heaven is not glorious for the saint but awaits the eschaton. He does not because all of heaven declares the glory of God, and therefore our heavenly presence without our glorious outer robes is an affront to Christ's work, and absurd. The lost are defined as those at the judgment seat without the proper outer garment, and this curse must not remain assigned to the sons of God in heaven.

Section 3: 1:13-15

> I think it is right to refresh your memory as long as I live in the tent of this body, because I know that I will soon put it aside, as our Lord Jesus Christ has made clear to me. And I will make every effort to see that after my departure you will always be able to remember these things. (NIV)

Peter ties his coming death and departure from this world and his current residing in his earthly body to his receipt of resurrection life in the body and his future glorious arrival in heaven. Note, Peter already stated previously that the time reference of this transformation was upon entrance into heaven. He is clearly contrasting his present time in his mortal body with the time of his death and the future time in his new glorious body. He describes this time of death as a setting aside of his body and he does not follow with a description of the time delay where he will be without a body in heaven which would naturally follow this statement if the intermediate state were true. The natural reading of the text is his setting aside of the body of death and putting on the new body.

Section 4: 1:16-19

> For we did not follow cleverly devised stories when we told you about the coming of our Lord Jesus Christ in power, but we were eyewitnesses of his majesty. He received honor and glory from God the Father when the voice

came to him from the Majestic Glory, saying, "This is my Son, whom I love; with him I am well pleased." We ourselves heard this voice that came from heaven when we were with him on the sacred mountain. We also have the prophetic message as something completely reliable, and you will do well to pay attention to it, as to a light shining in a dark place, until the day dawns and the morning star rises in your hearts. (NIV)

Peter begins with a reference to the transfiguration of Christ in verse 16. Why does he do this? And what tie does this event have with the topic of his looming death and departure and his topic of their calling to glorious inheritance in heaven? We recall the transfiguration consisted of these things, 1) the manifestation of Christ in his future glorious state of outer glory, 2) the location was the mountain of God, 3) the affirmation by God the Father of his pleasure in his son. In short, the transfiguration was a revelation of Christ's future glory to the three witnesses which also showed them the future glory to be manifested by his elect upon their final destination in heaven. Christ instructed them not to tell of this experience until after his resurrection (to heaven) as then the meaning would be clear to them. The transfiguration occurred "on the holy mountain" or the earthly typological example of heaven, also indicating the location of the actual transformation to heavenly glory is in the true mountain of God in heaven. The text here refers to their current status as "a light shining in a dark place" (v.19), describing their current residence on earth until "the day dawns and the morning star rises in their hearts"(v.19) indicating their future transformation to heaven where no darkness exists and they will be transformed from a lamp in a dark place to one of the glorious day stars showing forth the full glory of Christ in heaven where no night exists.

Section 5: 3:1-18

Dear friends, this is now my second letter to you. I have written both of them as reminders to stimulate you to wholesome thinking. I want you to recall the words spoken in the past by the holy prophets and the command given by our Lord and Savior through your apostles. Above all, you must understand that in the last days scoffers will come, scoffing and following their own evil desires. They will say, "Where is this 'coming' he promised? Ever since our ancestors died, everything goes on as it has since the beginning of creation." But they deliberately forget that long ago by God's word the heavens came into being and the earth was formed out of water and by water. By these waters also the world of that time was deluged and destroyed. By the same word the present heavens and earth are reserved for fire, being kept for the day of judgment and destruction of the ungodly. But do not forget this one thing, dear friends: With the Lord a day is like a thousand years, and a thousand years are like a day. The Lord is not slow in keeping his promise, as some understand slowness. Instead he is patient with you, not wanting anyone to perish, but everyone to come to repentance. But the day of the Lord will come like a thief. The heavens will disappear with a roar; the elements will be destroyed by fire, and the earth and everything done in it will be laid bare. Since everything will be destroyed in this way, what kind of people ought you to be? You ought to live holy and godly lives as you look forward to the day of God and speed its coming. That day will bring about the destruction of the heavens by fire, and the elements will melt in the heat. But in keeping with his promise we are looking forward to a new heaven and a new earth, where righteousness dwells. So then, dear friends, since you are looking forward to this, make every effort to be found spotless, blameless and at peace with him. Bear in mind that our Lord's patience means salvation, just as our dear brother Paul also wrote you with the wisdom that God gave him. He writes the same way in all his letters, speaking in them of these matters. His letters contain some things that are hard to understand, which ignorant and unstable people distort, as they do the other Scriptures, to their own destruction. Therefore, dear friends, since you have been forewarned, be on your guard so that you may not be carried away by the error of the lawless and fall from your secure position. But grow in the grace and knowledge of our Lord and Savior Jesus Christ. To him be glory both now and forever! Amen. NIV

Peter begins this section by reminding the readers of the Lost's disregard of the warnings of the final judgment to come on the Last Day by referring to both the prophets of the Old Testament and Christ's declarations of that day.

Does Peter direct the readers future hope to the Day of Judgment or to the final renewal of the heaven and the earth, which occurs after the Day of Judgment? This has been a repeated theme throughout the book as I have made the point that Christ's work in redemption is always our focus and future hope, rather than Judgment Day. With Peter's warning in verses 15 and 16 regarding the difficulty of understanding some of Paul's writings, "which the ignorant and unstable twist to their own destruction, as they do the other Scriptures", I believe the focus of the church has been moved from Christ's work of resurrection life at death for the individual and the final renewal of the heavens and earth to a focus on Judgment Day as a glorious day for the saints where they are resurrected to glory.

The error lies in the fact that there are places in scripture where the saints do long for the Day of Judgment to arrive, including here. We look towards this day only because we understand this day must take place in order to eliminate death from the cosmos, and that our hope of the future renewal is the true Blessed Hope. My point is that the day of destruction is a horrific event and there is no rejoicing for the saint in the death and misery which will occur. God is patient and longsuffering in order to bring repentance, thus when his patience has ended it results in his return to judgment. As there is no joy for us when a person dies and we suspect there was no repentance or faith in Christ evident in their life, we long for this day with reservation due to our desire for those we love to avoid judgment. Likewise, God only arrives on judgment upon the exhaustion of his patience and therefore his day of wrath and anger has arrived.

Peter begins this section by referring to the Day of Judgment in verses 1-12, using the terms "day of the Lord" (v.10) and "the day of God" (v.12) as well. Then in verse 13 he gives the ultimate day to which these saints now under persecution, are to look forward to, saying, "But in keeping with his promise we are looking forward to a new heaven and a new earth, where righteousness dwells" (v. 13). The day the saints are to look forward to and keep their sights upon is the renewed age in which sin and death has been purged, while at the same time being aware of the need for the Day of Judgment to destroy the Satanic Kingdom.

Peter emphasizes the points I have repeatedly made. The first is the comparison of the period of salvation which he refers to here as "last days" with the singular "Day of Judgment." We see the contrast of a period of multiple days where the gospel is available for salvation with a singular day of judgment. Peter is highlighting the two periods here using the differing amounts of time for each: long for the gospel era and short for the Day of Judgment. None of the descriptions of the Day of Judgment assign the judgment activity to the saints. It is described as a day of fire, destruction of the ungodly, exposure, perishing, and passing away. The two sequential time periods reveal two separate fates for two different kinds of residents of two separate kingdoms. Therefore, there is not a resurrection of the elect nor a judgment of the elect on the Last Day.

Peter also uses the phrase "one day is as a thousand years, and a thousand years as one day" (v.8) to contrast these two different events, salvation and judgment, in a similar manner as "last days" is contrasted with a "day". Equating 1000 years and one Last Day serves to highlight these time frames using the images of daytime identifying the gospel period, as when the light of the gospel is available, versus the Last Day judgment, which is a day of total darkness. Two different days, one full of light and another with total darkness, emphasize the difference, not the intermediate state's common resurrection and judgment activities for the lost and the elect. One is for the elect and the other is for the lost. The thousand-year period is also contrasted with a "day", thus the "1000 years" and the "last days" represent the same time period, which is the interadvent gospel period. The thousand years description is also used repeatedly by John in Revelation 20 to indicate the church age or the time ending with the final judgment. This is another textual proof of the last days or thousand years where the saints come to Christ in regeneration and then by resurrection life in the glorious body preceding the Last Day resurrection of the lost to judgment. The thought Peter is expressing is that although the period of trials for the saints may seem long, God will fulfill his promise to come in judgment. The time periods are contrasting events in order in time, not at the same time. The end of the gospel period is followed by Judgment Day for the lost.

All of mankind will experience one or the other, either the renewal of the cosmos for the saints, or Judgment Day for the unbeliever. There is no joy in looking forward to the wrath of God being poured out on the lost, but we understand it is the only means by which death can be defeated for eternity.

CONCLUSION

I hope that this book will lead to a serious look at the doctrine of the resurrection. My fear is that church leaders today will remain in the same frame of mind as that of the leaders of the Old Testament at the end of the old covenant. Those church leaders relied more on their traditions, writings, and common interpretations, rather than what the Old Testament foretold, so much so that they could not recognize Christ. I pray the New Testament church era will not end in the same manner, and rely on writings of the early church, esteemed men throughout the age, and church councils and cannon, rather than on the scripture. Today we live in an age where the science in certain areas has become settled and there is no longer any allowance for the questioning of majority opinions, but science is never settled. The same holds true for our quest for the knowledge to be gained through our study of the scriptures, the reformation is ongoing.

To God be the glory.